Loretta MacAlpine has been covering the children's video
industry since 1986. As managing editor for *Video Insider*,
she wrote a column on children's video. She has also written
reviews and articles on children's video and entertainment
for other publications, including *TV Guide*, *Video Business*,
Metro Kids, and *Video Software Magazine*. A founding member of the National Advisory Board of the Coalition for Quality Children's Video, Loretta MacAlpine now lives in Lincoln
University, Pennsylvania.

INSIDE KidVid

▪ The Essential ▪
Parents' Guide to Video

Loretta MacAlpine

Penguin Books

PENGUIN BOOKS
Published by the Penguin Group
Penguin Books USA Inc., 375 Hudson Street,
New York, New York 10014, U.S.A.
Penguin Books Ltd, 27 Wrights Lane,
London W8 5TZ, England
Penguin Books Australia Ltd, Ringwood,
Victoria, Australia
Penguin Books Canada Ltd, 10 Alcorn Avenue,
Toronto, Ontario, Canada M4V 3B2
Penguin Books (N.Z.) Ltd, 182–190 Wairau Road,
Auckland 10, New Zealand

Penguin Books Ltd, Registered Offices:
Harmondsworth, Middlesex, England

First published in Penguin Books 1995
1 3 5 7 9 10 8 6 4 2

LIBRARY OF CONGRESS CATALOGING IN PUBLICATION DATA
MacAlpine, Loretta.
Inside kidvid: the essential parents' guide to video / Loretta
MacAlpine.
p.   cm.
Includes index.
ISBN 0 14 01.7341 2 (pbk.)
1. Video recordings for children.   2. Video recordings for
children—Catalogs.   3. Children's films—Catalogs.   I. Title.
PN1992.945.M23   1995
028.1'37—dc20   95–14876

Printed in the United States of America
Set in Century Old Style
Designed by Virginia Norey

To my mother and father, who always believed in my talents and told me that I'd be happiest doing what I loved most—you were right

And to the children and their loving parents, without whom there would be no need for this book

■

ACKNOWLEDGMENTS

So many people goaded me into sharing my peculiar talent for recognizing and promoting good children's programming that I must apologize if one or two of my supporters are not specifically named.

Long ago, Mom and Dad encouraged me when things looked bleakest; I could not have dreamed of becoming a writer without their love and support.

For all his patience, fortitude, and unflagging encouragement (and constructive nagging), and for putting up with the angst and long hours of the freelance writer, my husband deserves more than a mere acknowledgment—he deserves a medal. He encouraged me to take a risk and follow my dream.

Thanks to my family and all my closest friends, who accepted that I was incommunicado at times during the writing and research phases of my book, among them Eileen Muller, Bill Hopper, David Feske, Beth and Art Stephano, Debbie Rowland and Margie Cummings, the Womers, and the MacAlpines.

Many thanks to Douglas Kirschner, who's responsible for giving me my first big break as a writer and a magazine professional. And to Steven Apple, who gave me such encouragement early in my video career. And to Jon DeKeles, who convinced me this was a viable project.

A special thank-you goes out to Joanne Singer and Adrian Hickman, whose guidance, expertise, and passion for the genre are inspirational beyond words.

It took a child to help me see the value in some programs, so my central corps of young reviewers—and their patient and appreciative parents—deserve much praise: Marty, Stuart, and Christopher Armstrong; Margie, Jimmy, Rachel, Rebecca, and Jamie Cummings;

Ellen Ziemer and Jerry Waddel, and Erica and Mark; Donna, John, Jacquie, and Jaimie Reichert; Betsy, Howard, and H. G. Thompkins; Michele, David, Kira, and Caylan MacAlpine; Bob, Kathy, Shannon, and Stephen Miller; Joe, Sharon, and Taylor Dombroski; Bobbie, Davey, Davey Jr., Zach, and Amber Harris; Ron, Lisa, Zach, and Matt Casalvera; Lori Walker and Linda Smith and their children; and all the children these people shared my review copies of videos with.

Thanks also to those who have edited and continue to edit my magazine articles and parenting-paper articles, and in doing so helped hone my reviewer's voice, particularly Nancy Lisagor, Myles Callum, Andy Wickstrom, and Gayle Carter.

My gratitude goes to all those in the video industry who encouraged me to "go for it" and who provided me with information, research, and their expertise, especially Ranny Levy, Diana Huss Green, Peggy Charren, Karen Tucker, Jane Murphy, Andrea Blaine, Shari Lewis, Shelley Duvall, Martha Dewing, David Archibald-Seiffer, Linda Leszynski, Cindy Spielvogel, Georgia Cave, and Doris Wilhousky.

A most heartfelt thanks goes to Frederick Glasser for providing the entrée into publishing.

And my deepest gratitude is to Caroline White, my editor at Viking Penguin, who believed in and nurtured my potential and abilities, and provided a strong base of support that many first-time book authors probably don't get.

Thanks, finally, to all the children's video producers and their helpful publicists: Please continue to produce and promote the excellent programming that is the subject of this book.

CONTENTS

INSIDE
KidVid

■

INTRODUCTION

In the years since 1986, when I began covering the children's video industry, technology has changed so greatly that now kids are more likely to be teaching us adults how to program the VCR. Children have always clamored for the newest gadget, the latest toy; now those toys—videos, CDs, even TV—are employed as educational adjuncts and found in most homes. When it comes time for a trip to the video store, how can parents keep up with the overwhelming number of videos being released monthly, let alone know which of the more than 7,000 children's tapes on the market today are quality productions?

If you're concerned by the statistics from the American Academy of Pediatrics that indicate today's child has watched more than 11,000 hours of TV by the time he or she reaches senior year in high school, you can do something about it. Make the choice to offer your children an alternative to the mind-numbing, overcommercialized fare passing for children's entertainment on today's weekday and Saturday-morning lineups. While TV networks ponder how to use the Children's Television Act enacted in 1990, your choices are multiplying on video store and library shelves: Buy, rent, or borrow a video. You and your child can choose when, where, and how frequently to watch it, and whether to pause and discuss the action or content on the screen or have a pre- or post-viewing chat. This book is intended to help make choosing easier.

Many of the programs recommended here fit into more than one chapter category in this book. You won't find such well-recognized favorites as Bugs Bunny and the Roadrunner, or every single one of Disney's films. That's not to say they aren't among the best in their genres; most people are already familiar with those famous names, however, and they're easily found on cassettes at video specialty stores as well as your local discount store or supermarket. I've chosen to give airtime to some less familiar, even forgotten video options.

I hope you find that at least 90 percent of what you discover here is "evergreen": programs that are watchable years from now with your second, third, and fourth child, maybe even with your grandchildren (though they may not be watching what we know as VHS!). You can use this book as a resource as well, to explore other means of finding high-quality children's entertainment; that's why I've tried to include many book-based videos and make reference to other media that are available.

The experts I've consulted have years of experience and are well known in children's entertainment and/or education circles. I hope you appreciate their expertise and the opinions they've shared, which may open your eyes to new ways of thinking about the TV and VCR and new ways of using current technology to your and your children's advantage. Our present TV and VCR may be only a stepping stone to technologies that are just now being developed, such as CD-I (CD-Interactive), CD-ROM (CD-Read Only Memory), 3DO (three-dimensional, full-motion video), and video-on-demand (programming delivered over phone lines, established pay-per-view cable networks, and digital broadcast satellite).

I originally intended to give prices for every tape included here, but just in the time it took me to write a single chapter, many prices were lowered. You can now buy most children's programs for under $15, the average price being $12.99. Tapes that at press time were still priced above $29.99 and intended for rental are marked as such. But please note: If you see a $2.99 cartoon compilation at a checkout counter, consider whether you'd rather apply the $2.99 to something you've read about here or risk it on a poor substitute that probably was duplicated on thin, easily broken tape.

In addition to the words of respected authorities and renowned celebrities interviewed for each chapter, a "tip sheet" on how to choose quality entertainment for your children appears at the end of this Introduction.

How to Use This Guide

Chapters are divided into the most recognizable genres in children's entertainment: live-action feature-length films (generally longer than 60 minutes); animated feature-length films; musical fun (concerts, sing-alongs, and other productions in which music plays an integral part); "discovery" tapes (including a broad range from science and nature to self-awareness and reference material); sports, health, and fitness (bloopers, how to improve your game, safety, and exercise/dance videos); activity tapes (usually designed to entertain children by teaching them to make things); and storytelling and book-based videos (from contemporary stories to traditional fairy tales to the works of famous authors). Within each chapter, tapes are arranged alphabetically. You might not find all of the episodes in a series in separate entries; for some, I've chosen to review what I consider the most outstanding volume and simply mention the rest in the series.

Where I felt it necessary or useful to parents, I included information on prequels and sequels, and references to titles with similar plots or themes. I hope you find such information leads you to some previously undiscovered gems.

After each title, the following information appears:

■ *MANUFACTURER.*   You'll find most of the manufacturers' addresses and phone numbers listed in Resources. Use the information to order a tape through your local video store, or to call or write the manufacturer directly.

■ *YEAR.*   In most cases, this indicates the year the film or video was produced; sometimes, however, the production year was not available. In that case, what's listed is the year the title was released on video, if that information was available.

■ *RUNNING TIME.*   This is a factor to consider when you want to get the most from your rental dollars or when buying videos. The youngest children will often find a feature-length film more accessible if you serialize the movie into several segments over one or several days.

■ *MPAA RATING.*   The Motion Picture Association of America established its rating guidelines and the Classification and Rating Administration (CARA) in 1968; prior to that year, no ratings were issued

by the MPAA. CARA is composed of parents from across the country who screen films prior to their theatrical releases. As defined by
the MPAA, current ratings are:

G for General Audience (all ages admitted)
PG for Parental Guidance Suggested (some material may not
be suitable for children)
PG-13 for Parents Strongly Cautioned (some material may be
inappropriate for children under 13)
R for Restricted (under 17 requires accompanying parent or
adult guardian)
NC-17 for No Children Under 17 Admitted (age may vary in
certain areas).

Contrary to popular belief, there really is no "X" rating now that
there's an NC-17 designation, and the MPAA has never given an
"XXX" rating. Recently, the MPAA began to assign qualifiers with
its PG, PG-13, and R ratings; for example, if it gave a film an "R," it
noted in its media releases whether the film's content reflected material of a sexual nature, violence, language, drug use, and so on.
The MPAA intends that the public use its ratings for guidelines only;
parents are the ones who are fully qualified to judge what's best for
their children.

■ *AGE RANGE.* This is another subjective qualifier. It's based on a
number of factors: What the company literature suggests, if anything (you might find such information on the box cover); what
other sources, such as the MPAA and Parents' Choice, have recommended; screenings with my network of child reviewers; and my
own recommendation, based on my years of experience in the industry and watching children watch my preview copies. Like the
MPAA ratings, please use the suggested age range as a guideline
only; if you have the opportunity to screen a video ahead of time,
you'll be able to judge whether your child is too young or too old
for it. While this book covers videos for children of all ages, the
emphasis is on programming for preschoolers, elementary-school
aged children, and preteens.

■ *PRICE.* As I mentioned earlier, with all the manufacturers changing pricing every six months, the information became impossible to

record accurately. The only exception is when videos were intended to be rented, carrying wholesale prices of anywhere from $64 to $109. In that case, the word "rental" appears.

■ *DIRECTOR.* When available and listed in the video's credits, the director is listed. For many original programs or animated half-hour videos, however, directors are unknown to the general public; in those cases, it seemed a better use of space to eliminate directors' names.

■ *STARS.* The most prominent cast members are listed, as are narrators (who appear in voice-overs only or as animated caricatures of themselves), hosts (who appear as themselves), and for animated programs, the actors who supplied the voices.

One thing I eliminated from my original game plan was the list of all the awards won by each entry in this book. Some of these programs have been so decorated by various film festivals and the Academy of Motion Picture Arts and Sciences (AMPAS, which awards the Oscars) that were I to list all their awards, I'd have no room left for descriptions! I have listed as many notable awards as possible, however, and have compiled the following list of the most frequently mentioned awards for films.

Interpreting a Video's Awards

Some of the best videos on the market boast starbursts, trophies, seals, and ribbons on their boxes, denoting award-winning programs. Here's a partial list of who bestows these awards and what they mean for consumers.

Generally, videos that are singled out for an award by one or more of the following groups are worth renting and even buying. Often, several groups will honor the same tape, especially highly original, lovingly animated programs and unique concepts in special-interest programming, like life lessons. Children's and family films are eligible for far too many awards to mention here (considering that many are based on award-winning books, too), but here's an explanation of the most frequently seen kudos, and several sources parents can reference.

■ *OSCARS.* Given annually in March by the Academy of Motion Picture Arts and Sciences, the Academy Awards are considered the pinnacle of a film's achievement. Walt Disney's **Beauty and the Beast** broke new ground as the first animated film nominated for Best Picture; it was also nominated in several other categories, including score.

■ *EMMYS*. The best television programming is put on this pedestal by the Academy of Television Arts and Sciences.

■ *GRAMMYS*. You'll see this old Victrola graphic on videos featuring children's musical performers such as Raffi or Joanie Bartels. These awards are given out by the National Association of Recording Arts and Sciences each February.

■ *ACE*. Each January, the National Academy of Cable Programming honors non-network programming.

■ *PARENTS' CHOICE*. Announced annually during Thanksgiving week, the prestigious awards from this nonprofit foundation that reviews all types of children's media honor a score of notable toys, books, music, and video programs. The best rate a Gold Award or Silver Honors, while the rest receive "approved" seals, still quite an honor for an original program. Critics and parents across the country are judges. To subscribe to the foundation's quarterly guide, call or write Box 185, Newton, MA 02168; 617-965-5913.

■ *ACTION FOR CHILDREN'S TELEVISION*. This organization, a watchdog for children's media for over twenty years, was disbanded at the end of 1992 and will no longer give out its awards. There are still plenty of videos on store shelves, however, that will display ACT's coveted seals with pride for years to come.

■ *COALITION FOR QUALITY CHILDREN'S VIDEO*. This nonprofit group's admirable goals are to educate parents and caregivers about the availability of high-quality children's videos and to enhance public awareness of this product via a national publicity campaign. The coalition honors high-quality children's programs by giving them its Kids First! seal of approval. Those videos bearing the Kids First! seal are listed in the coalition's *Kids First! Directory*, first published in 1994 (to order, call 505-989-8076).

■ *OPPENHEIM TOY PORTFOLIO*. Noted author and child-development expert Joanne Oppenheim publishes an independent quarterly guide to noteworthy toys, books, and videos, and has described the best of them in a recently published book (see Resources). Products that receive a Gold Award are also nominated for the Platinum Awards announced each November. Subscribe by calling 800-544-TOYS or 212-598-0502.

■ *CALIFORNIA CHILDREN'S BOOK AND VIDEO AWARDS.* A consortium of six California-based parenting publications offers awards to media that enrich the educational experience of children. The group chooses four winners in each of six categories: Baby/Toddler, Preschool, Early Elementary, Family, Informational, and Sing-Along.

■ *THE FILM ADVISORY BOARD.* This organization affixes its starburst seal of approval to award-winning films that teach lessons as well as entertain. In addition, the FAB has an alternative ratings system to the MPAA's that denotes in letters the content of a film (M for mature, MM for very mature, etc.).

■ *CINE GOLDEN EAGLE.* This honor is handed out each December by the Council on International Nontheatrical Events (CINE). The winners are considered the most suitable films to represent the United States in international film competitions.

■ *CHILDREN'S VIDEO REPORT.* Although CVR does not hand out awards, a nod from this newsletter is the equivalent of an award. Former teacher Martha Dewing, also a judge in the California Children's Book and Video Awards, rounds up reviews of video programs from child development and media experts in this guide, published eight times a year. For subscription information, call 718-935-0600.

■ *PARENT'S VIDEO RESOURCE CENTER.* The PVRC is a clearinghouse for more than fifty tapes for expectant parents, new parents, and parents of youngsters up to age eight. It does not hand out awards, but its programs are well-endorsed titles difficult to find outside hospitals, doctor's offices, and some libraries. Included in the mix: **Baby Alive,** a lifesaving tape approved by the American Academy of Pediatrics, and **Safe and Sound,** which provides information for parents as they choose a child's day-care center. For information, call 800-756-8792.

Ten Tips to Choosing Quality KidVid

1. Read the box. Video manufacturers will shout the praises of their product on the box art. They'll happily list many of the AWARDS the program has won, from Grammys to Parents' Choice honors, and will usually name well-known cast members or directors. Skim the SYNOPSIS: What elements in the video will draw your children's attention? Will the viewer engage in any activities while watching, and

do the activities mentioned require supervision? Check the RUNNING TIME: Toddlers may find it tough to sit through a Disney feature-length time, so you may want to have them view it in installments. And a 30-minute documentary may not allow enough time to broach the subject for a 10-year-old. Does the box display an AGE RANGE? If not, ask the video store manager or librarian to look it up on the sales materials. Play it by ear: What may terrify one 6-year-old may be hilarious to another.

2. If there is a lack of adequate information on the box, preview the tape without your child. As you watch, ask yourself: What can the viewer learn from this video? Is the subject thought-provoking or likely to raise questions? Does the program support your family's values? Is the tape repeatable? (Children, as you well know, are likely to watch a tape so many times it snaps from overplay.) Will your child be emotionally satisfied? If your children are preschoolers, watch an episode of *Sesame Street* beforehand to get yourself in the right frame of mind; often, the silliest things are those that are most endearing to a youngster. Your local library should be able to lend you a video by the American Library Association on choosing children's videos. You don't need to be a video-educated parent or have a degree in early childhood education to know quality from junk. A quality tape tells your children something you want them to hear; it portrays the world in a way that informs or changes the way you think about it; it tells you something you need to know. It's easy to separate that kind of program from those that contain stereotypic, mass-made, violent, meaningless, or convoluted messages. And talk to your children to develop their values and make them discriminating reviewers. The dialogue about what you are watching is as educational as any dialogue you have with your children.

3. Find out what others think. Word of mouth can make or break a video, and that's often the way a hit succeeds in the children's video industry. Talk to other parents you know or might meet browsing at the local video store or supermarket. Ask teachers and librarians for recommendations. Make a friend of your video store's manager by asking for his or her opinion; ultimately, you could influence the inventory of the store as you make requests to include more and better kidvid.

4. Do your homework and research before you buy, just as you would for a major purchase. However innocuous the package looks, what your children watch somehow impacts them positively or negatively. Get to know and respect certain reviewers in newspapers and magazines, as well as books like this one, to help you choose only the best. You might want to collect and save reviews in a scrapbook in case your children are not yet ready for some videos that sound worth trying.

5. Trust the classics. Are the books you loved as a child now on video? Many probably are. Look for live-action fairy tales from Shelley Duvall **(Faerie Tale Theater)** and animated nursery rhymes and fairy tales from a score of companies, as well as adaptations of works by Maurice Sendak, Dr. Seuss, Rudyard Kipling, Beverly Cleary, and many other notable authors. Enhance the viewing experience with a trip to the library; books and videos naturally complement each other, as do videos and music. The best video doesn't have to be new; educate your kids as they grow old enough to appreciate the joys of black-and-white classics.

6. Learn a few industry names, and don't be afraid to try something new. Become familiar with dependable producers such as Jim Henson (although he's passed away, his family is continuing his tradition of providing engaging programs for children through Henson Associates, known as HA!) and Rock Demers, companies like CC Studios and Rabbit Ears, entertainers like Shari Lewis and Rory, authors like Leo Lionni and the Berenstains. Don't settle for fool's gold—programming that's shown on TV. Find something that hasn't been shown before.

7. Find alternative sources for videos. Not every video store has the room to stock every good children's title, although most video store owners will gladly special-order a certain title for you. Investigate bookstores, specialty children's stores, educational stores, even catalogues for the best product. (For a selection of sources, see Resources.)

8. Look for added value. Many of today's video stars are also singers or authors. Extend the video experience beyond the TV medium to companion books, audiocassettes or CDs, and coloring books by choosing tapes that either are packaged with these little extras or mention their availability on the box. Within a few years, plenty of video suppliers will also have augmented their product lines with CD-ROMs.

9. Be on the lookout for new and different video solutions. You don't feed growing children a steady diet of peanut butter and jelly sandwiches at every meal, so why let them watch the same old things on video? Be adventurous in using the above guidelines. Yes, there are bound to be a few lead balloons, but remember your joy when you first watched **The Red Balloon.**

10. Learn how to use and program your VCR so that you and your children can enjoy the best programming whenever you wish, not just when it's broadcast.

Using Video Wisely

If you'd like to learn how to use video in a constructive manner, here are a few resources, some of which you'll find in the appendixes in this book as well:

The American Library Association has produced a 35-minute videotape entitled *Choosing the Best in Children's Video*. Host Christopher Reeve (of the **Superman** films) lets parents and children ask questions and provide their own solutions to finding good, entertaining videos. In addition to clips from award-winning programs, the video offers a list of recommended programs categorized by age and genre. If your local library does not have a copy, send $1 to the ALA, 50 East Huron, Chicago, IL 60611. (At press time, another version of this parenting aid was being re-edited by the Coalition for Quality Children's Videos.)

The International Reading Association offers the free guide *You Can Use Television to Stimulate Your Child's Reading Habits,* which demonstrates the beneficial connection between books and video materials. Its guidelines easily translate to the video experience. Their address is 800 Barksdale Road, P.O. Box 8139, Newark, DE 19714; 302-731-1600.

Kidsnet is a not-for-profit electronic clearinghouse used by teachers, librarians, and parents to cross-reference video and audiotapes and TV and radio programming for media-structured learning experiences. Parents can tap into its on-line services via computer. They can be reached at 6856 Eastern Avenue, NW, Suite 208, Washington, DC 20012; 202-291-1400.

The National Education Association offers a free pamphlet called *Family Viewing: An NEA Guide to Watching TV with Your Children.* Tips on using TV to your advantage transfer easily to the home video experience. Contact NEA at 1201 16th Street NW, Washington, DC 20036; 202-833-4000.

Chapter 1

■

FEATURE FILMS

Included here are not only such live-action theatricals as **Cheetah,** but also **Anne of Green Gables,** the **Tales for All** gems from Rock Demers, and other programming that encompasses comedy, drama, sci-fi, adventure, and biography.

All films in this chapter run longer than 60 minutes and are rated G (General Audience, suitable for all ages) by the Motion Picture Association of America unless otherwise noted. Where "rental" is indicated, tapes were priced above $29.95 at press time; otherwise, all titles are available at prices lower than $29.95. Age ranges are given to be used as guidelines only; the information included here should help you to judge best what types of programs and content are suitable for your child.

Peggy Charren of ACT suggests that parents take advantage of the variety of programming offered on video, instead of simply being dissatisfied with what's available just on TV.

As founder and president of Action for Children's Television (ACT), the organization that for more than twenty years lobbied for quality programming for children first on TV and later on home video, Peggy Charren has become renowned as the foremost caretaker of children's media interests. When she closed ACT at the end of 1992, citing the completion of its goal to advance the quality of children's programming with the passage of the Children's Television Act, those of us with our hearts in this industry felt a great loss. Who will watch out for children's best interests in broadcast and home video viewing in Charren's absence?

"Parents," Charren replies emphatically, noting that there are two ways parents can ensure their children watch the best on TV and video: First, police the airwaves, and second, monitor your child's viewing.

"The most important element of the [Children's Television] act is the language that requires every television station to provide some programs *specifically designed to meet the education and information needs of children*—or else risk losing their license. The law won't work unless the public lets the stations know they understand this new obligation; unless parents tell networks, and by extension, video stores, you're here, you're educated, and you want the choice. The law requires stations to include information on what they're doing for kids in a public file, and the public has the right to inquire of each station what they're doing for kids."

As for monitoring your children's viewing diets, "The only appropriate form of censorship occurs in the home, when the parent uses the off button to turn off a terrible program," Charren instructs. "We all have to be more conscientious than we were twenty years ago; there's a wider choice and more technology available. *ACT was always pro-choice in programming. And the VCR has made choice the name of the game. A VCR is the most important adjunct to TV that you can buy.* What's special about so many videos is that video is the only medium they're available on."

Charren advocates learning how to program your VCR so you can censor *in* the good stuff. (Since there are so many different VCRs on the market, we'll leave that step up to you; just don't throw out the instructions to your machine!) "Video is a terrific option for families who are fed up with broadcast choices and the overcommercialization of children's media. ACT took a videocassette approach to children's TV: We suggest that parents tape what they love from public and cable TV." She also suggests considering the VCR-Plus or similar programming options, or even a lock box, to exert more control over what TV brings into your home.

How would she draft a "A Video Bill of Rights for Children"? It should begin, Charren recommends, with the understanding that "children are vulnerable human beings." She asserts there are two basic tenets to children's rights regarding video:

1. *"Children have a right to commercial-free programs; it's their right not to be manipulated."* Video enables parents to shelter young viewers from commercial manipulation (including that which airs during cable-delivered programs in schools, she reminds us). Char-

ren has always advocated fairness, and TV creates an unfair environment of "buy this, gotta have it," ignoring the fact that some families may not be able to afford what they see. Keep advertising off videos, she asserts.

2. *"Children have a right to choice and diversity. That puts an obligation on producers to create better programs."* The fact that many producers have reduced the amount of violence or foul language in certain programs does not mean that they have improved the content.

There won't be any silencing the vocal Peggy Charren until the final credits roll. Without ACT, she's now become a children's media consultant and is hoping that her efforts will net for children's electronic media (video, audio, multimedia, and computer software) the same level of attention that it bestowed upon children's books. To that end, she remains active on the National Board of Directors for the Coalition for Quality Children's Video.

"The coalition is the essence of what should be happening with children's video, and I see their collection as a way to get the message out to parents that there's life after killer tomatoes. Here's a group of people who care about terrific video and who have organized to do something about it. The names of much of the terrific stuff are not familiar to parents or kids; commonplace video reinforces what's on TV. By organizing to focus on the kinds of programs that are not on TV and to help make those available where video is bought and sold, the coalition has found a beautiful way to begin." (Check out the interview with Ranny Levy, Director of the Coalition, in Chapter 5: Sports, Safety, Health, and Fitness.)

Used intelligently, video can lead children to books, Charren adds, and what better place to find these videos than your local library? Many of the videos listed in this book will be found not in the local video rental store, but in libraries or through special-interest catalogues. "Our library system is the envy of many countries," Charren states. "We should make sure every family has access to what's available in home video by getting libraries to stock terrific video, free for the borrowing."

Charren's influence will stretch on. She promises to ensure that "the organizations ACT has handed the torch to will get to the finish line by using the Children's Television Act of 1990 to make things better on TV."

The Adventures of Baron Munchausen (Columbia TriStar, 1989, 125 m., PG, 8–up, rental; director Terry Gilliam, stars John Neville, Eric Idle, Sarah Polley, Robin Williams, Oliver Reed)

Terry Gilliam of Monty Python fame stretches his imagination further in this fabulous adventure surrounding the legendary eighteenth-century storyteller. Known for his bizarre special effects, Gilliam treats viewers to eye candy worth savoring, though there are a few slow parts. Let young viewers exercise their imagination by trying to top this madcap adventurer's tall tales. Check out the animated version, **The Fabulous Adventures of Baron Munchausen,** in the Animated Films chapter. See also Gilliam's **Time Bandits** in this chapter.

The Adventures of Milo & Otis (Columbia TriStar, 1989, 76 m., G, 4–up)

Dudley Moore's lively narration keeps this one-trick pony trotting squarely along. Although there's not much of a plot, that fact won't deter young viewers as they revel in the adorable antics of a pug dog and a tabby cat who wander from their farm into what is for them the great unknown. Some wise parents have used the video as an analogy to teach children who are beginning to explore the world beyond their front doors that although they are young, they can partake in wonderful adventures. There are a few moments of danger, but there is very little nightmare material in this innocuous cross-country trip. For similar titles, look up **The Incredible Journey** and **Homeward Bound: The Incredible Journey** in this chapter.

The Adventures of Robin Hood (MGM/UA, 1938, 102 m., 8–up; directors Michael Curtiz, William Keighley, stars Errol Flynn, Olivia de Havilland, Basil Rathbone, Claude Rains, Alan Hale)

Errol Flynn has so much fun in this film, described by Leonard Maltin as "the definitive swashbuckler," that it's an infectious experience for the entire audience, regardless of age. If it piques a child's curiosity about history, archery, or medieval times, so much the better. Compare it with the updated, less critically successful 1991 version with Kevin Costner and the wonderfully comic Alan Rickman, **Robin Hood: Prince of Thieves.** Families who want more medieval adventure may look up another great swashbuckler, **The Black Arrow** (reviewed later in this chapter).

The Adventures of Tom Sawyer (Fox Video, 1938, 77 m., 6–up; director Norman Taurog, stars Tommy Kelly, Jackie Moran, Ann Gillis, Walter Brennan, Victor Jory)

Huck Finn, Disney's 1992 film of Mark Twain's Mississippi tales, could not compete with this David O. Selznick–produced, slapstick-silly version of Twain's classic novel. Victor Jory's portrayal of Injun Joe is the epitome of a screen villain, particularly memorable in the cave scenes. Have Twain's book on hand for an interesting comparison.

Amadeus (HBO, 1984, 158 m., PG, 10–up; director Milos Forman, stars F. Murray Abraham, Tom Hulce, Elizabeth Berridge, Simon Callow)

This eight-time Oscar winner portrays one mediocre composer's jealousy of the genius that was Mozart. Antonio Salieri, Vienna's conservative court composer, is threatened by the arrival of the talented young upstart Wolfgang Amadeus Mozart, who seems to compose almost without effort, and to live a dangerously decadent lifestyle, seemingly without respect for anyone or anything. At two and a half hours long, it's a bit much for very young children to sit through, but it shouldn't be too difficult for children over ten to stick with: The plot is intelligently wrought, the music is fantastic, the cinematography and sets are beautiful (it was shot in Prague), and the lesson it teaches in the downfalls caused by pride and envy is well worth the wait. For those to whom sex is a tricky issue, be forewarned that Mozart dallies with women a bit openly. For something similar from a child's perspective, check out **Beethoven Lives Upstairs** in Chapter 3: Musical Fun.

And You Thought Your Parents Were Weird (Vidmark Entertainment, 1991, 92 m., PG, 10–up, rental; director Tony Cookson, stars Marcia Strassman, Alan Thicke)

A little poignant, a little silly, but basically harmless fun. After their father passes away, two young boys discover his ghost has taken up otherwordly residence in a robot they've built. Stars Strassman and Thicke give it a game shot, and there's plenty of off-the-wall humor, but the very thought of losing one's father may be too painful for some children.

Anne of Green Gables (Disney, 1985, 195 m./2 cassettes, 6–up) and **Anne of Avonlea** (Disney, 1987, 195 m./2 cassettes, 6–up)

Both made-for-Canadian-TV miniseries star Megan Follows and Colleen Dewhurst, with Richard Farnsworth as the bachelor farmer who adopts the orphan Anne Shirley, featured in the first volume. Both are set on idyllic Prince Edward Island in the early 1900s. The first installment follows teenaged Anne as she adapts to life on the farm, with Dewhurst her strict taskmaster and Farnsworth her rather smitten guardian. The second volume picks up with Anne at 18 becoming a teacher in the school at Avonlea and learning the ways of love. Fans of Lucy Maud Montgomery's books will thrill to these beautiful adaptations of her work. And for anyone who doubts that a successful sequel can be made, here's proof from director Kevin Sullivan. The admirable series currently running on the Disney Channel features weaker characters and at times stretches the plots into sitcom territory, straying from the feel of Montgomery's books.

Baby . . . Secret of the Lost Legend (Disney, 1985, 95 m., PG, 6–up; director Bill Norton, stars William Katt, Sean Young, Patrick Mc-Goohan, Julian Fellowes)

For those who are still too squeamish or impressionable for **Jurassic Park**, here's a fantasy about the discovery of a family of brontosaurs alive in Africa. There's more than enough violence in here to warrant the PG rating, so parents of children under 6 may want to screen the video first before deciding whether it's appropriate for their children. Parents should also be aware of some overt sexism and racism that bring the quality of the film down a notch. Another children's dinosaur fantasy is **Prehysteria,** reviewed later in this chapter.

Bach and Broccoli (Family Home Entertainment, 1986, 90 m., 7–12)

When Fanny, a young orphan, moves in with her bachelor uncle, a concert pianist, she wreaks havoc with his lifestyle, yet adds a missing dimension to his life. But wait till he gets a load of her pet (descented, of course) skunk! Fanny is the keystone in this production, from the opening scenes in which she symbolically waves goodbye to her deceased parents, to the triumphant ending, in which she makes a lasting impression not only on her staid uncle but also on the boys who are her friends. Poignant and touching, the film was created by French-Canadian producer Rock Demers, who attempts in his **Tales for All** series to address the needs and feelings of "tweeners," those children in between the ages of 7 and 12. Other titles in the **Tales for All** series, some of which are reviewed here, that are available on video are **The Dog Who Stopped the War, Tommy Tricker and the Stamp Traveler** (both reviewed here), and **The Peanut Butter Solution.**

Back to the Future (MCA/Universal, 1985, 116 m., PG, 6–up; director Robert Zemeckis, stars Michael J. Fox, Christopher Lloyd, Lea Thompson, Crispin Glover, Thomas F. Wilson)

This trilogy of teen sci-fi adventures is a bit violent, yet it's also fun and challenging in a far-fetched, wacky way, especially the first and third installments. The original installment of the three-part adventure begins slowly but picks up speed once young, 1980s average teen Marty McFly warps back to his parents' teenaged years. While in the 1950s, he must make certain he does nothing to disrupt his parents' falling in love, or he'll fade right out of existence. A spectacular finale, lots of special effects, and great performances, especially from Christopher Lloyd as the "mad" scientist, add up to fun family entertainment.

Back to the Future, Part II (MCA/Universal, 1989, 107 m., PG, 8–up; director Robert Zemeckis, stars Michael J. Fox, Christopher Lloyd, Lea Thompson, Thomas F. Wilson, Harry Waters, Jr.)

With more than its share of dark visions of the future, this second installment in Steven Spielberg's three-part sci-fi adventure falls short of most audiences' expectations. It's violent, frightening, and humorless in parts, and becomes a challenge to follow at the end, where parallel universes are created. How bleak is the future? Bad guy Biff is now a powerful casino owner who's virtually enslaved and degraded Marty McFly's parents. Aside from the depressing scenario, it's really not unacceptable entertainment, but be prepared for the teaser ending that strands Christopher Lloyd in time, setting up **Part III.** We've enjoyed this installment more when combined in a double feature with the more lighthearted **Part III.**

Back to the Future, Part III (MCA/Universal, 1990, 118 m., PG, 6–up; director Robert Zemeckis, stars Michael J. Fox, Christopher Lloyd, Lea Thompson, Thomas F. Wilson, Mary Steenburgen)

The series returns to its powerful, frenetic comedy roots and goes way beyond the unbelievable at the film's "uplifting," corny conclusion. Stranded in the Old West of 1885, Doc finds himself looking over his shoulder for a bad guy, as well as for Marty's arrival—and what an entrance he finally makes in the DeLorean! Together, the pair vanquish the bad guys and change history for the better, and Doc even finds himself involved with an intelligent, forward-thinking woman. Loads of outlandish fun, this is a treat not to be missed by anyone looking for clever, far-fetched entertainment.

The Bear (Columbia TriStar, 1991, 93 m., PG, 6–up, rental; director Jean-Jacques Annaud, stars Jack Wallace, Tcheky Karyo, Andre Lacombe)

Wordlessly, this film tells the tale of a bear's adventurous life, from the incident that orphaned him through his ascension to a royal role in wilderness life. Wonderful cinematography and scenes that may evoke a desire to travel to the wilds of the American West strengthen the production. Because there is no narrative in this selection, parents may want to watch along with their children to help explain situations and challenge young viewers with thought-provoking questions. Inspiration for the film came from the early-twentieth-century book *The Grizzly King,* by James Oliver Curwood.

Bingo (Columbia TriStar, 1991, 90 m., PG, 8–up, rental; director Matthew Robbins, stars David Rasche, Cindy Williams)

What happens when a highly intelligent circus dog is misunderstood by his insensitive trainer? He runs away from the circus to join a family. Irreverent and smart-alecky, this film will appeal to boys and girls who are troubled by a sense of not fitting in or not belonging to a group, and it shows that one good friend is sometimes far better than a group of acquaintances with ulterior motives. No award winner, this somewhat mediocre film delivers a decent message in an offbeat way.

The Black Arrow (Columbia TriStar, 1948, 76 m., b&w, 8–up, rental; director Gordon Douglas, stars Louis Hayward, Janet Blair, George Macready, Edgar Cavanaugh)

Another great swashbuckler for fans of the genre, and of extravagant filmmaking, 1940s-style. It's hero against villain in medieval England, where knights compete for the honor of their kings and the hands of beautiful maidens. Mysterious black arrows point to clues to the murder of a crusader's father. The jousting tournament at the finale is a classic scene; make certain you don't fall off the edge of your seat!

The Black Stallion (CBS/Fox Video, 1979, 118 m., G, 6–up; director Carroll Ballard, stars Mickey Rooney, Kelly Reno, Teri Garr, Hoyt Axton)

Just for the celebration of the bond between a child and his found horse, and the dance they revel in on a tropical island beach, every family should watch this video. Only a theater's large screen can do the proper justice to the cinematography, but enough of the theatrical proportions remain to make video viewing pleasant. The story, based on Walter Farley's book of the same name, revolves around Alec, a preteen boy whose adventures begin when the ship he's traveling on sinks, and only he and a horse survive. The two befriend one another on a deserted island, and once rescued, the boy decides to race "the Black." Okay, the horse race is corny and contrived, but it provides the necessary excitement for the denouement of the film. The youngest of viewers may be troubled by the frightening, fiery ship-sinking scene, the horse entangled in ropes, and a boy—who also loses his father in the disaster—fighting against drowning. Rooney is the only link between this tale and the series aired on the Family Channel. This fabulous adventure was followed by the not-so-exciting **The Black Stallion Returns** (Paramount, 1983, 103 m., PG, 6–up; director Robert Dalva, stars Kelly Reno, Teri Garr, Vincent Spano, Woody Strode, Allen Goorwitz), in which Alec has pursued the native chieftains who've stolen his horse to Arabia. Fans of the first film will want to sample this, but should not expect to marvel at anything other than beautiful settings and well-trained horses.

The Boy Who Could Fly (Warner/Lorimar, 1986, 114 m., PG, 8–up; director Nick Castle, stars Jay Underwood, Lucy Deakins, Bonnie Bedelia, Fred Savage, Fred Gwynne, Colleen Dewhurst)

A woman who recently lost her husband relocates with her son and daughter to a small town, where neighborhood bullies torment the son (Savage), and next door there's an orphan boy who sits out on the roof, pretending to fly. The sensitive young girl, who has difficulty fitting in with her classmates, befriends the "flying" boy, who she discovers is autistic but really *can* fly. It's that supernatural capability that gets the boy—and, in a way, the film—in hot water, because it weakens otherwise strong performances and the film's credibility. Still, it's a terrific story about interdependence, the building of relationships, and asserting your own persona, regardless of peers' or anyone else's preconceived ideas.

Boyz N the Hood (Columbia TriStar, 1991, 107 m., R, 12–up; director John Singleton, stars Laurence Fishburne, Ice Cube, Cuba Gooding Jr., Nia Long, Morris Chestnut)

Kids who think violence is funny and a gun is power should watch what violence does to this promising group of teenagers in riot-ripped and violence-torn Los Angeles. It's a powerful, thoughtful examination of the inner-city life of African-Americans, their hopes, dreams, and daily lives—though admittedly, it's not for all tastes. A divorced mother and father try to imprint their teenage son with positive values that will help him rise beyond the wasted lives some of his friends succumbed to so easily. He tries to keep his feet firmly planted in reality, even among the senseless murders, drive-by shootings, and sirens that daily disrupt their lives. The film contains a lot of violence, much of it graphic, but parents who need to make a point can watch and discuss with their children the ignorance and senselessness portrayed here.

Breaking Away (CBS/Fox Video, 1979, 101 m., PG, 12–up; director Peter Yates, stars Dennis Christopher, Daniel Stern, Dennis Quaid, Jackie Earle Haley, Barbara Barrie)

During the summer following their high school graduation, four friends contemplate what to do with their lives, considering their working-class existences in sharp contrast to the university students invading their town (Bloomington, Indiana). One ponders becoming the average local blue-collar man with a family; a high school quarterback faces his lack of prospects after not winning the scholarship he expected; an unwittingly intelligent boy, whose abusive father has damaged his psyche, begins to rediscover himself. The fourth is so enamored of bicycle racing that, in honor of his favorite team, the Italians, he speaks Italian and eats only Italian food. The foursome are loyal to one another and exhibit positive, supportive qualities, so viewers will recognize that whatever they choose to do with their lives, these will be honorable young men. Together, they pin their hopes on a bike race for locals, in which they seem unevenly matched against privileged college frat boys; their efforts and team attitude pay off. The screenplay won an Academy Award.

Cloak and Dagger (MCA/Universal, 1984, 101 m., PG, 7–12; director Richard Franklin, stars Henry Thomas, Dabney Coleman, Michael Murphy, John McIntire, Jeanette Nolan)
When an imaginative youngster becomes embroiled in a real-life espionage scheme, complete with a murder, will his imaginary hero, Jack Flash, come to the rescue? No one but Flash believes the boy's story, since he's known for his overactive imagination. Interestingly, the boy creates a fictitious hero who's an uncanny duplicate of his father (Coleman is great in both roles). For a similar story, check out **The Window** (Turner Home Entertainment, 1949, 73 m., 8–up; director Ted Tetzlaff, stars Bobby Driscoll, Barbara Hale, Arthur Kennedy), in which a boy witnesses a murder but no one believes him.

Close Encounters of the Third Kind (Columbia TriStar, 1977, 132 m., PG, 8–up; director Steven Spielberg, stars Richard Dreyfuss, Teri Garr, François Truffaut, Melinda Dillon)
Steven Spielberg proved his ability to captivate families with this wonderful fantasy, a precursor to his next film about aliens, **E.T.**, (reviewed later in this chapter). Unlike the sci-fi horror stories of the 1950s, this film portrays the aliens not as threatening monster invaders but as childlike, supremely intelligent beings who want to learn from us, teach us, and share with us. And, if the analogy could be adapted to real life, viewers might infer that not all that's unfamiliar is necessarily bad, evil, or untrustworthy; such encounters

can be the beginning of expanded relationships, deeper learning, a higher consciousness. Yes, there are several scary parts, but as a whole, this is superb, uplifting entertainment suitable for almost the entire family.

Dances with Wolves (Orion, 1990, 181 m., PG-13, 10–up; director Kevin Costner, stars Kevin Costner, Mary McDonnell, Graham Greene, Rodney A. Grant)

Long but luscious, this old-fashioned western with a 1990s twist follows the life of a man who turns his back on one culture in favor of another, simpler one. A cavalry officer assigned to a remote out-post on the uninhabited plains following the Civil War develops a special relationship with a tribe of Native Americans, who, at first reluctantly, teach him their ways. In their village, he meets and falls in love with a white woman who has been raised by the clan and has nearly forgotten her origins. His immersion in Native American culture opens his eyes to the often wasteful, cruel, and greedy white world, and he chooses to abandon his post and flee as the tribe is hunted down by his former colleagues in the cavalry. Heartbreaking and tear-jerking at times, this film also helped open doors in Hollywood for Native American actors and crew. Its celebration of Native American life and careful attention to period details make the entertainment part history and social studies lesson, part civil rights primer. Parents may want to watch this with their children, as much for a discussion of intolerance and/or civil rights as for the exceptional piece of filmmaking it is. It captured seven Oscars, including Best Picture. For more on Native American life and culture, look up **Island of the Blue Dolphins** in this chapter, and in Chapter 7, **Squanto and the First Thanksgiving** and **Princess Scargo and the Birthday Pumpkin.**

The Dog Who Stopped the War (HBO, 1984, 91 m., 8–13, rental; director Andre Melancon, stars Cedric Jourde, Maripierre A. D'Amour, Julien Elie; dubbed)

From the magical French-Canadian producer Rock Demers comes this antiwar statement featuring children on their winter holiday. The kids decide to occupy themselves with war games, but after establishing rules and lobbing the first snowballs, the group discovers the painful realities of innocent victims, property damage, personal injury, and strained relations. The film is the first in the

Tales for All series Demers created to address that often misunderstood and ill-addressed group called "tweeners"—ages 7–12 (see **Bach and Broccoli** in this chapter). Don't be put off by the dubbing; it didn't matter to my young previewers, and the story holds up beautifully.

The Electric Grandmother (LCA/New World, 1982, 50 m., 8–12; director Noel Black, stars Maureen Stapleton, Edward Herrmann, Robert MacNaughton)

Excellent little films like this gem find a following regardless of when they were produced, what language they're shot in, or who stars in them. The premise here is fascinating: Satisfaction-guaranteed robot grandmoms who do it all for their families, much like Mary Poppins. Maureen Stapleton is dropped by helicopter into a family of three children who've recently lost their mother. She turns the most mundane tasks into magical moments: pouring hot cocoa from her finger, hanging wash out to dry from the tail of a kite. Her efforts at being available for the children, who come to trust this robot replacement for her comfort, judgment, and kindness, win her the family's respect and turn withdrawn, depressed "robot" children once again into loving, feeling, real kids.

E.T. The Extra-Terrestrial (MCA/Universal, 1982, 115 m., PG, 6–up; director Steven Spielberg, stars Henry Thomas, Dee Wallace, Drew Barrymore, Peter Coyote, Robert MacNaughton)

This classic friendly-alien scenario builds on Spielberg's previous masterwork, **Close Encounters of the Third Kind.** Children, particularly one fatherless boy, Elliot, befriend a squat, alien horticulturist who's mistakenly left behind when his ship must leave Earth in a hurry. Children are portrayed as the heroes here, courageously protecting their alien friend; they learn from him, and in return show him the very best of the human spirit. As a film, **E.T.** touches all the right heartstrings, just as E.T. himself cannot hide his "heartlight." It's a tremendous tearjerker, too, and parents of children who still fear being left alone may want to wait another year before sharing this lovely film with them. It won three Oscars—for musical score, sound, and special effects.

The Ewok Adventure (MGM/UA, 1984, 100 m., 5–10; director John Korty, stars Eric Walker, Warwick Davis, Fionnula Flanagan, Guy Boyd, narrator Burl Ives) and **Ewoks: The Battle for Endor** (MGM/UA, 1985, 100 m., 6–12; directors Jim and Ken Wheat, stars Wilford Brimley, Warwick Davis, Aubree Miller, Sian Phillips)

Two TV movies were made based on the wonderful furry creatures that made their debut in **Return of the Jedi,** the third film in the **Star Wars** trilogy. In the first adventure, the Ewoks help two little space travelers in their search for their missing parents. In the sequel, a hermit and a girl help the tribe defend their planet from invasion by dark forces by tracking down an evil sorceress. Though far from the epic adventure of the **Star Wars** trilogy, both Ewok films contain the same types of technical magic and good-versus-evil fairy-tale contests that made the **Star Wars** films so popular. They're suitable alternatives for children who aren't quite ready for the intergalactic firepower of the **Star Wars** trilogy.

Flight of the Navigator (Disney, 1986, 90 m., PG, 8–up; director Randal Kleiser, stars Joey Cramer, Veronica Cartwright, Cliff De Young, Sarah Jessica Parker, Howard Hesseman, voice of Paul Reubens, a.k.a. Pee Wee Herman)

Talk about an evergreen adventure! Children have made this one of the best-renting tapes of all time. After a potentially frightening (for the littlest viewers) opening (a child falls and is knocked unconscious and wakes up to find his family no longer lives in his home), the film becomes a mystery about what happened to a boy who was missing for eight years, yet did not age. Seems an alien craft abducted him, and another one is still on Earth, waiting for him to fly it back to its own planet. The voice of the ship's on-board computer, which puts a real comic spin on the second half of the film, is supplied by Reubens.

Free Willy (Warner, 1993, 112 m., PG, 8–up; director Simon Wincer, stars Jason James Richter, Jayne Atkinson, Michael Madsen, August Schellenberg, Lori Petty)

In one of the better family films of recent years, the "boy and his pet" theme takes on a new relevance when the animal in question is a performing whale in an aquatic circus. It is inspiring to see such a determined youngster, a role model for other children, succeed in spite of adult doubts, concerns, and practicalities. A viewer would have to be empty-hearted not to thrill at the dramatic conclusion. In this era of sensitivity to the environment and living things, this film touches a nerve in all of us, and the video company plucks that nerve with its inclusion of the 800-4-WHALES charity, the Earth Island Institute, in a public service announcement at the tape's opening.

George's Island (New Line, 1991, 89 m., rental, PG for mild profanity, implied violence, depiction of an alcoholic, 8–up with discretion)

Pirates, treasure, and ghost stories make for a wonderful, sometimes spooky tale from the National Film Board of Canada. It's a family film that upholds family bonds, stresses how deceiving appearances can be, and debunks outdated, insensitive authority figures. This fantasy revolves around the legend of Captain Kidd and his treasure, believed to be buried on an island off Halifax, Nova Scotia, and 10-year-old orphan George, who lives with his crusty old seafaring grandfather, a disabled drunk. George's teacher has designs to remove him from his grandfather's questionable influence, but the grandfather proves too feisty a match for her, and an attempt at relocating George to a foster home is foiled. Meanwhile, George fantasizes about finding the buried treasure and creating a more comfortable life for his grandfather. A less exciting middle section, which deals more with relationships and less with pirates, is sandwiched between a fantastic opening, set in 1733, at the burial of the treasure, and a lively denouement. Encourage young viewers to bear with the middle; they'll be rewarded, just as young George was.

Goonies (Warner, 1985, 111 m., PG, 8–13; director Richard Donner, stars Sean Astin, Josh Brolin, Corey Feldman, Jeff Cohen, Martha Plimpton, Ke Huy Quan)

Wild, wacky, and at times genuinely irritating (though admittedly more to adults than to children), this pirate adventure follows a group of kids whose homes are slated for demolition as they pursue an adventure with a treasure map on their last weekend together. Since it's a Steven Spielberg production, it carries some of his signature marks: homage to past adventures, wild rides, and stunts, a la the Indiana Jones trilogy. For another pirate tale with a supernatural twist, check out **Treasure** in this chapter.

Gremlins (Warner, 1984, 111 m., PG, 10–up; director Joe Dante, stars Zach Galligan, Phoebe Cates, Hoyt Axton, Frances Lee McCain, Judge Reinhold) and **Gremlins 2: The New Batch** (Warner Home Video, 1990, 106 m., PG-13, 10–up; director Joe Dante, stars Zach Galligan, Phoebe Cates, John Glover, Christopher Lee)

For a "family" film, the initial movie in this pair is pretty violent, so a parental pre-screening is recommended. When an inventor and collector of exotic pets gives his teenage son an adorable furry gremlin, he warns the boy not to get the animal wet or feed it after midnight. Gizmo is a terrific pet, but of course those warnings are violated, and the creature births legions of ugly, evil gremlins who wreak havoc on the town, torment little old ladies, set fires, and generally make life a mess—sort of like teenagers run amok. They get their due in the end (one meets his maker courtesy of a blender—eeuuuw!), but the town pays a high price. Young viewers might find the gore a bit much, while parents might feel there's too much dangerous behavior depicted here for impressionable, crea-tive young minds. And adults more than children may enjoy the high volume of film-buff in-jokes. In the sequel, Gizmo spawns a new litter of little monsters, who terrorize New York. This installment is a bit less violent, spending more time spoofing itself and the genre, yet it still warranted a PG-13 rating. Keep the VCR rolling at the film's close; the action and gags don't stop until *after* the credits.

Hamlet (Warner, 1990, 135 m., PG, 10–up, rental; director Franco Zeffirelli, stars Mel Gibson, Glenn Close, Alan Bates, Paul Scofield, Ian Holm, Helena Bonham-Carter)

Shakespeare was never so accessible as in this adaptation. For any child aspiring to the stage or interested in Shakespeare or Eliz-abethan England, and for parents who'd like to introduce their chil-dren to culture without the shock, handsome Mel Gibson makes it easy. A reading of the play before or after viewing the film may help clarify the language and multiple meanings, especially for those who are new to or unfamiliar with Shakespeare. And for serious students and film aficionados, try the epitome of all **Hamlet** interpretations: the four-time Oscar-winning 1948 version, directed by and starring Sir Laurence Olivier. If it's romance your preteens are hungry for, set them upon the most romantic of Shakespeare's filmed plays, Franco Zeffirelli's **Romeo and Juliet.**

Heidi (Fox Video, 1937, 88 m., 5–up, b&w; also available colorized; director Allan Dwan, stars Shirley Temple, Jean Hersholt, Arthur Treacher, Helen Westley) and **Heidi** (GoodTimes, 1968, 120 m., 5–up; director Delbert Mann, stars Maximilian Schell, Jean Simmons, Michael Redgrave, Walter Slezak, Jennifer Edwards)

Of three live-action versions of Johanna Spyri's classic available on video at press time, these are the best, with the Shirley Temple version the more memorable. The classic story celebrates Heidi's infectious optimism, which changes the people she encounters, beginning with her coldhearted grandfather. When she joins him in his isolated mountain house high in the Alps, he doesn't even speak to the people in town, much less to his new charge. By the time her mean aunt claims Heidi and packs her off to become the invalid Clara's companion, grandfather's icy attitude has melted. The two miss each other desperately and are eventually reunited. Tearjerker material is abundant, but like Heidi herself, each film is wonderfully uplifting. In the second entry here, the script by Earl Hamner (who created *The Waltons* for TV) elevates the 1968 TV production beyond the realm of the average TV movie. It's a classy production, and its full color will appeal to those who don't easily cotton to black-and-white films.

Homeward Bound: The Incredible Journey (Disney, 1993, 84 m., G, 6–up; stars Robert Hayes, Kim Greist, voices of Don Ameche, Sally Field, Michael J. Fox)

A dog's loyalty to its young master has been sung in many films, but not in such a current fashion. Thirty years after the original was made, another trio of pets find themselves trekking across the Western United States to find their owners. It takes all their energy to avoid becoming anyone else's meal and evade the perils of the wilderness, but through love, companionship, and teamwork, they succeed. Viewers might be less inclined to treat pets just as possessions after watching this adventure. Also check out the original, **The Incredible Journey,** in which two dogs and a cat follow their family of humans across the Canadian wilderness.

Honey, I Shrunk the Kids (Disney, 1989, 93 m., PG, 6–up; director Joe Johnston, stars Rick Moranis, Marcia Strassman, Kristine Sutherland, Matt Frewer, Thomas Brown, Jared Rushton, Amy O'Neil, Robert Oliveri)

Crazy, klutzy inventor Rick Moranis unwittingly lets his children become the guinea pigs in his latest experiment, when they accidentally trigger a device that shrinks them to roughly the size of a pinhead. Although they find themselves only in their backyard, it's a hostile place when you're smaller than an ant (sprinklers are like being *in* Niagara Falls, and the lawnmower—Help!), and they seem to have little hope of ever being found. Dad's doing his best, but it takes the family dog to bring them in, and they're finally restored to the proper size. What makes this entry outshine its sequel is the fact that the kids must use their ingenuity to survive and return to the house, putting them in a powerful position and giving young viewers some creative role models to emulate. In the sequel, **Honey, I Blew Up the Kid** (Disney, 1992, 89 m., PG, 6–up; director Joe Johnston, stars Rick Moranis, Marcia Strassman, Lloyd Bridges), our intrepid inventor has created a machine that causes things to expand in size, and of course, his youngest son strays into the beam. Unforgettable segments include contemplation of changing that diaper, which could blanket all of Rhode Island, and Junior traipsing happily amid the neon lights of Las Vegas, unaware of the havoc he's creating down below. With more emphasis on adults and less on children (except the baby, who, once he's zapped, upstages everyone), this sequel is not as strong as its predecessor.

Hook (Columbia TriStar, 1991, 142 m., PG, 4–up; director Steven Spielberg, stars Robin Williams, Dustin Hoffman, Julia Roberts, Maggie Smith, Bob Hoskins)

Did Peter Pan ever grow up? It's easy to imagine that if he did, he might be embodied in the manic comic Robin Williams. In this version, Peter has grown up to become an ultrasuccessful businessman with barely enough time for himself, let alone his family. Captain Hook remedies that by kidnapping his two children, and Wendy Darling, now quite elderly, convinces Peter that he must fly with Tinkerbell to Neverland to rescue them and vanquish Hook. The Lost Boys (updated with skateboards and Rollerblades) reawaken Peter's memory, imagination, and courage, and team with him to carry out the quest. Children under 6 may be distressed by the evil Hook and the death of a main character; otherwise, the fact that this is fantasy is never far from mind. Lavish sets and costumes, unexpected twists, drama in a magic setting: Spielberg uses it all to make believers out of a willingly captive audience.

Hoosiers (LIVE/Vestron, 1986, 114 m., PG, 11–up; director David Anspaugh, stars Gene Hackman, Barbara Hershey, Dennis Hopper, Sheb Wooley, Fern Parsons)

In rural Indiana in the early 1950s, a down-on-his-luck former basketball coach is given one last chance to coach by an old friend, the principal of a tiny school out in the boondocks. Through hard work, he develops a team for which there weren't enough players at first, then carries them to the state championships, redeeming himself in the bargain. Fairly predictable, it pushes all the right buttons, yet the solid performance and all-American atmosphere keep it entertaining. The film does not hide the negative side of keeping the pressure on: Dennis Hopper's role as an alcoholic father/fan creates an issue that receives sensitive treatment. But the main focus is on the value of honest hard teamwork to realize dreams.

The House of Dies Drear (Public Media, 1990, 116 m., 8–up; director Alan Goldstein, stars Howard Rollins, Jr., Moses Gunn, Shavar Ross, Kadeem Hardison)

Part ghost story, part history lesson, this tale from the award-winning **WonderWorks** collection (see Chapter 4, Discovery and Learning, for a complete list) lets a pair of African-American children play detectives as they unravel the mystery of their new home, a historic Ohio house that seems to be haunted. It was once owned by a wealthy Dutch immigrant, Dies Drear, an abolitionist. There's some present-day rivalry between the house's caretaker and a family of oddballs who constantly tear up their property in search of Drear's map to his treasure. The new family stumbles upon clues leading to the treasure while learning more about local history, folklore, and the Underground Railroad. This film is worth a trip to the video store, and although a little spooky in parts, it should be entertaining and educational for any child 8 or over.

The Incredible Journey (Disney, 1963, 80 m., 6–up; director Fletcher Markle, stars Emile Genest, John Drainie, Tommy Tweed, Sandra Scott)

Anyone who loves animals will enjoy this adventure in which two dogs and a cat set off across Canada in search of their owners. There's danger from both nature and man, but narrator Rex Allen is quick to explain that everything will be fine. This classic, long unavailable on the home video market, inspired a 1993 remake, **Homeward Bound: The Incredible Journey** (also reviewed in this chapter).

Island of the Blue Dolphins (MCA/Universal, 1964, 93 m., 6–16; director James B. Clark, stars Celia Kaye, George Kennedy, Ann Daniel, Carlos Romero)

When an Indian girl is abandoned on an island, she develops a bond with the wild dogs that live there and finds ingenious ways to make her lot in life bearable, even fun. The story—a true one set in the early nineteenth century—is an engaging one and gives a girl the chance to shine in a rough situation, even though this production is not as top-notch as it could be. Suggest that kids look up the book by Scott O'Dell upon which this film was based, and don't be too harsh a judge; it certainly delivers a well-intentioned message about survival and meaningful coexistence with others.

The Karate Kid (Columbia TriStar, 1984, 126 m., R, 10–up; director John G. Avildsen, stars Noriyuki "Pat" Morita, Ralph Macchio, Elisabeth Shue, Martin Kove, Chad McQueen)

Arguably, this is the film that launched a thousand children into the martial arts, long before they'd heard of the Teenage Mutant Ninja Turtles. Take one thin, fatherless boy, a new school in a new city, and a tough bunch of kids, and you have the perfect recipe for lessons in karate and self-confidence. It's far better than its two successors, thanks mainly to the freshness and sincerity between Macchio and Morita. If your children are interested in learning more about the martial arts, check out the **Karate for Kids** series (see Chapter 5: Sports, Safety, Health, and Fitness).

Labyrinth (New Line/Columbia Tri-Star, 1986, 101 m., PG, 8–13; director Jim Henson, stars David Bowie, Jennifer Connelly, Toby Froud)

"Be careful what you wish for; your wish might come true" is the moral here. A girl's wish that the Goblin King kidnap her baby brother does come true, and only she can rescue him by completing a terrifyingly complex maze in the Goblin King's land. The Muppets that round out the cast often seem more intelligent than our young heroine, and at times the story does slow considerably, but it's a delightful fantasy movie to share with your children. Watch for the fascinating M. C. Escher–inspired scene. The screenplay of this *Alice in Wonderland*–like story was written by Terry Jones, a member of the Monty Python troupe, and the epic treatment comes courtesy of executive producer George Lucas.

Ladyhawke (Warner, 1985, 124 m., PG-13, 10–up; director Richard Donner, stars Matthew Broderick, Rutger Hauer, Michelle Pfeiffer, Leo McKern)

An evil curse binds and separates two lovers, one of whom turns into a hawk by day, while the other turns into a wolf by night, preventing them from ever being together as humans. The only way to break the spell is to kill its creator, and to accomplish the task, the lovers need a third person to assist. That's where the narrator, a teenaged thief, steps in to aid the knight/wolf. Stick with the story, although it's long, and you'll be rewarded with fine performances from Hauer and Pfeiffer, neither of whom were as well known in 1985 as they are today.

Lady in White (Video Treasures, 1988, 112 m., PG-13, 10–up; director Frank LaLoggia, stars Lukas Haas, Len Cariou, Katherine Helmond, Jason Presson, Jared Rushton)

Super supernatural adventure set in 1962 on Halloween. Haas, who's accidentally locked in the school coatroom, witnesses the restless spirit of a child reenact her own murder, complete with hints as to the identity of the killer. The ghost begs Haas to help justice be done so that her spirit can rest. Along the way, there are encounters with the mysterious Lady in White, as well as close calls with the killer. With some parental guidance, this is a wonderful substitute for more gory Halloween fare.

The Land of Faraway (Prism, 1987, 95 m., PG, 5–13, rental; director Vladimir Grammatikov, stars Timothy Bottoms, Susannah York, Christopher Lee, Nicholas Pickard, Christian Bale)

Although this fantasy opens in Stockholm, the actors have American accents, so the material, based on Astrid Lindgren's book *Mio, My Son*, is wonderfully accessible. Preteen orphan Mio, known as Bosse to the hardened aunt and uncle he lives with, runs away when he overhears his aunt complain that he is too much like his wicked father. When he rescues a magic spirit that was trapped in a bottle, Mio is transported to the Land of Faraway, where his father, who had disappeared from the real world, is enthroned as king. The rest of the action may not seem suitable for a youth as young and small as Mio: He has to battle evil knights, and his life is threatened at every turn. But he's not alone or unprepared, and with the help of a magic cape and a sword, he vanquishes the evil, saving his land and making the universe a safer place. It's a weighty quest for young Mio, but he rises to the occasion and may inspire young viewers to overcome seemingly impossible odds to do the same.

A League of Their Own (Columbia TriStar, 1992, 90 m., PG, 8–up; director Penny Marshall, stars Geena Davis, Lori Petty, Tom Hanks, Rosie O'Donnell, Madonna)

Just about anyone can enjoy this film, which combines a little history, a story of finding oneself, and a lot of great ball playing. During World War II, America didn't lose its passion for baseball when the men shipped out, so managers replaced battle-bound boys with talented women on the diamonds. The manager of the Georgia Peaches is a washed-up drunk, so one woman, a born leader (Davis), takes the reins and calls all the plays, surprising him out of his stupor. Although the women take the game seriously, the ball club owners know that sex sells, so they persuade the women to charm the crowds, wearing skirts on the field and blowing kisses to the fans. Regardless of their championship status and their newfound talents and desires, the women lose their baseball jobs as soon as the men return home. Years later, they reunite when the Baseball Hall of Fame pays tribute to the women's leagues. This film is a great one for mothers and daughters to watch together and discuss their dreams, realized or not, and the promise of each individual's potential. If you or your child are interested in the background for this film, look up **A League of Their Own: The Documentary,** which gives a short history of the women's leagues, in Chapter 5: Sports, Safety, Health, and Fitness.

The Long Walk Home (LIVE, 1980, 98 m., PG, 8–up; director Richard Pearce, stars Sissy Spacek, Whoopie Goldberg, Dwight Schultz, narrated by Mary Steenburgen)

For an eye opener about the Montgomery, Alabama, bus boycotts and their effect on two families, sample this program that accurately details the civil rights movement in the 1950s. The central characters are a privileged Southern woman (Spacek) and her black housekeeper. As the housekeeper, Goldberg awakens in her employer a sense of equality not only between races, but also between sexes. Children are involved directly in the confrontations between black and white people, and since young viewers can watch their peers handle the pressure, they may understand the anguish. The film is a powerful essay on the value of the struggle for what one believes is right. For another look at the era, look up the **WonderWorks** title **And the Children Shall Lead** in Chapter 4: Discovery and Learning.

The Man from Snowy River (FoxVideo, 1982, 115 m., PG, 8–up; director George Miller, stars Tom Burlinson, Sigrid Thornton, Kirk Douglas, Jack Thompson)

The boy from Snowy River becomes a man in this simple but terrific family film based on an Australian epic poem. He gets a job as wrangler for an aggressive cattle rancher (Douglas in one of two roles he plays) and falls in love with his boss's daughter. He has his hands full with a particularly handsome and spirited brumby (Aussie for "wild horse") and winds up winning not only the girl, but the respect of the rancher as well. Wonderful adventure, thrilling horseback riding and stunts, and breathtaking scenery may make you want to schedule your next vacation in Australia. The sequel, **Return to Snowy River** (Disney, 1988, PG, 10–up; director Geoff Burrowes, stars Tom Burlinson, Sigrid Thornton, Brian Dennehy, Nicholas Easie, Bryan Marshall), is another rousing wonder from Down Under that never quite measures up to its predecessor. There's a bit more violence here than in the first film, as Burlinson battles an evil rival who'll stop at nothing to steal his girl, his land, his horses— everything that has meaning to the outback horseman. Since it contains more fisticuffs and romance, it's suited to a slightly older audience.

Mary Poppins (Disney, 1964, 140 m., 4–up; director Robert Stevenson, stars Julie Andrews, Dick Van Dyke, David Tomlinson, Glynis Johns, Ed Wynn, Hermione Baddeley, Karen Dotrice)

Julie Andrews as Mary Poppins infuses this classic with so much magic per minute: visual magic of Mary and chimney sweep Bert dancing with animated penguins (the Visual Special Effects captured an Oscar long before Roger and Jessica Rabbit were a twinkle in an animator's eye); musical magic, with an Oscar-winning score and song ("Chim Chim Cheree"); storytelling magic about children who find themselves the ideal nanny when no one else can. This is a collectible classic. Compare it with **The Electric Grandmother.**

The Mighty Ducks (Disney, 1992, 114 m., PG, 8–up; director Stephen Herek, stars Emilio Estevez, Lane Smith, Heidi Kling, Joss Ackland)

Ice hockey, one of the only team sports in which fans encourage players to pummel one another, maybe even draw blood, is the sport that in this fantasy redeems an underhanded lawyer. That very irony should entertain adults, who may at times sympathize with the "winning is everything"–mottoed lawyer, as he struggles to maintain his patience while coaching his misfit team. The on-ice action and teamwork of the very ordinary children on this peewee league will hold young viewers' attention. In an interesting turn of events, the movie spawned a National League Hockey team in California, complete with its own ice rink, the Duck Pond. The sequel, **The Mighty Ducks II,** features essentially the same cast but loses some of the pizzazz the second time around.

My Girl (Columbia TriStar, 1991, 102 m., PG, 10–up, rental; director Howard Zieff, stars Macaulay Culkin, Anna Chlumsky, Dan Aykroyd, Jamie Lee Curtis)

Culkin, the imp from the **Home Alone** films, takes a serious turn here and shows that he can do more than slapstick comedy. But the real headliner is Chlumsky, who stars as preteen girl coming of age and understanding life and death in her father's funeral parlor home in the early 1970s. A bit of a tomboy, she share some adventures, lots of conversation, and a first kiss with an allergy-ridden, bespectacled boy. There's an untimely death depicted here, but it's handled tactfully, not graphically, and if that's a subject that you need to address with your children, then this video may be an icebreaker. **My Girl 2** features a more independent Chlumsky in a story that focuses on more upbeat topics.

National Velvet (MGM/UA, 1944, 125 m., 6–up; director Clarence Brown, stars Elizabeth Taylor, Mickey Rooney, Donald Crisp, Anne Revere, Angela Lansbury)

The ultimate girl-and-her-horse movie has aged well and is still a phenomenal story of what one can do if one really tries. Author Enid Bagnold's tale of a girl who enters her beloved horse in the grueling Grand National Steeplechase in England in the early part of this century is a tearjerker and a triumph. It also bespeaks the heritage handed down from a determined mother who swam the English Channel to a determined daughter who'll beat the odds as a female to enter a men-only horse race.

The NeverEnding Story (Warner, 1984, 92 m., PG, 6–up; director Wolfgang Petersen, stars Noah Hathaway, Barrett Oliver, Tami Stronach, Moses Gunn, Gerald MacRaney)

Here's a tie-in parents are certain to like: a film that promotes reading. A boy who's often left on his own is so caught up in the magical book he's reading that he's actually drawn into it, so much so that he becomes crucial to the outcome, in which The Nothing threatens to absorb the kingdom of Fantasia. It's up to him and his young parallel in the book to preserve the mystical land. In the weaker sequel, **The NeverEnding Story II: The Next Chapter** (Warner, 1990, 89 m., PG, 6–up; director George Miller, stars Jonathan Brandis, Kenny Morrison, Clarissa Burt), which has none of the original stars, the boy is again drawn into the book, this time to rescue a child princess.

Prancer (Columbia TriStar, 1989, 102 m., G, 3–12; director John Hancock, stars Sam Elliott, Rebecca Harrell, Cloris Leachman, Abe Vigoda, Rutanya Alda)

If, as an innocent child, you'd seen an injured reindeer hanging around your neighborhood during the holidays, wouldn't you believe it might be one of Santa's own? In spite of taunts from other children and the practical disbelief of adults, the strong-willed, independent 9-year-old girl who finds the animal believes this so strongly that she's rewarded in more ways than one. Simplistic at times, the film still manages to tug those sentimental strings, even in adults. Rebecca Harrell, in her first film role, is an absolutely delightful, natural actress. **Prancer** is definitely worth a look for holiday family viewing.

Prehysteria (Paramount/Moonbeam, 1993, PG, 86 m., 8–up, rental; directors Albert and Charles Band, stars Austin O'Brien, Brett Cullen, Colleen Morris, Samantha Mills)

In his first children's film, a lighthearted adventure, horror director Charles Band pays homage to Steven Spielberg's **Raiders of the Lost Ark** in the opening scene. A greedy treasure hunter steals five apparently petrified dinosaur eggs from a native South American sanctuary. Back in the States, his precious find is accidentally switched with a bag belonging to an amateur rock hound and his two children. The fun begins when the eggs are hatched by the motherly family dog; the mutant pygmy dinosaurs that emerge are uncannily intelligent, protective, and cute. But the greedmeister wants his treasure back—and he'll stop at nothing to get it. The 10-year-old star is convincing as the central character in a close-knit family; a weak subplot concerns his widowed father's infatuation (sometimes comic, sometimes a little risqué for preteens) with a pretty gemologist who works for the villain. This film should appeal to families with children who aren't ready for the intensity of **Jurassic Park**. Also take a look at **Baby . . . Secret of the Lost Legend**, reviewed in this chapter. **Prehysteria 2**, released on video in 1994, shares only the dinosaurs with its predecessor, and vacillates so frequently between morality play and slapstick comedy that it becomes difficult to follow. Stick with the original.

The Princess Bride (New Line, 1987, 98 m., PG, 6–up; directed by Rob Reiner, stars Peter Falk, Fred Savage, Cary Elwes, Robin Wright, Mandy Patinkin, Chris Sarandon)

A story within a story, much like **The NeverEnding Story**, this film begins and returns periodically to a grandfather telling his home-with-the-flu grandson the story of a woman, the lowly stablehand she loves and believes is lost, and her impending marriage to a heartless nobleman. Based on the novel by William Goldman, who also wrote the screenplay, the film has plenty of swashbuckling ad-

venture, a little romance, and some comedy, and since it's all a tale
Falk invents on the spot, anything can happen—and does. Carol
Kane and Billy Crystal have hilarious cameos as magicians, whose
comic interruptions soften the fact that the hero has apparently died.
Regardless of the feminine sound of the title, this is a fantasy that
will attract as many boys (and adults) as young girls.

Raiders of the Lost Ark (Paramount, 1981, 115 m., PG, 8–up; director
Steven Spielberg, stars Harrison Ford, Karen Allen, Wolf Kahler,
Paul Freeman, John Rhys-Davies, Denholm Elliott)
    In this raucous, rollicking roller coaster of a film—the definitive
modern matinee movie—Spielberg pays homage to the Saturday
matinee serials that he grew up with. Around the beginning of
World War II, a college archaeology professor named Indiana Jones
is called upon by the government to retrieve a religious artifact before the Nazis get to it. He makes a stop in Nepal, picks up his old
flame, and heads to the Middle East, dodging bullets, scimitars,
bombs, and bad guys all the way. This is edge-of-your-seat, don't-
drop-the-popcorn fun. Considering the recent furor over excessive
violence in the media, the humor in several violent scenes (such as
Indy comically shooting a huge, scimitar-wielding adversary after
fighting off others with his infamous bullwhip) may seem a little
stretched, but take the movie for what it is: entertainment, not a
moral statement. The film took four Oscars, **Raiders** spawned a prequel, **Indiana Jones and the Temple of Doom** (Paramount, 1984, 188 m.,
PG, 8–up; director Steven Spielberg, stars Harrison Ford, Kate Cap-
shaw, Ke Huy Quan, Amrish Puri, Dan Aykroyd); the violence and
"gross-out" factor in the prequel inspired the Motion Picture Association of America to create the PG-13 rating. Not half as much fun
as the original, it features an enslaved workforce of children, much
peril to the hero and heroine, and a terrifying sequence in which a
man's beating heart is ripped from his chest—not for the squeamish. The sequel, **Indiana Jones and the Last Crusade** (Paramount, 1989,
127 m., PG-13, 8–up; director Steven Spielberg, stars Harrison Ford,
Sean Connery, Denholm Elliott, John Rhys-Davies, River Phoenix,
Alison Doody), although not as powerful as the original, is much
fresher and more upbeat than the second installment. Indy's inter-
play with his archaeologist father is terrific, and although there

are fewer cliffhangers than in **Raiders,** this film still delivers thrills and fun.

Remote (Paramount/Moonbeam, 1993, 80 m., PG, 8–up; director Ted Nicolaou, stars Chris Carrara, Jessica Bowman, John Diehl, Tony Longo)

Like some of the comedies of the 1960s and '70s (such as **The Pink Panther** films), this kids' comedy caper features crazy animation "helping" its opening credits roll. Ten-year-old Randy is a remote-control enthusiast, as are his best buddies, Judy the softball queen and Jamal. They spend their free time navigating their remote-control cars and airplanes around a model home in an undersold subdivision. Randy faces expulsion from elementary school after a prank with a favorite remote-control airplane backfires, even though the real culprit is the class bully. To avoid losing his collection of models, Randy takes them to his hideout in the vacant subdivision. But when three bumbling thieves hole up there, unwittingly trapping him overnight, he has to rely on his resourcefulness with his clever models to avoid being caught. Although they're trespassing in the empty house, Randy and his friends haven't really damaged property (unless it's in self-defense); they do, however, distract a guard dog by feeding it hot dogs with the plastic wrappers intact— don't try this at home! With very little violence and only one instance of "bad" language, **Remote** achieves a level of family comedy similar to that of the **Home Alone** films without actually endangering the lives of the villains.

The Right Stuff (Warner, 1983, 193 m., PG, 10–up, 2 tapes, rental; director Philip Kaufman, stars Ed Harris, Scott Glenn, Dennis Quaid, Sam Shepard, Fred Ward, Barbara Hershey, Veronica Cartwright, Pamela Reed)

Children who are fascinated by astronauts and space travel may be captivated by this long but engrossing chronicle of the early years of America's space program. The focus is on the career and private life of test pilot Chuck Yeager (who has a cameo as a bartender), whose bravery in breaking the sound barrier set the stage for myriad other technological developments that enabled humans to set foot on the moon. The mix of passion, adventure, love, admiration, respect, and fear in recent real-life heroes made for a best-selling book (by Tom Wolfe) and this excellent movie. For other space-related tapes, check out **Astrodudes** and **Astronomy 101**, both reviewed in Chapter 4: Discovery and Learning.

Robin Hood: Prince of Thieves (Warner, 1991, 138 m., PG-13, 8–up; director Kevin Reynolds, stars Kevin Costner, Mary Elizabeth Mastroantonio, Alan Rickman, Morgan Freeman, Christian Slater)

This modern version of the Robin Hood legend begins unevenly and challenges viewers to focus on the action and ignore Costner's blatantly out-of-place American accent. The very modernness, however, is what draws today's young viewers. The central theme of an ousted nobleman's uprising against tyranny is effectively played out, including near-mutiny by Robin's right-hand man, Will Scarlett, who shares a unique relationship with Robin not explored in any other version of the tale. Aside from the special effects, the most wonderful scenes are those in which the adroit "Dick Dastardly"–like Alan Rickman postures as the Sheriff of Nottingham. Though it probably won't become a classic, this **Robin Hood** is thoroughly modern and punchy.

The Rocketeer (Buena Vista, 1991, 108 m., PG, 10–up; director Joe Johnston, stars Bill Campbell, Jennifer Connelly, Alan Arkin, Timothy Dalton, Paul Sorvino)

Fun, adventure, and romance highlight this film that, regardless of its clichéd villains (Nazis), will appeal to preteens rather than preschoolers. There's nothing not to like, although a vehicle this formulaic, after receiving lots of pre-release promotion, turned off many critics. Set in the 1930s, when air travel was still an infant industry and the threat of World War II hovered over the country, the tale revolves around a rocket pack that lets its wearer fly, and our handsome young pilot hero certainly has fun with it. Younger viewers' interest may wane when the dialogue slows the action with explication and romantic interludes, but the Saturday-matinee flavor is, for the most part, worth waiting for. Also check out the more memorable **Raiders of the Lost Ark**, reviewed in this chapter.

The Sound of Music (CBS/Fox Video, 1965, 174 m., 5–up; director Robert Wise, stars Julie Andrews, Christopher Plummer, Eleanor Parker, Peggy Wood, Richard Haydn)

Another "wow" film that pleases the senses: The scenery is almost too beautiful to be believed (the small screen unfortunately can't do the Alps justice); the music, from Rodgers and Hammerstein ("Climb Ev'ry Mountain," "Edelweiss," "Do Re Mi," "My Favorite Things"), is lush and memorable; the sentimental but truly moving story is based on the real-life exploits of the Von Trapp family, who escaped Nazi-occupied Austria. Another collectible classic, it garnered five Oscars, including Best Picture, and continues to be a favorite today. Like many classics, it's best viewed on video, since television airings invariably butcher the film for commercials.

Superman (Warner, 1978, 145 m., PG, 6–up; director Richard Donner, stars Christopher Reeve, Margot Kidder, Marlon Brando, Gene Hackman, Ned Beatty, Jackie Cooper)

The first is the best in this series of four films based on the comic book superhero. Heroes with an irreverent sense of humor have become the norm in the 1990s, but this hero is played by Reeve with a rather reverent tongue in cheek as a real geek—until he whisks into that red cape! Part of the reason this film works so well for kids is its depiction of a boy's growth and coming of age, particularly since this boy is so different from his peers. He feels he won't fit in, then discovers his extraordinary powers, which really separate him from the crowd. When he's old enough to leave the farm, he becomes a reporter on a big city paper, finds a love interest who only notices him when he's Superman, and saves the world from Lex Luthor's diabolical plans. This **Superman** is loaded with Oscar-winning special effects—and fun.

Swiss Family Robinson (Disney, 1960, 128 m., 4–up; director Ken Annakin, stars John Mills, Dorothy McGuire, James MacArthur, Tommy Kirk, Janet Munro, Kevin Corcoran)

Romance, fun (who'll forget the ostrich in that all-animals race?), a treehouse to die for, and danger (Pirates, ho!) make this film good family fun with a moral—the family stays together through good times and bad. To the idyllic setting and premise, add glorious cinematography and appealing characters, and you have the stuff that really fires a child's imagination. The only drawback: The two women (mother McGuire and friend Munro) have ultratraditional roles as nurturers and objects of desire. The film is based on Johann Wyss's book of the same name.

Time Bandits (Paramount, 1981, 110 m., PG, 8–up; director Terry Gilliam, stars David Rappaport, Jack Purvis, Mike Edmunds, Sean Connery, Shelley Duvall, Michael Palin, John Cleese, Katherine Helmond, Ian Holm)

From the manic minds of some members of the Monty Python clan comes this time- and space-tripping sci-fi fantasy starring a group of dwarf bandits who've stolen the map of creation. They arrive in a young boy's bedroom in present-day England and proceed to take him on a whirlwind tour of time. Among the dignitaries the loony group encounters are King Agamemnon (Connery), Robin Hood (Cleese), and Napoleon (Holm). Though not quite a history primer, this is an imaginative exploration of the hypothetical (or are they?) holes in the universe that let travelers who know how to find them slip in and out of eras. Also look up **The Adventures of Baron Munchausen** in this chapter.

The Time Machine (MGM/UA, 1960, 103 m., 10–up; director George Pal, stars Rod Taylor, Yvette Mimieux, Alan Young, Sebastian Cabot)

Adapted from H. G. Wells' story of the same name, this film takes a scientist from the early twentieth century to the year 802701 (that's not a typo!), where he finds things are vastly different from anything he'd imagined. His adventures are not so much full of wonder as of frustration, and he's happy to return to his contemporaries. The film won an Oscar for special effects, which seem primitive by today's standards. Less fun and more adult-oriented than **Time Bandits** and the **Back to the Future** saga, it's still worth a look for the perception of time travel from almost 100 years ago, interpreted through a 1960 filter.

Tommy Tricker and the Stamp Traveler (Family Home Entertainment, 1988, 101 m., 7–14; director Michael Rubbo, stars Lucas Evans, Anthony Rogers, Jill Stanley, Andrew Whitehead)

In another of the terrific Rock Demers **Tales for All** series, "Tricker" aptly describes the budding conman of the title, even though he's only 12. Tommy convinces timid young Ralph to trade him one of his father's valuable stamps, and the action escalates as Ralph and two friends try in vain to retrieve the stamp. Presto! Let film magic intervene! Ralph discovers a way to shrink so that he can travel on a postage stamp to Australia to get a replacement stamp. It won't be easy, though, as he finds when he is accidentally mailed to China. When he finally reaches Australia, Ralph finds Tommy, who *had* to get in on the action, is also there and needs his help. The children depicted in this fantasy either are or become strong characters through their own actions. The film also touches on the romance and armchair adventure of stamp collecting, which has become America's top-ranking hobby.

Treasure (Vidmark, 1993, 85 m., 7–12, rental)

Three young teens—Freddy, David, and his nerdy cousin John —are in for real adventure when they stumble upon clues to the solution of a 30-year-old mystery at a lighthouse. Cap, an aging fisherman, tries to help them reconstruct the questionable events around a boat's unexplained explosion in 1959 and the simultaneous disappearance of the lighthouse keeper. The boys learn to take nothing at face value when they encounter a shadowy figure digging for treasure beneath the town's abandoned lighthouse. Three ex-cons, also snooping for clues, pose a real threat to the boys, especially when, to their dismay, the kids discover a connection between the potential thieves and a trusted friend. Although many of the mysteries remain unsolved at the film's close, this is still an adventure that lets children's imaginations run wild. For more pirate adventure, see **Goonies** and **George's Island,** in this chapter.

A Tree Grows in Brooklyn (FoxVideo, 1945, 128 m., 10–up, b&w; director Elia Kazan, stars Dorothy McGuire, Joan Blondell, James Dunn, Lloyd Nolan, Peggy Ann Garner)

This exquisite tale of an early-twentieth-century girl's struggle to succeed regardless of her downtrodden life in a New York tenement was adapted from the wonderful book by Betty Smith. Though the premise is depressing, especially as the tension increases between her black-sheep, liquor-loving father and her tight-lipped, workaholic mother, the girl's brightness keeps the woe in line. For anyone who loves a good story, as well as for anyone who wants insight into immigrant life, it's a winner; the Academy bestowed two Oscars upon it.

Tron (Disney, 1982, 96 m., PG, 10–up; director Steven Lisberger, stars Jeff Bridges, Bruce Boxleitner, David Warner, Cindy Morgan, Barnard Hughes)

Dazzling special effects are as much a character as the humans in this precursor to virtual reality. While checking out his company's electronic security, a computer whiz is sucked inside a computer, where he must compete in a life-or-death video game. Though the plot fades and the story flounders next to the technical wizardry, it's worth checking out just for the pioneering special effects.

Wild Hearts Can't Be Broken (Buena Vista, 1991, 88 m., G, 8–up; director Steve Miner, stars Gabrielle Anwar, Michael Schoeffling, Cliff Robertson, Dylan Kussman)

Back in the Great Depression, people were willing to go to new heights to make ends meet. In this historical drama, Sonora Webster, an ambitious young woman with nowhere to go but up, sets her sights on becoming a "diving girl," one of the women who rode horses off four-story platforms into a tank of water. Sonora's ambition carries a steep price, but it becomes an element that strengthens her character. Anwar is captivating as Sonora. There's an innocent love interest, tastefully and believably developed, and true to the era in which this film was set. And although the stunts look dangerous, no animals actually jumped from that high-dive for the cameras. This is a fantastic family film.

Willow (Columbia TriStar, 1988, 125 m., PG, 8–up; director Ron Howard, stars Val Kilmer, Joanne Whalley, Warwick Davis, Jean Marsh, Billy Barty)

This is another fantasy with a quest taken up by a man who must safeguard an orphaned baby until it can conquer an evil queen. His disadvantage is his short stature. Unlike some of the other "quest" adventures, however, this entry benefits from its genesis as a powerful story by **Star Wars** creator George Lucas. The special effects and adventure are topflight.

Willy Wonka and the Chocolate Factory (Warner, 1971, 100 m., G, 4–up; director Mel Stuart, stars Gene Wilder, Jack Albertson, Peter Ostrum)

Based on the book *Charlie and the Chocolate Factory*, by Roald Dahl, this film is delicious entertainment for the whole family, although it has a bitingly sarcastic edge that might be frightening to the younger viewers. A candymaker takes five prizewinning children on a tour of his fantastic, mysterious candy factory and teaches each one a sometimes humiliating or painful lesson. Musical numbers feature the factory's Oompah Loompahs, Wonka and his wry wit, and earnest young Charlie and his beloved grandfather.

The Witches (Warner, 1990, 91 m., PG, 8–up, rental; director Nicolas Roeg, stars Anjelica Huston, Mai Zetterling, Jasen Fisher, Rowan Atkinson, Bill Paterson, Jane Horrocks)

In an oceanfront hotel in the English countryside, a coven of witches is holding a convention. Unfortunately, a 10-year-old guest at the hotel is discovered spying on them—witches detest the foul smell of children—and they turn him and another boy into mice, which is the fate they've planned for all the children of England. Even as a mouse (magnificently crafted by Jim Henson's Creature Shop), the hero enlists his loving grandmother to find a way to foil the witches' plans. As in other Roald Dahl stories, including *Charlie and the Chocolate Factory,* there's an undercurrent of cruelty. But never fear: there are good witches as well. The scarier aspects, including the costumes, might not sit well with the youngest viewers, but taken as a whole, the video makes for a suspenseful, spooky night's viewing.

The Wizard of Oz (MGA/UA, 1939, 101 m., 4–up, partially b&w; director Victor Fleming, stars Judy Garland, Ray Bolger, Jack Haley, Bert Lahr, Margaret Hamilton)

What list of the best in family entertainment would be complete without this phenomenal Technicolor wonder? The film, based on L. Frank Baum's story, is timeless and needs no explication, but the Wicked Witch of the West and those flying monkeys may provoke nightmares in the wee-est of wee ones. Focus instead on the unforgettable music ("We're Off to See the Wizard," "Over the Rainbow)," and keep reminding children that "There's no place like home, there's no place like home. . . ."

Chapter 2

■

ANIMATED FEATURE FILMS

Walt Disney's classic animated films cannot be ignored; there are, however, many other treasures, such as **A Journey Through Fairyland** and **Scamper the Penguin,** that deserve attention. In this chapter I focus more on gems that you might not have heard of, films off the beaten track. There are numerous films that don't enjoy wide distribution or attention, and some of them may really intrigue you.

Unless they're of particular significance, no compilation tapes (for example, four episodes from the *Bugs Bunny* TV series combined to make a 90-minute tape) are listed in this chapter. The animated programs included here are either theatrical releases or successful TV series pilots. Also, when available, I have listed the MPAA rating; some films are unrated, but those included here are suitable for family viewing. Still, I advise you to check the age-appropriateness for your child by previewing the program.

John Sirabella, National Film Board of Canada Non-Theatrical Marketing Manager, encourages parents to "push the envelope" to try alternative videos that will amuse and challenge both them and their children.

John Sirabella does not consider himself "an animation connoisseur." He allows, however, that he's "an ardent fan of animation." He was unable to narrow down all the feature-length animated films to identify a favorite, opting instead for a 12-minute short called "The Big Snit" (available from Whole Toon Catalog on the tape **Incredible Manitoba Animation**) and "The Street," another short (also from Whole Toon, on the tape **Hollywood Salutes Canadian Animation**).

As the person who convinces video distributors and consumers to try National Film Board of Canada product, Sirabella has developed a discriminating taste for high-quality animation. Here's one of the ways he distinguishes the best from the rest: "Look for films that provoke thought for many themes and topics. A good film doesn't have to be highbrow or didactic to be educational; a good story can do the job well."

In addition, he agrees with other experts quoted in this book in recommending that parents should consider a variety of elements when choosing kidvid or family titles, whether animated or live action. Among the factors he suggests parents and caregivers consider are morals and social value, educational content, production quality, and indications that the tapes have won awards. "Award-winning films are generally those that push the envelope in terms of animation technique, subject matter, tone, and approach. They'll be the films that most often both amuse and challenge both adults and children."

He also joins other experts in advising parents to "do your homework. Ideally, you should watch the tapes before you purchase them, and watch them with your child instead of using the TV as a babysitter."

Animation of the quality and nature that the National Film Board of Canada releases can draw families together. "It works across generational boundaries," Sirabella believes. "Parents can easily be convinced by the educational merit of the material; these pieces have won Oscars and other awards. And I think children are more open to trying new things than parents think they are." So even if children are clamoring for the same cartoons they regularly watch on TV, they might be convinced to give something different a try—and they just might like it.

As for resources, he mentioned "a good children's librarian, and the coalition" (for Quality Children's Video—see the Resources appendix). Many animated short films are collected on compilation videos available from such sources as Smarty Pants Video and Whole Toon Catalog, and on laser disc from Lumivision.

Does video, even animated programs, have any educational merit? Sirabella's 4-year-old nephew is already receiving only the best in animated product, and is learning to read by following a book as he watches a story unfold on the screen. "He knows the stories, but sometimes, he'll make it up, or alter it."

The Adventures of the Great Mouse Detective (Disney, 1986, 74 m., G, 4–up; voices of Vincent Price, Barrie Ingham, Candy Candido, Alan Young, Melissa Manchester)

Basil, the rodent supersleuth, matches wits with his cunning adversary, Professor Ratigan, to save all of Mousedom from the professor's evil plans. Cleverly drawn, appealing characters and a quick pace propel this story, although it is not one of Disney's greatest accomplishments. With parallels to Sherlock Holmes, this entry could satisfy young mystery lovers; if they're hungry for still more sleuthing, check out **Encyclopedia Brown, the Boy Detective** in Chapter 7.

The Adventures of Mark Twain (Paramount, 1985, 90 m., 8–up; director Will Vinton; voices of James Whitmore, Chris Ritchie, Gary Krug, Michele Mariana)

A legendary animation technique—Will Vinton's Claymation— complements the imaginative stories by legendary author/wit Mark Twain. Be forewarned, however, that this feature film is no picnic; it shows a dark side of Twain, and features two characters in particular (an angel named Satan and Injun Joe, who's always been a threatening figure) that might cause nightmares for younger viewers, even though it's only Claymation. Twain finds three of his characters (Huck Finn, Becky Thatcher, and Tom Sawyer) stowed away on his souped-up hot-air balloon, which he intends to pilot to Halley's Comet. Born in a year when the comet was sighted (1835), this fictitious Twain hopes to meet his destiny there. The twisty plot combines snippets of Twain's stories with his sardonic commentary.

The Adventures of Sinbad the Sailor (Family Home Entertainment, 1973, 88 m., 5–up)

Sinbad, the mythical adventurer, rescues damsels in distress, battles evil cyclops and other monsters, and in general, provides young viewers with plenty of fantasy for their imaginations. A shorter version of the story is available through MGM/UA (47 m., 5–up).

Alice in Wonderland (Disney, 1951, 75 m., 5–up; voices of Sterling Holloway, Kathryn Beaumont, Ed Wynn, Richard Haydn)

There are plenty of potentially frightening sequences in Lewis Carroll's original tale, but in Disney-animated form, they're not as scary for young viewers. The illogical, irrational events and people, such as the "Drink Me" bottle, the Mad Hatter, and the Queen of Hearts, may unsettle youngsters who read the book or see a live-action adaptation. But here there's more room for comedy, with the help of the eminently entertaining Mad Hatter and Cheshire Cat.

Aladdin (Disney, 1993, 87 m., G, 4–up; voices of Robin Williams, Scott Weinger, Linda Larkin)

Robin Williams absolutely *makes* the film as the shape-shifting, scene-stealing genie. This updated approach to the old *Arabian Nights* tale is particularly satisfying because its young, modern-thinking Princess Jasmine boldly takes matters into her own independent, royal hands. There are a few unsettling moments for the youngest children, among them Aladdin's experiences in the cave where he finds the lamp, and the battleground climax. But the animation is mesmerizing, the setting is romantic, the adventure is unparalleled, the hero and heroine are lovable, the villain is the embodiment of evil, and the theme is universal (with a lot of hard work and a little luck, all things are possible)—all make for a quintessential Disney film. Disney also created a movie exclusively for home video, **The Return of Jafar,** that picks up where **Aladdin** leaves off. Check out another version of the **Aladdin** story in Chapter 7.

All Dogs Go to Heaven (MGM/UA, 87 m., G, 5–up; director Don Bluth, voices of Burt Reynolds, Loni Anderson, Dom DeLuise, Vic Tayback, Melba Moore)

For an animated tale, this film has a dark theme—death and the afterlife—that may put off younger children. The story skips around, following a recently deceased "gangster" dog who gets a second chance when he has to find his record of good deeds on Earth before he's admitted to Heaven. A young orphan girl provides the perfect way for the former puppy thief to complete enough good deeds to enter Heaven. Because of its heavy themes, good deeds performed in a selfish way, and the questionable motives of some characters, parents may want to screen this film before letting their children watch it. Then again, some children may not catch the morbid drift and may enjoy this simply for its story of redemption.

An American Tail (MCA/Universal, 1986, 80 m., G, 6–up; director Don Bluth, voices of Christopher Plummer, Dom DeLuise, Madeline Kahn, Nehemiah Persoff) and **An American Tail: Fievel Goes West** (MCA/Universal, 1991, 75 m., G, 6–up; director Phil Nibbelink, voices of James Stewart, John Cleese, Dom DeLuise)

In these Steven Spielberg–produced films, the Eastern European immigrant rodent named Fievel Mousekewitz represents our collective experiences as nonnative Americans. Audience warmed easily to this "everymouse," and the sequel was well received. Both films parallel the Disney formula of song and production numbers to encourage the protagonist on his learning odyssey. Both films are also saccharine-sweet, lacking the punch that today's young viewers are beginning to expect from filmed entertainment. Both the original and its sequel have dangerous moments (among them encounters with felines, a near-drowning, and Fievel's separation from his family), and each may raise some questions in very young viewers that parents should be around to answer. But our hero also has the opportunity to learn and grow. Fievel always finds a way to surmount his troubles, making this a truly all-American fairy tale.

Around the World in 80 Days (Prism, 1975, 80 m., 8–up)

For those not ready for the live-action adventure version of Jules Verne's classic, here's an easy animated introduction. Colorful and fantastic in the extreme, this tale follows Phineas Fogg as he circumnavigates the Earth in all manner of vehicles.

Asterix (Disney, 1985, two titles, 4–8)

Asterix the Gaul is one of Europe's most popular animated characters, and it's easy to see why from his brave adventures depicted here. In the first installment, **Asterix and Cleopatra** (72 m.), he and his sidekick Getafix match wits with Cleopatra, Queen of the Nile. In **Asterix the Gaul** (67 m.), Asterix and Obelix keep the Roman armies, led by the inept general Phonus Balonus, at bay while defending their home turf. Although the animation does not reach the typical Disney pinnacle, the stories are quite good, and the hero is an upstanding little fellow. Two more of his adventures are also available from another video company in the **Asterix** series (Just for Kids, 1985, two titles, 85 m. each, 4–8). In **Asterix in Britain,** the clever Gaul uses magic potions to keep Caesar and his armies from capturing

Britain. Asterix's loyal friend Obelix manages to assist in any way possible. The adventures continue in **Asterix Versus Caesar,** wherein Asterix befriends a prince and princess and saves them from the Roman practice of throwing one's enemies to the lions. For additional background, look up his adventures in your local library.

Babar: The Movie (Family Home Entertainment, 1989, 79 m., G, 3–10)

Laurent De Brunhoff's classic, classy elephant takes viewers to his roots in Africa, where he battles the angry rhinoceros ruler Rataxes for control of his homeland. The style is almost "Indiana Babar." There are some pretty serious fight scenes when elephants and rhinos clash, and unlike Bugs Bunny–style violence, the battle scenes here are choreographed as if humans were fighting. But it's all animated, so most children should not be disturbed by the violence.

Beauty and the Beast (Disney, 1991, 90 m., G, 2–up; voices of Robby Benson, Paige O'Hara, Angela Lansbury, Jerry Orbach, David Ogden Stiers)

When an animated film competes with live-action dramas in non-animated Oscar categories, consumers should understand there's something very special about that film. This two-time Oscar winner delighted theater and video audiences of all ages, and will prove its evergreen nature in years to come. It's embellished somewhat from the original fairy tale, but all for the better: Belle is a bookworm, a beautiful girl who knows bravado when she sees it in Gaston, the village hunk who wants to possess her, not truly love her. His rival is a curious beast, not really an ugly creature but definitely a sad one. There's magic not only in the story but also in the production, with wonderful music and fantastic computer animation bringing a ballroom breathtakingly to life. This gem is worth collecting and treasuring.

Bon Voyage, Charlie Brown (And Don't Come Back!) (Paramount, 1980, 76 m., G, 3–12; director Bill Melendez, voices of Daniel Anderson, Casey Carlson, Patricia Patts, Arrin Skelley)

I don't know if anyone ever outgrows Charles Schulz's timeless comic strip, with its gentle, intelligent comments on today's world.

In this adventure originally made for TV, the Peanuts gang travels on an exchange program to France, where Charlie Brown, Linus, Peppermint Patty, Lucy, and Snoopy find adventure, romance, history, and some lessons worth learning.

A Boy Named Charlie Brown (FoxVideo, 1969, 85 m., G, 3–12; director Bill Melendez, voices of Peter Robbins, Pamelyn Ferdin, Glenn Gilger, Andy Pforsich)

This was the first fully animated adventure featuring Charles Schulz's Peanuts gang from the newspapers' comic pages. Somehow, it's withstood the test of time. Charlie Brown, the world's favorite loser, is preparing for baseball season, but first he has to clear the pitcher's mound of its dandelion crown. There are a number of musical interludes; songs are by poet Rod McKuen.

The Brave Little Toaster (Disney, 1987, 96 m., 2–12; director Jerry Rees, voices of Jon Lovitz, Tim Stack, Timothy E. Day, Deanna Oliver, Phil Hartman)

A toaster named Slots leads his fellow appliances (five altogether) on a jaunt to find the little boy that plugged them all in to love. They've been relegated to the vacation cabin in the country, while their little master goes back to school in the big city. Will they find him before they suffer a power failure—or before the cord runs out? Look for the Thomas M. Disch book upon which this is based in your local library or bookstore.

The Care Bears Movie (Facets Multimedia, 1985, 75 m., G, 2–6; director Arna Selznick, voices of Mickey Rooney, Georgia Engle)

If you can hack the sugarcoated attitudes of this group of cuddly bears, more power to you! In all fairness, there's nothing insidious about the Care Bears, but their overbearing sweetness may not appeal to all viewers. Also, if you're wary of entertainment that's based on a toy line, then beware of this series, and avoid the compilation tapes of the TV series. Three movies were made: In the first, when a young boy unwittingly unleashes an evil spirit, even the Care Bears cousins turn out to assist. In **The Care Bears Movie 2: A New Generation** (Columbia TriStar, 1986, 77 m., G, 2–6; director Dale Schott, voices of Maxine Miller, Pam Hyatt, Hadley Kay), a little girl is tricked into trapping the Care Bears, but once she learns the truth, she changes her attitude and sets them free. In **The Care Bears Adventure in Wonderland** (MCA/Universal, 1987, 76 m., G, 2–6; director Raymond Jafelice, voices of Bob Dermer, Eva Almos, Dan Hennessy, Jim Henshaw), the Care Bears and Alice rescue the princess of Wonderland, proving that everyone is special.

Charlotte's Web (Paramount, 1972, 94 m., G, 4–up; director Charles A. Nichols, Iwao Takamoto, voices of Debbie Reynolds, Henry Gibson, Paul Lynde, Agnes Moorehead, Charles Nelson Reilly)

The production team of Joseph Hanna and William Barbera adapted E. B. White's barnyard novel into this entertaining cartoon with a conscience. Some of the mysteries of life—birth, death, and friendship—are made more understandable by paralleling animals' lives with our own. A young farm girl saves the runt of a litter of piglets when she asks, "If I had been very small, would you have killed me?" Her father decides to let his daughter raise the undersized piglet, and all goes well until Wilbur, healthy, fat, and happy, is sold for slaughter. While awaiting his fate, he befriends Charlotte the spider, who tries to save Wilbur by spinning messages about him into her web. Soon, Wilbur is famous across the countryside, but Charlotte's days are numbered by Nature. The animation is basic, but the story, even with its sadness, is uplifting.

Cinderella (Disney, 1950, 76 m., 4–up; director Wilford Jackson, voices of Ilene Woods, William Phipps, Eleanor Audley, Verna Felton)

This classic is pure fantasy and pure entertainment in traditional Disney style; that means some helpful critters—in this case mice—ensure that for the human contingent, love and romance succeed. Some of the most memorable Disney tunes are featured here, including "Bibbidi Bobbidi Boo" and "A Dream Is a Wish Your Heart Makes." Catch it with the kids, and if a little girl dreams of being the prince, the doer, instead of being rescued, as most fairy tale heroines were, so much the better.

Clementine (Just for Kids, 2 titles, 95 m. each, 3–10)

In two tapes, a wheelchair-bound girl dreams herself into all sorts of adventures, freeing her body as well as her spirit. **A Young Girl and Her Dreams** finds Clementine and her kitten skipping across the centuries to help those in need. She meets children's literary figures as well as ordinary folk. In **Clementine's Enchanted Journey,** Clementine transfers from wheelchair to magic bubble to time-travel back to Leonardo da Vinci's era, and meets the model for Pinocchio as well. These unusual films are inspiring and sensitive without being patronizing.

The Dark Crystal (HBO, 1983, 94 m., PG, 4–up; voices of Jim Henson, Frank Oz)

In this "all-creature" fantasy, Henson makes his first foray into other-than-Muppets features, combining elements of fairy tales and mythology with an alien world. The film centers on two young adults who embark on a quest to find a missing Dark Crystal and prevent evil from taking over their world. The simple story is secondary to the fantastic creatures and props that "morph" into living beings when you least expect it. If you hear exclamations of "Eeeuww" and "Yech," viewers are probably being introduced to the evil antagonists, a crusty bunch of withered, roachlike critters. Henson throws in a few plot twists and some terrific special effects to keep viewers "engrossed." This is one of those videos that parents will enjoy watching beside their kids.

Dot And . . . (Family Home Entertainment, 1986–87, 4 titles, 75 m. each, 2–12)

Before **Captain Planet** wowed American preteens with environmental awareness in cartoon form, there was this Australian series that combined live backgrounds with animated characters. It's a fascinating piece of production, and most of the titles deliver powerful lessons on how even a small child can help the environment or another living creature. **Dot and Keeto** (1986) tells of Dot's encounter with a mosquito, when she is magically shrunk to the size of a bug so she can explore the insect world with her newfound friend. **Dot and the Koala** (1986) teams Dot with Australian bush inhabitants to protect the environment from unchecked advancing technology and the pollution and overcrowding it wreaks. In **Dot and the Smugglers,** our young heroine uncovers the real wildlife smuggling operation behind a fake circus. **Dot and the Whale** finds Dot exploring the depths of the oceans and helping a beached whale regain its will to live. Fox Video also has two Dot titles: **Dot and Santa Claus,** in which she searches for her lost pet kangaroo, and **Dot and the Bunny,** in which Dot meets the unusual rabbit named "Funny Bunny." Its affiliated label, Playhouse, has **Dot and the Kangaroo,** in which Dot becomes lost in the Australian Outback, but a loving kangaroo takes her on a fantastic journey to subdue her fears.

The Dragon That Wasn't (Or Was He?) (MCA/Universal, 1983, 96 m., 3–10)

Can Ollie Bear manage to keep his pet dragon, Dexter, as Dexter experiences a terrific growth spurt and outgrows his home and town? Ollie realizes that his only recourse is to return his beloved dragon to his rightful home beyond the Misty Mountains. This entry offers a less painful way to introduce the issue of separation anxiety.

Dreaming of Paradise (Just for Kids, 1987, 82 m., 8–up)

European animation like this production tends to be heavy-handed in its treatment of such serious subjects as nuclear holocaust, destruction of the environment, and people's unjust treatment of one another. You'll have to preview this one to determine whether your children are ready for a lesson this serious: despite its euphoric-sounding title, this is *not* an upbeat adventure. In the post-Apocalyptic future, a segment of society has developed a subterranean culture whose inhabitants pass on stories of their former lives in embellished oral tradition. Their enemies, rats as big as humans, torment them, but the elders believe one day a bird like the phoenix will show them the way to paradise. Spike, a clever girl, and Dum Dum, a mute boy, are up for the adventure of finding and following the bird, but the journey is dangerous, grueling, and frightening, and the climax presents an open-ended question: What are the survivors to do once they reach Paradise? Parents who feel their children are ready to view this piece of social commentary will want to be available to answer questions and help lift viewers' spirits.

DuckTales The Movie: Treasure of the Lost Lamp (Disney, 1990, 74 m., G, 2–10)

This video pays homage to **Raiders of the Lost Ark** and other adventure movies. Huey, Dewey, and Louie provide the brains—and the silliness—behind the adventure of finding Collie Baba's (yes, he's portrayed as a dog) treasure, complete with a magic lamp, and then losing it all. Scrooge McDuck and Webbigale VanderQuack are also in on it and provide more comic relief. There are lots of parallels to **Aladdin,** but the participants in this adventure learn the lesson that you can't take it with you.

Dumbo (Disney, 1941, 64 m., 4–up; director Ben Sharpsteen, voices of Sterling Holloway, Verna Felton, Edward Brophy, Herman Bing)

For a fantastic lesson in the triumph of inner beauty over physical beauty, watch this old-fashioned gem from Disney's golden years of animation. More than 50 years after it was first released to theaters, **Dumbo** is still a vibrant, colorful depiction of circus life, even if the presiding perspective is that of the performing animals. In the most touching scene, Dumbo's mouse friend, Timothy, helps him reunite with his mother. The most fascinating scene is the dream segment, featuring those wonderful pink elephants. Since the film was made back in the 1940s, though, there are several racial stereotypes you might want to explain to your children. For example, most of the circus hands doing the manual labor are black, and the crows that are depicted speak in a colloquial Southern black dialect. The film won a 1941 Oscar for Scoring for a Musical Picture.

The Fabulous Adventures of Baron Munchausen (Family Home Entertainment/Vestron, 1979, 78 m., 5–10; director Jean Image, voice of Claude Lemesle)

Baron Munchausen was an eccentric eighteenth-century soldier who regaled his friends and other guests at his castle with far-fetched stories of fantastic adventures. This animated interpretation of his exploits allows young viewers to imagine themselves participating in Munchausen's feats: encountering a rabbit whose extra feet on its back allow it to hop twice as fast as any ordinary rabbit; meeting five superhuman men whose special features are useful when Munchausen decides to steal a treasure belonging to a neighboring baron; escaping from prison by hopping on a cannonball and riding it into the clouds, where he naps. Also check out the live-action version, **The Adventures of Baron Munchausen,** featuring the work of several members of the Monty Python comedy team, in Chapter 1: Feature Films.

Fantasia (Disney, 1940, 120 m., 3–up; score by Leopold Stokowsi and the Philadelphia Orchestra)

Walt Disney's personal favorite is slated to be changed by the studio periodically with the addition of a new segment; the first new version was announced in 1993 for release in 1996. Walt's vision was a marriage of classical music with the best animation his talented teams could produce. Few viewers, once they see "The Sorcerer's Apprentice," will forget Mickey Mouse in his magical hat commanding ordinary brooms to clean—and then becoming swept up in the magic. "The Dance of the Hours" has never been the same since the Disney animators allowed alligators and hippos to dance their way through it. Check out the "Night on Bald Mountain" segment before showing it to your young viewers; some children under 6 may find the demon and other supernatural elements make for terrifying nightmare material.

FernGully: The Last Rainforest (FoxVideo, 1992, 72 m., G, 4–up; voice of Robin Williams)

Deep in a rainforest that is targeted for lumbering, there's an evil presence holed up in a twisted specter of a tree. When one of the timber crew members unleashes it, all of the lovely rainforest is threatened. Can the wood nymph Chrysta save her homeland from destruction? She accidentally reduces one of the construction workers to her almost-microscopic size, which gives him quite a different perspective on cutting trees and endangering an environment he never realized existed. Robin Williams gives an exuberant performance as a laboratory-altered bat that foreshadows his Genie in **Aladdin.**

The Fox and the Hound (Disney, 1981, 83 m., G, 2–up; directors Art Stevens, Ted Berman, Richard Rich, voices of Pearl Bailey, Kurt Russell, Mickey Rooney, Jack Albertson, Sandy Duncan, Corey Feldman)

Can a foxhound befriend the creature he's been bred to hunt and kill? This Disney movie investigates that premise in animated form, and proposes that a solid friendship can override inherent differences. Borrowing backgrounds from **Bambi** and an age-old odd-couple story line, this more recent of Disney's "classics" addresses a phase that most of us have experienced: growing apart from one's friends, identifying differences, and resolving them. With minimal parental input, this movie could give young viewers a terrific example of how people get along and why they have to.

Gallavants (Just for Kids, 1985, 100 m., G, 4–10)

An ant colony serves as an allegory for human society in this interesting production from Europe. Ideally, everyone works together, but there are lazy members of society even among those who labor tirelessly. The Gallavants' motto is "Anything is possible," and that belief buoys them even in tough times. The story is an acceptable, modern adjunct to Aesop's fables.

Gay Purr-ee (Warner, 1963, 85 m., 6–up; director Abe Levitow, voices of Judy Garland, Robert Goulet, Red Buttons, Mel Blanc, Hermione Gingold, Morey Amsterdam)

In an era when musicals were still all the rage, talented felines cavort on screen in an animated love story, somewhat dated by today's standards. Mewsette, a lovely country-bred cat, longs for the excitement of the "City of Lights" and travels to Paris, pursued by her plain but loving suitor, who wants to protect her and provide for her in a cozy, rural home. Like Dorothy in **The Wizard of Oz,** this curious cat (as portrayed by Judy Garland) learns all too well that "there's no place like home." Much of the dialogue and plot twists are beyond the faculties of children under 10, and the intricacies of the musical score and its attendant animation are entirely lost on children, yet viewers as young as 6 may find the eye-pleasing characters appealing.

The Great Muppet Caper (Disney/Jim Henson, 1981, 95 m., G, 3–up; voices of Jim Henson, Frank Oz)

It's tough to know whether to put the Muppets in the live-action category or leave them here. On this, their second outing, the Muppets discover that a priceless British gem, the Baseball Diamond, is missing, and it's Miss Piggy and the crew to the rescue. Musical Miss Piggy aids in Kermit and Fozzie's search, and the ensuing gags and puns should have most under 10-year-olds—and their parents, no doubt—in stitches. (Look under "M" in this chapter for other Muppet mania.)

Grendel, Grendel, Grendel (Family Home Entertainment, 1980, 90 m., 8–up; director Alexander Stitt, narrator Peter Ustinov, voices of Arthur Dignam, Keith Mitchell, Bobby Bright)

This Australian production is based on John Gardner's novel about the monster from medieval times who wonders why he's considered such a horrible beast when men pillage, plunder, and murder their own kind. The animation is very basic, though this film is a bit mature for some children, but the story should provoke thought in observant viewers.

Gulliver's Travels (Video Yesteryear/Turner, 1939, 77 m., 3–12; director Dave Fleischer, voices of Lanny Ross, Jessica Dragonette)

None of the film versions does justice to Jonathan Swift's classic tale of a shipwrecked sailor washed up on the shores of various strange lands. This animated offering, however, despite its wandering plot and lackluster details, may entice older children to read the original.

The Hobbit (Warner/Facets Media, 1977, 76 m., 6–12; director Arthur Rankin Jr., voices of Orson Bean, John Huston)

J.R.R. Tolkien's wonderful fantasy gets a fair shake in this production directed by half of the Rankin/Bass animation team that brought you those model-animated holiday specials. Although the film is lovingly produced, it's no match for the intricacies of Tolkien's novel; it may, however, provide a timely opportunity to get older children hooked on a mythical fantasy.

It's the Great Pumpkin, Charlie Brown (Paramount, 1966, 76 m., 2–12)

While the rest of the Peanuts gang is out trick-or-treating, Linus camps out in the pumpkin patch, awaiting the arrival of the legendary Great Pumpkin, who, tradition claims, will rise up out of one special pumpkin patch and give toys and candy to all the good boys and girls. While most of the other TV specials featuring Charles M. Schulz's Peanuts crew are shorter than this (generally 25 to 30 minutes), this was one of the first holiday TV specials to feature the comic strip characters. Also check out the familiar favorites **A Charlie Brown Christmas, A Charlie Brown Thanksgiving,** and **You're a Good Sport, Charlie Brown.**

Jetsons: The Movie (MCA/Universal, 1990, 82 m., G, 2–10)

Will bumbling George Jetson become a hero when he discovers a way to benefit both Spaceley Sprockets and what's left of the environment, without eradicting an entire race of creatures? Parents who used to watch the TV show as youngsters may want to watch along with their children. This wacky family of the future still rings true as they deal with an elementary-school boy genius, his hormone-happy teen sister, and Rosie, that unfailingly service-oriented robot with the New Yawk accent. The Jetsons may not have the powerful draw they did 20 years ago, but they still provide a creative look at our potential future.

The Jetsons Meet the Flintstones (Turner/Hanna-Barbera, 1987, 93 m., G, 2–10)

In this outing, Elroy creates a time machine as a science project and whisks the family off to prehistoric times, where they meet and are befriended by the Flintstones and the Rubbles. The tables turn when Elroy transports the prehistoric quartet to the future for an out-of-this-world experience.

Journey Back to Oz (MGM/UA, 1974, 88 m., G, 2–10; director Hal Sutherland, voices of Liza Minnelli, Milton Berle, Margaret Hamilton, Danny Thomas, Ethel Merman, Mickey Rooney, Paul Lynde)

This star-studded sequel to the live-action classic that starred Minnelli's mother, Judy Garland, is a fitting tribute and surprisingly successful. Also on hand is Margaret Hamilton, who portrayed the witch in the 1939 version. Green elephants threaten and terrorize the inhabitants of Oz, and Dorothy and her trio of friends travel back to Oz to see if they can help.

A Journey Through Fairyland (Just for Kids, 1989, 88 m., 6–12)

Only **Fantasia** surpasses this European creation at marrying music and free-form animation. The story line involves a talented young musician and his flute and the muse who guides him to a higher plane, where he can learn to truly appreciate and understand music. Children with any musical inclination will find this excursion through classical music and art fascinating.

The Jungle Book (Disney, 1967, 78 m., G, 2–12; director Wolfgang Reitherman, voices of Phil Harris, Sebastian Cabot, Louis Prima, George Sanders, Sterling Holloway)

This is the last picture Walt Disney himself had a hand in producing. As told here, Rudyard Kipling's tale of Mowgli, the boy raised by wolves in India's jungles, is at times funny, frightening, and terrifically entertaining. To safeguard him from the sinister tiger Shere Khan, Mowgli is to be sent back to live with the rest of Mankind, but the independent-minded boy does not want to go. That's when the musical fun begins, as Baloo the amiable bear teaches Mowgli "The Bare Necessities," and Mowgli meets and is befriended by apes and vultures—all to memorable Disney songs, of course!

Katy and the Katerpillar Kids (Just for Kids, 85 m., 2–8)

A cautionary tale about the perils of growing up too quickly, this well-intentioned European import features several antagonists that may be off-putting to the littlest viewers. Two young caterpillars, desperate to become butterflies so they can fly, venture away from mom's cocoon in search of adventure. Along the way they encounter a little danger, some new friends, and several shady characters among Nature's creatures. When their frantic mother butterfly does find them, she teaches them to appreciate that all things come in due time.

Lady and the Tramp (Disney, 1955, 75 m., 5–up; directors Hamilton Luske, Clyde Geronimi, Wilfred Jackson, voices of Peggy Lee, Larry Roberts, Stan Freberg, Barbara Luddy)

Scruffy but lovable Tramp narrates this love story/adventure, featuring himself and a respectable spaniel, Lady, whom he rescues and woos. (They're the only canines able to make eating spaghetti look so romantic!) Terrific musical numbers include the slinky Siamese cats meowing "We Are Siamese If You Please." Disney films always have at least one message; here, the moral is that divisions between social classes are really only in one's mind. Family is all-important, regardless of social status. This was Disney's first animated feature filmed in Cinemascope, which is why the small screen can't do it justice. If you have the chance to see it in a letterbox, or widescreen, version, you'll see a more fluid, less choppy film.

The Little Mermaid (Disney, 1989, 76 m., G, 2–up; directors John Musker, Ron Clemente, voices of Jodi Benson, Pat Carroll, Samuel E. Wright, Kenneth Mars, Buddy Hackett)

Disney rewrites—with record-breaking results—Hans Christian Andersen's story of a mermaid who falls in love with a human. Wayward and independent, lovely young Ariel sets her sights on getting a landlubber prince to kiss and love her. The latter is easy; it's the kiss that he must deliver on deadline that establishes the cliffhanger tone in this fairy tale. In typical Disney fashion, the producers know when to tug at the heartstrings, break into song, or escalate the tension. This film won Academy Awards for Best Original Score (Alan Menken) and for the Song "Under the Sea," by Menken and Howard Ashman. If you and your children enjoy this film, chances are you'll also like **Ariel's Undersea Adventures,** the videos from the TV series (two episodes per tape). Although this book lists very few TV series that were released to video, this series deserves mention. It's several steps ahead of any of its competitors, even many other Disney series, because it consistently imitates the film on which it's based in musical storytelling finesse and animation expertise. And in the TV series, Ariel becomes a protector of endangered species and sets a moral example for her peers.

The Muppet Movie (Disney, 1979, 94 m., G, 2–up; director James Frawley, voices of Jim Henson, Frank Oz, stars Charles Durning, Austin Pendleton, cameos by Edgar Bergen, Mel Brooks, Milton Berle, Steve Martin, and other stars)

In their first adventure beyond the confines of the television screen, the Muppets follow their leader Kermit the Frog when he leaves his Southern swamp home for the greener pastures of Hollywood. With musical power to equal any Disney animated feature, this movie proves why people can easily fall in love with a bit of green felt.

The Muppets Take Manhattan (FoxVideo, 1984, 90 m., G, 2–up; director Frank Oz, stars Dabney Coleman, Art Carney, James Coco, Joan Rivers, Gregory Hines, Linda Lavin)

In this outing, the Muppets think the lights are brighter on Broadway, where they try to make it big. As in the first film, lots of enjoyable musical numbers keep the audience humming. And if you're still in a Muppet frame of mind, you can try the feature films **The Muppet Christmas Carol** (Disney, 1992) or **The Great Muppet Caper** (reviewed earlier in this chapter), or **It's the Muppets! Vol. 1** and **Vol. 2** (classic scenes from *The Muppet Show,* Disney), **Jim Henson's Muppet Babies** (cartoons, not Muppets, also Disney), or **The Muppet Video Series** (ten hour-long videos that compile scenes from *The Muppet Show,* FoxVideo).

Once Upon a Forest (FoxVideo, 1993, 71 m., G, 2–12; voices of Michael Crawford, Ben Vereen)

A trio of young animals in a forest threatened by pollution from a runaway chemical truck embarks on a quest to save the life of their friend. Abigail the wood mouse, Edgar Mole, and Russell the hedgehog learn through their generosity on behalf of their friend that much more can be accomplished when friends work as a team, and when they admit that nothing is impossible if you set your mind to it. The music is good (by the team of Oscar-winner James Horner and Oscar-nominated lyricist Will Jennings), if not as memorable as music from many of Disney's animated films. William Hanna, half of the Hanna-Barbera team, served as executive producer.

101 Dalmatians (Disney, 1961, 80 m., 4–up)

This true classic is also a terrific anti-fur statement: You know someone has a screw loose if she covets Dalmatian fur coats. When loving Dalmatian parents birth fifteen adorable puppies, and inadvertently add almost ninety other orphan pups to their clan, they find they must protect them from Cruella De Ville's plan to make a fur coat of them. Dashing heroes from the countryside, the nightly "bark" through which the dogs communicate to one another over distances, and the love evident both between Pongo and Perdita and the humans who own them help to dispel the dark element Cruella and her henchmen bring to the film.

The Phantom Tollbooth (MGM/UA, 1969, 90 m., G, 9–12; stars Butch Patrick, voices of Mel Blanc, Hans Conried, Daws Butler, Candy Candido)

Although it begins and ends with live action, this adventure in learning is more fittingly placed in the animated category. MGM chose director/animator Chuck Jones to helm its first animated feature based on the Norton Juster book about Milo, a boy who's so bored with learning he's completely lost his curiosity. On a trip through the Phantom Tollbooth, where he becomes an animated character in the Kingdom of Wisdom, Milo finds himself on a mission—which he cannot complete without an understanding of numbers and words—to reunite the lands of Digitopolis and Dictionopolis by restoring the princesses Rhyme and Reason to their thrones. He comes to understand that without knowledge, life would be chaotic, and he'd be in the doldrums. The plot is well developed and enhanced with music, but there may be too much story for early elementary-school children.

Pinocchio (Disney, 1940, 87 m., 4–up; director Ben Sharpsteen; voices of Dickie Jones, Cliff Edwards, Christian Rub)

"When You Wish Upon a Star" is just one of the numerous highlights of this classic Disney masterpiece that features top-notch musical numbers, glorious animation, memorable and lovable characters, and dazzling special effects. The toymaker Geppetto carves the son he never had from a piece of wood. After trials and tribulations that might reduce lesser puppets to splinters, Pinocchio earns his way into real life. The special effects are what might give the wee ones nightmares; although they're softened by being animated, scenes such as boys morphing into donkeys and a chase with an immense, malevolent whale are potentially frightening. The film was adapted from Carlo Collodi's story.

The Point (LIVE/Vestron, 1971, 73 m., 7–up; director Fred Wolf, narrated by Ringo Starr)

Those who differ from the norm are not welcome in the land of Point. One boy whose head is round instead of pointed learns this with difficulty when he's banished to the Pointless Forest. There he learns that, actually, everything has a point, and with this revelation, he grows his own point. Young viewers involved in an episode of intolerance or prejudice at school or elsewhere may find it easier to digest a lesson on the topic via this innocuous and accessible video, rather than a lecture. The score is by Harry Nilsson. This video is also available in audio formats.

Samson and Sally: Song of the Whales (Just for Kids, 1988, 70 m., 8–12)

Environmentally conscious in the extreme, this animated feature is just too grim for many young children. Tempered, however, with a parent's thoughtful insights on how children can change the world, this program could be of interest to children who are mature enough to understand that it is simply one view of the world. In the tale, two young whales in search of the legendary Moby Dick encounter a seascape literally littered with man's waste, toxic and otherwise. Skeletons, flaming oil slicks, harpooners, and killer whales nearly prevent the duo from completing their quest. Lovingly wrought animation and some welcome musical interludes try to make the serious subject matter easier to digest. **Samson and Sally** is based on the book "Song of the Whales," by Bent Haller.

Scamper the Penguin (Just for Kids, 1989, 85 m., 5–up)

Few films that try so hard to get a message across are as successful as this Enoki Films production. In animation that rivals Disney's, humans, seen from the perspective of penguins in Antarctica, are painted in both good and bad light. First the scientists come to study and protect the penguins, who befriend a good-hearted dog accompanying the expedition. Like children, these young penguins learn their survival skills in the classroom and grow attached to others of their kind, giving the animators a chance to stretch their skills at making expressive, emotive characters. When a few penguins are captured by men other than the scientists, they are saved only by the human beings' stupidity. The narrator tells viewers some interesting things about penguins, such as the fact that the male is responsible for building the family's nest and incubating the eggs. Ideally, a film like this will inspire children to learn more about a topic, like life at the South Pole, penguins, and endangered species; it may lead to a trip to the library.

The Secret of NIMH (MGM/UA, 1982, 82 m., G, 5–up; director Don Bluth, voices of Derek Jacobi, Elizabeth Hartman, Dom DeLuise, John Carradine, Peter Strauss)

Don Bluth's first feature-length cartoon, based on Robert O'Brien's children's book, is social commentary at its best. Bluth crafted this gem lovingly, with care and attention to detail, in classic cel animation style, without the fast-moving images generated by today's computer animators. It's not hard to see the difference between the quality here and standard Saturday-morning cartoons. The plot focuses on a mouse who must relocate her family; on her quest for a new home, all the elements of fantasy come into play, from betrayals and challenges to secret treasures and long-lost relatives. With all the adventure, viewers of all ages will find plenty to keep them involved, and parents may want to share the fun.

Tiny Toon Adventures: How I Spent My Vacation (Warner, 1991, 80 m., 4–up)

The puns, inside jokes, and sight gags in this film will keep the entire family—regardless of age—rolling in the aisles. When Babs and Buster Bunny, relatives of the lanky Bugs, get together with their producer, Steven Spielberg (in his first full-length, made-for-video animated production), expect intelligent humor, above-average animation, and plenty of fun. These cartoon characters captivate viewers by speaking directly to them and winking into the camera. And they're quick to remind us that they never get hurt and can always rewind themselves to change the plot, since they're just cartoons.

Twice Upon a Time (Warner, 1983, 75 m., PG, 8–up; director John Korty; voices of Lorenzo Music, Judith Kahan Kampmann, James Cranna, Marshall Efron)

For anyone who appreciates the humor of *Bullwinkle* and the off-beat techniques (like this cutout style) found in animation festivals, here's a clever production with a similar ambiance. Producer George Lucas (the **Star Wars** trilogy) tries his hand at animation and does quite well with this enjoyable romp. In this tale of warring dream creators (the Frivoli induce sweet dreams, while the Murkworks create nightmares), one evil being plans to turn all dreams into nightmares by stealing the Cosmic Clock and freezing time. Fast-paced puns and complex layers of cerebral comedy might escape children under eight, though younger children may enjoy watching the animation and cheering for the heroes.

Watership Down (Warner, 1978, 92 m., PG, 8–up; director Martin Rosen, narrator Michael Hordern, voices of John Hurt, Ralph Richardson, Denholm Elliott, Richard Briers, Zero Mostel)

An allegorical representation of a family's escape from Nazi Germany, fraught with danger, terror, blood, and death, this is not a cartoon that children should watch alone. Viewers younger than the recommended 8 years old may not understand the mature themes, and the violent depictions of blood and death, handled straightforwardly, may unnerve them. Still, the adventure is spectacular, and the illustration-style animation, so realistic and natural, is beautifully wrought. Also, check out the book by Richard Adams.

We're Back (MCA/Universal, 1993, 72 m., G, 5–up; directed by Dick Zondag, Ralph Zondag, Phil Nibbelink, Simon Wells, voices of John Goodman, Rhea Perlman, Jay Leno, Walter Cronkite, Martin Short)

Aside from a few scary predators and a sinister circus ringmaster, this children's film contains none of the nail-biting suspense and bloodshed Steven Spielberg applied to his other 1993 dinosaur flick, **Jurassic Park.** In this adventure based on Hudson Talbott's book *We're Back! A Dinosaur's Story*, a time-traveling scientist tampers with the natural order by imbuing a quartet of lovable prehistoric critters with human-level brains. He transports them to modern-day New York City, intending that they should take up residence at the Museum of Natural History to teach dinosaur lovers how it really was when they roamed the Earth. But the scientist's brother has his evil eye on them to add to his "Eccentric Circus." If only Spielberg could have as much irreverent fun with his feature-length fare as he does in his animated TV series *Tiny Toons* and *Animaniacs,* this could have been a terrific movie. Instead, it's passably enjoyable entertainment.

Who Framed Roger Rabbit? (Disney, 1988, 103 m., PG, 6–up; director Robert Zemeckis, stars Bob Hoskins, Joanna Cassidy, Christopher Lloyd, Stubby Kaye, Alan Tilvern, voices of Charles Fleischer, Lou Hirsch, Mel Blanc, Mel Questal, June Foray)

A film this full of quick-moving visual one-liners warrants a second and even a third look. Though not the first to combine live action and animation (see **Mary Poppins**), it's one of the first to incorporate animated special effects successfully onto and around a live-action star in nearly seamless scenes—and the first to make the viewer feel that the human element really is interacting with an animated entity. It won four Oscars, including one for Visual Special Effects —not surprising, since it was a coproduction between Disney and Steven Spielberg's companies.

The Wind in the Willows (Disney, 1950, 47 m., 5–up; narrator Basil Rathbone)

In this compilation of three Disney shorts, the automobile is the glue that binds them together. A delightful version of Kenneth Grahame's book leads off the trio. Toad of Toad Hall, landed gentry in amphibious form, insists on driving his car dangerously fast down rural roads, threatening not only his own life but that of everyone else on or near the road as well. It takes some friends from the other side of the tracks to settle the rich toad down and help him learn his lesson. Children should be able to relate Toad's wild ride not with the amusement ride at Disney World but with their own experiences with excess. Also on the tape is the Chip and Dale short "Trailer Horn," in which Donald Duck is bedeviled by the mischievous chipmunk pair. Goofy comes down with "Motor Mania" when he takes the wheel of a car. There is also a four-tape HBO series available you may want to investigate called simply **The Wind in the Willows;** for a review, see Chapter 7: Storytelling and Literature-Based Videos.

Yellow Submarine (MGM/UA, 1968, 85 m., G, 6–up; director George Dunning, voices of John Lennon, George Harrison, Paul McCartney, Ringo Starr)

The Beatles are enlisted to save Pepperland (where Sgt. Pepper lives, of course) from the Blue Meanies, who stomp the joy and color out of Pepperland's inhabitants. A phenomenon in its time, this trip through the Sea of Holes and Nowhereland is one that still hasn't gone out of date, thanks to classic popular songs by the Beatles. Surreal, Peter Max–created/inspired fantasylands and creatures delight the eyes, while one-liners, puns, and the Beatles' singular sense of humor delight the ears. This is a superb way to reminisce while introducing young children to terrific music and animation.

Chapter 3

■

MUSICAL FUN

From **Barney & the Backyard Gang, Wee Sing,** and **Don Cooper** to such concert tapes such as **Tickle Tune Typhoon, Fred Penner,** and Raffi's two tapes, children's video choices are expanding, thanks to a proliferation of audio artists now making the transition to video.

Music video has been one of the fastest growing genres in the children's video industry, almost since the medium's inception in the 1980s. The reason is easy to see if you reflect on how many mainstream audio artists are looking for movie roles: Entertainers can double their exposure, and sometimes their profits, by producing videos as well as audiocassettes.

How can you know what kinds of music videos your child might like? A good rule of thumb is to base your selections on your own musical tastes, especially where toddlers are concerned. Then choose programs that are based on your child's favorite musical performers, even if *you'd* rather not have your toddler watch, for example, a Barney tape. Remember, those tapes were intended for children; to understand how a child views them, you have to put aside all your preconceived adult notions and sensibilities.

Opt to collect a variety of musical styles to suit your child's various moods. Remember, you'll have to listen to these ditties at least twenty to thirty times before your child wants something different, so make sure at least *some* of the music is in a style or by a performer *you* enjoy.

Even though most of these programs are pure entertainment, many incorporate songs with educational messages about socializing, the environment, nature, and other topics. Choose programs that reflect subjects, attitudes, and music you want your child to learn, adopt, and enjoy.

Programs are live-action unless otherwise noted.

Diana Huss Green, editor-in-chief of Parents' Choice Foundation's quarterly publication, discusses the benefits of adding video to your children's entertainment diet.

"The VCR costs little and gives a lot," Diana Huss Green is quick to establish in any conversation about the validity of video as worthwhile family entertainment. "It gives families, both parents and children, choices and control of content as well as time."

As editor-in-chief of the periodical for Parents' Choice, the nation's premiere nonprofit parenting group, Green knows about the validity of many forms of children's entertainment. Parents' Choice annually hands coveted awards to only the best children's books, videos, toys, TV programs, audio releases, computer programs, video games, and rock-and-roll music. Since more than one book or video usually receives a Gold, Silver, or Classic Award in a given year, the lists of winners often reflect the wonderful diversity of product available in the market.

A Parents' Choice Award for a video is the equivalent of an Oscar for Children's Video. But Parents' Choice Award winners are selected differently than many other organizations' awards: they are chosen by children, parents, and grandparents. The adults are experts in the field: teachers, librarians, and TV, video, or film critics and producers. Explains Green, "They make choices thinking, 'Does this fulfill my standards as a parent? Does it fulfill my standards as a critic?' We set the children up in the groups so that we see a variety of responses."

As for the criteria, Green says the jurors consider that "Successful children's videos entertain and teach with first-rate skills and talent. That's really the key. Good material for children speaks virtuously and instructively to them. This is the way we pass on the standards and mores and morals of each generation, one to the next."

How should the consumer judge children's video? How can any parent or grandparent distinguish real gold from fool's gold? Green admits it's not always easy, and "You can't always go by the cover or the company," since not all of a particular company's videos will appeal to any one individual.

Her best advice is "Use previews, reviews, and word of mouth." Read the reviews in your local paper, and in particular in your local parenting papers. (See Resources for the address of the Parenting Publications of America, which can put you in touch with your local parenting papers.) "Also, go to the library and ask for *Booklist* and the publication *Video Librarian,* and of course, *Parents' Choice,* which contains product that will be in stores as well as in the library."

Previews can be a bit time-consuming, but in the long run, it's worth it to invest your time making certain you are buying or renting something that will satisfy both you and your child. Green recommends asking your local video store manager to play a title in question on a Saturday, a time when children are usually in the store, or at an off time. Otherwise, you'll just have to rent the film and skim through it before letting your child watch it.

As for word of mouth, Green suggests speaking with the local experts, including your children's librarian, as well as language-arts teachers, who may be able to point you in the right direction.

"There *is* a problem in getting the information," she acknowledges. "The problem is being so busy and exhausted that you really want to say, 'Just go turn on the TV.' That's not such a terrible thing; it should be a reasonably guilt-free process if you've looked at the TV show or the videotape first. Do just a little bit of homework, a little bit of research, and you'll free yourself up for months." Sometimes it might take getting together with neighbors, or people with whom you share babysitters, or PTA groups to share ideas and information about which videos children really seem to like, and which teach something as well as entertain viewers.

Why should parents watch videos with their children when they can, instead of letting the TV babysit them? "You watch video as a family so you can pass on to your children your responses, which maybe you can't do verbally. . . . It sets up a family memory, like watching the annual spring showing of the **Wizard of Oz.** It allows parents to interact, to prompt their children to think, to respond, to learn values, to judge between fantasy and reality. It can ignite imagination and spark discussion."

I asked Green to compile a short list of the ten essential videos she'd include in the ideal children's video library. All the people we asked, including Green, had a hard time limiting themselves to only ten. She tried instead to compile a list that was "balanced." Here's what she suggested (following each suggestion, you'll find the chapter in which each is mentioned): "The **Raffi** video, since he's the Pied Piper of children's video [Chapter 3]; **Baby Songs** and **More Baby Songs,** but not the others in the series, since the first two were a fresh concept [Chapter 3]; **Stories from the Black Tradition** [Chapter 7] introduces children to fabulous books they might not read otherwise; the story 'The Three Robbers' because it teaches viewers universal ethical concepts and teaches them lovingly [the tale is included on two videos from CC Studios: **The Tomi Ungerer Library,** which is not reviewed here, and **What's Under My Bed?,** found in Chapter 7]; **Sesame Street Visits the Hospital** is remarkable in the way it dispenses information [Chapter 4]; **Pecos Bill:** Robin Williams is pure tall-tale American humor, and it appeals to all ages [Chapter 7]; **Granpa,** for its sensitive approach to death [Chapter 7]; **The Red Balloon,** which is a classic gem [Chapter 7]; the **Preschool Power** tapes [Chapter 6]; **The Wind in the Willows** [Chapter 7] because it leads children to chapters in a book most children don't read anymore. The Disney version, however, is sassy and crispy as fresh celery." Green added **Sounds Around** [Bo Peep Productions, not reviewed here], a live-action video for toddlers to 6-year-olds that includes such surprising sounds as snoring and wagon wheels rolling across gravel, as well as **Mouse Soup** and **Frog and Toad Together** (both in Chapter 3), two of Golden Book Video's puppet/stop-motion videos based on the work of the late children's author Arnold Lobel. "They are sweet-natured and full of gentle humor; besides, they'll lead your child to reading the books." What more could you ask of a special video?

All Aboard: A Collection of Music Videos (The Learning Station, 800-458-3417 or 407-727-1428, 30 m., 3–8)

Following *Sesame Street*'s lead, the producers of this program aim for the post-diaper set with songs, fun, and games that will help them adjust in society, gain self-confidence, and learn new social and motor skills. The Learning Station is the name of an earnest musical troupe (two men, one woman) who've produced six education-oriented audio releases. All-original music may be unfamiliar at first, but soon young viewers will be reciting the words as easily as they'll learn their ABCs. **All Aboard** also covers such developmental issues as learning about body safety and recognizing trouble, improving one's ability to follow directions, and learning to express oneself. You may want to have a beanbag on hand for the segments that work on a child's muscle development with beanbag movements and songs.

The Animal Alphabet (LIVE/Scholastic, 1985, 30 m., 2–6, live-action/animation)

Original songs put a new spin on learning the alphabet for preschoolers. Here, animation is combined with footage of exotic animals from the National Geographic archives to make for a highly creative way to help children understand language and remember the alphabet. Geoffrey the Giraffe, the mascot from retail toy giant Toys "R" Us, appears in animated form to encourage children to sing along and recite the alphabet (rest assured, Scholastic did not include an ad for the toy store on this tape). The tape not only helps children learn the alphabet but also opens their minds to the vast variety of creatures that are living on the planet.

Baby Songs, More Baby Songs, Turn On the Music!, Even More Baby Songs, John Lithgow's Kid-Sized Concert, Baby Rock, Follow Along Songs, Baby Songs Christmas (Hi-Tops/Video Treasures, 30 m. each, infant–6)

Live-action toddlers mean viewers have humans to connect with on-screen, and they do connect in this beautifully produced series. It's magical to watch that happen, especially when the accompanying music (by renowned children's entertainer Hap Palmer) is as clever as "Today I Took My Diapers Off," "Sittin' in a High Chair," or "My Mommy Comes Back." Growing up couldn't be easier or more natural, thanks to the comfort Palmer's songs bring to each new and different experience. What sets this series apart from its competition is the use of high-quality shots of children that seem as natural as your own home videos. The first two tapes, as well as **Even More Baby Songs,** are for toddlers and contain plenty of footage of babies and kids who are just beginning to crawl, as well as toddlers. The John Lithgow entry is a sedate video that features the actor showing his musical side; the children in his on-screen audience, however, appear less than enthralled with his soft mannerisms. Give slightly older kids a taste of the rock-and-roll classics in **Baby Rock,** which features some original tunes as well as old standbys. **Turn on the**

Music! is skewed slightly older, for ages 3–7, and encourages children to experiment with movement as well as music. **Follow Along Songs** reaches children who are ready to learn colors, sequences, and rhythms as it invokes participation. The holiday tape, which includes familiar carols, shows lots of happy children frolicking in the snow, helping older siblings and parents decorate their homes and trees, and making certain Santa has a snack on Christmas Eve. Another series, **Original Tales & Tunes** (reviewed in this chapter), was also produced by the Backyard Productions team, and although it is not all live-action, it is a clever collection for preschoolers and young elementary-school children.

Barney & Friends (The Lyons Group, 13 tapes, 30 m. each, 1–8)

Adults seem to either love or hate Barney, but many toddlers agree that he's their favorite "dinostar." He's included in this chapter since he relies mostly on music to make his points about learning, loving, and respecting one another, and simply having a great time using one's imagination. Through 1991, the original series was called **Barney & the Backyard Gang** and featured eight videos. Now episodes culled from his PBS-TV series, *Barney & Friends*, are also available on home video as **The *Barney & Friends* Collection.** The original set includes three titles hosted by Sandy Duncan: **Backyard Show, A Day at the Beach,** and **Three Wishes.** These establish the theme of "make-believe" play enhanced by Barney's suggestions about songs, learning, and acceptance of others. The original set also encompasses **Rock with Barney: Protect Our Earth** (a concert in which kids take on behind-the-scenes roles), **Barney in Concert** (which invites the audience on stage to sing their ABCs and introduces Baby Bop, Barney's "cousin," a toddler-aged dinosaur), **Barney Goes to School** (which teaches, as always, that learning is fun, especially if you can sing about it), **Barney's Campfire Sing-Along** (which focuses on learning from and about nature in songs and facts), and **Waiting for Santa** (How will Santa find Derek, who's new in town?). The following videos from the TV series include parent/child activity guides to help families get the most out of each viewing: **Barney's Magical, Musical Adventure, Barney's Birthday, Barney's Home Sweet Homes, Barney Rhymes with Mother Goose, Let's Pretend with Barney,** which introduces the newest dinosaur—freckled, yellow BJ, **Barney's Alphabet Zoo, Barney's Best**

Manners, Barney's Imagination Island, Barney Live! In New York City, Families Are Special, and **Barney Safety.**

Beethoven Lives Upstairs (BMG, 1989, 51 m., 7–up; director David Devine, stars Neil Munro, Illya Woloshyn, Fiona Reid, Paul Soles, Albert Schultz, Sheila McCarthy)

This little-known but exquisitely crafted TV production, set in nineteenth-century Vienna (though all the accents are American), details a different side of a famous composer, and is told from a young boy's point of view. A widow and her son in dire financial straits take in a boarder on their third floor. They are warned not to disturb the man, who paces and thumps and screeches and bangs away at a piano and other instruments at all hours. The boy, Christophe, becomes angry with this intruder, but his curiosity gets the better of him, and a special relationship develops between a composer who's battling deafness and a boy without a father. Without succumbing to sappiness, the film develops themes such as accepting those who are different; understanding that although your problems seem paramount, others have problems, too; and learning from and respecting one's elders. Its only weakness is its seemingly limited appeal to music- or history-loving viewers, but don't let the fact that it's a period drama turn off your young viewers. For other introductions to the works of famous composers, check out BMG's multiple-award-winning *Classical Kids* series of audio recordings, including an audio version of this video and *Vivaldi's Ring of Mystery, Mozart's Magic Fantasy, Mr. Bach Comes to Call,* and *Daydreams and Lullabies.* Older children who appreciate music might be ready for **Amadeus** (see Chapter 1: Feature Films).

Ben Vereen Sing Along series (Peter Pan Industries, 2 tapes, 30 m. each, 5–10; stars Ben Vereen, Savion Glover)

These performance tapes prove Ben Vereen has a healthy respect for the intelligence of children, as well as a powerful desire to share with them some of the things that make him happiest: dancing and singing. In **Welcome to the Party,** he adds new concepts to familiar tunes such as the "Hokey Pokey," which becomes a freeze dance for the audience, and brings children on stage to star in his song "Do the Dinosaur." **Around the World** is loosely structured to give children an overview of some of the music of other countries. Vereen sings "Day-O" from Trinidad and a rap version of "London Bridge" and encourages his audience to join him in clapping, imitating musical instruments a la Bobby McFerrin, and even harmonizing with him on stage. Glover is a young tap dancer who performs a dance number on each tape, and Vereen even breaks into a soft shoe. Vereen's energy and his penchant for making silly faces and drawing the children to him work beautifully.

Bethie's Really Silly Clubhouse (Discovery Music/BMG Kidz, 45 m., 2–8; stars Beth Marlin Lichter, Tommy Bertelson, George West Kellogg, Kristen Grammer, Leon McKenzi)

Add a children's musician to *Pee Wee's Playhouse*, and you have Bethie, an expressive, wonderfully wacky woman whose exuberance should get every couch-potato tot on his or her feet. Like *Pee Wee's Playhouse*, Bethie's silly clubhouse contains lots of furniture that comes alive to entertain and encourage three young visitors to join in and learn something new. The TV, for example, is a close-up of a heavily made-up woman, books on shelves flap their pages to get attention, and the Muppet-like doorknocker tells knock-knock jokes. There's a weak story line that tries to teach Bethie's guests about animals before they can adopt kittens from Kit E. Katman, a rhyming Rastafarian, but the tape is really a beautifully staged excuse to have fun and learn some original songs. The sets are professional, the caricatured humans and furnishings are delightfully silly, and the clever songs are easy for children to repeat and learn. Each video includes a mail-in offer for a free poster and a booklet on creating puppets. An audiocassette, *Bethie's Really Silly Songs About Animals,* is also available with a lyric book.

Bill Harley: Who Made This Mess? (A&M, 1992, 50 m., 4–8; stars Bill Harley)

Here's another children's entertainer who packs so much into his performance that you can rest assured children will sleep well that night. For his video audience, Harley sings, tells tall tales, clowns, and emotes, and he lets viewers know it's okay, even cool, to do the same. His delivery is witty and his songs, with such titles as "I Don't Wanna Wait Anymore," are infectiously funny. The youngest children in this age range may lose interest halfway through this rather long performance video, but encourage them to stick with the program; they will definitely be rewarded with clever plot twists in the story of Joey and Chloe, the twins with smelly sneakers, and Harley's humorous sound effects and funny faces. The program won a 1992 Parents' Choice Award.

Carnival of the Animals (Twin Tower, 1986, 30 m., 2–8, live action/animation; hosted by Gary Burghoff)

Children never seem to outgrow animals, and when their animated antics are combined with the clever rhymes of Ogden Nash, animals become irresistible entertainment. Plus, the tape is a subtle introduction to the joys and beauty of classical music; the work of the ingenious Camille Saint-Saens musically illustrates the animals, and makes it easy for children to hear the drama as the composer envisioned it. For example, when an animated lion plays the piano, he roars along with each crescendo he plays. This trip through the animal kingdom, shot at the San Diego Zoo, helps children see the relationship between a musical composition and its subject. And the fact that it's done in a lighthearted manner should keep viewers in good humor and ready to learn more.

A Child's Garden of Verses (Family Home Entertainment, 1993, 26 m., 2–10, animated)

Robert Louis Stevenson's book is set to music in this beautiful production, lovingly animated by Michael Sporn. It's just the sort of video you might want to plug in to introduce your child to a variety of media: art (Sporn's animation is fantastic), music (the songs complement the story, and may even inspire repetition), and the printed word (Stevenson's classic has delighted several generations of children). Try a read-along adventure, and maybe that will entice youngsters to sample some of Stevenson's other classic works.

Clifford's Sing-Along Adventure (Family Home Entertainment/Scholastic, 30 m., 2–6, animated)

Clifford the Big Red Dog, that wonderful learning hound from Scholastic, teaches preschoolers and young elementary-school children while they join him on an adventure. With such familiar songs as "She'll Be Coming Round the Mountain," "Old MacDonald," and "Skip to My Lou," Clifford encourages viewers to feel the music and participate by singing along, clapping, and even getting up off the couch to dance. Like other Clifford tapes (there are six others listed in Chapter 4: Discovery and Learning, under **Clifford**), this interactive musical video was designed by experts from Scholastic to motivate children to learn new things and be brave about acquiring new skills.

Dennis Hysom in the Wonderful World of the Wooleycat (Discovery Music/ BMG Kidz, 1994, 45 m., 2–10; stars Dennis Hysom)

Whether this program belongs in the storytelling chapter or here is debatable, but since Hysom has made his name as a musical performer like Bill Harley (also in this chapter), it's included here. In this video, Hysom portrays the curator of the Story Museum, who takes three young visitors to visit the Wooleycat in his Wishing Tree so they can write a creative story for school. An acrobat as well as a storyteller, the Wooleycat inspires them with his tales whenever "it's a perfect storytelling day"—and that can be any day. The Wooleycat is the perfect foil for Hysom, who accompanies the oversized kitty, usually on guitar and in song. With two audio releases that allow Hysom to alter nursery rhymes to create more pleasant endings (Humpty Dumpty puts himself back together again) or tell fabulous fairy tales, the Wooleycat is becoming a better-known character. Titles such as this one can easily be used as springboards to help young viewers develop their innate creative skills for storytelling and embellishment.

Disney's Sing-Along Songs (Disney, 11 tapes, 30 m. each, infant–14, live-action/animation)

It would be possible to write an entire chapter on the magic of Disney, but because of space limitations and because Disney is such a well-known commodity, just a few of the most memorable videos are highlighted here. Each video in this series uses songs from the company's live-action and animated features and blends them into an enjoyable music fest that showcases both music and animation. Children can easily follow along with the lyrics that are displayed in oversize type on-screen, so the tapes can also be used to help preschoolers with word recognition. Each program is dependable entertainment, and it's some of the best music you can find for children. **Be Our Guest,** one of the more recent, is "hosted" by Jiminy Cricket and comprises musical scenes from *Mary Poppins, Lady and* *the Tramp,* and *Sleeping Beauty,* as well as *Beauty and the Beast.* **Heigh-Ho** centers on the music of *Snow White,* which was just recently released on video for the first time. **You Can Fly!** showcases the upbeat song from *Peter Pan,* as well as numbers from *Bedknobs and Broomsticks* and *Lady and the Tramp.* **The Bare Necessities** contains the bouncy sound track from *The Jungle Book,* plus music from *Cinderella* and *Dumbo.* The other **Sing-Along Songs** tapes are **Friend Like Me, Alvin & the Chipmunks, Love to Laugh!, Disneyland Fun, Zip-A-Dee-Doo-Dah, Fun with Music,** and **Very Merry Christmas Songs.**

Don Cooper (Wood Knapp, 5 tapes, 1991–93, 30 m. each, 2–7)

This father of two has a gentle demeanor that attracts preschoolers like a mall attracts teens. Wood Knapp has released five of his musical compilations of original and familiar folk tunes, each of which showcases Cooper's vocal and instrumental talents, as well as the vocal stylings of the "Not Ready for Bedtime Players," a group of children. Cooper's love and appreciation for the great outdoors is evident in his use of the Montana wilderness for most of his tapes. **Mother Nature's Songs** is taped with the breathtaking Rockies as a backdrop; the environmental theme is echoed by such songs as "Trees" and "Singing Like a Bird." **Musical Games** should tickle the funny bones of preschoolers as they imitate animals, imagine they're butterflies, and bounce like balls. **Star Tunes** helps children understand the planets, stars, and astronomy. **A Pocket Full of Songs** showcases nine all-American tunes, including "Skip to My Lou," "Row Your Boat," and "She'll Be Comin' Round the Mountain," all performed with a small group of children as an audience in an outdoor setting. **Songs of the Wild West** features all original music, from "Potatoes and Beans" to "The Dance of the Indian Nations," and fun activities like horseback riding and campfire sing-alongs. In his press kits, Cooper has made his own suggestions to parents about how to make children's video a participatory experience: Make certain kids have room in front of the TV to dance and move about; look for programs that showcase children, since they relate to their peers; watch with your child and be there when your child has questions. Be alert to songs your children sing; if they're singing songs they heard on a video, the video probably has repeat value. Cooper also takes pride in reminding parents that original programs offer children something new and refreshing to imitate and learn from.

For an example of his earlier work, look up **Sing-Along Story Songs with Don Cooper,** reviewed later in this chapter.

Dr. Seuss Sing-Along Classics (CBS, 4 tapes, 30 m. each, 2–10, animated)

These are the video adaptations of the TV specials from Theodore (Dr. Seuss) Geisel that many of us grew up anticipating each year: **The Cat in the Hat, The Hoober-Bloob Highway, The Lorax,** and **Green Eggs and Ham and Other Stories** (you might find the original version listed under **Dr. Seuss on the Loose** in some video stores). CBS has added on-screen lyrics to help children follow the songs, which may promote reading readiness in the youngest viewers. Seuss wrote the lyrics specifically for these productions, and with the intention that they help children develop reading skills. If you'd like to find more Dr. Seuss books on video, look up his name in Chapter 7: Storytelling and Literature-Based Videos.

For Our Children (Disney, 1993, 85 m., 4–up)

The stars shine in this Disney-produced concert, proceeds of which were donated to the Pediatric AIDS Foundation, as were profits from the audio album and this video. The stars are as entertaining to adults as they are to children; Paula Abdul leads the cast, which includes Michael Bolton, Mayim Bialik, Melissa Etheridge, Kriss Kross, Bobby McFerrin, Jason Priestley, Salt 'N' Pepa, and others. Each of the musical entertainers gives a lively performance, while the actors among them add comments. It's innocuous fun that could prove entertaining for you and your children.

Frank Cappelli (A&M, 2 tapes, 30 m. each, 2–6; stars Frank Cappelli)

The Pittsburgh-based PBS-TV star of Nickelodeon's *Cappelli & Company* has two fantastic videos available: **All Aboard the Train** and **Slap Me Five,** both equally wonderful. A singer/songwriter, Cappelli exercises his talent for a variety of musical styles as he creates musical numbers based on the simplest things, such as setting the table and crossing the street. But the thickly mustached entertainer knows he's corny, so he plays it up to his young costars, and that's the attraction. He's having a great time entertaining them, and they're obviously enjoying themselves in a natural and uninhibited fashion. Children will cotton to his warmth and will easily recall in all styles of music, and her talent at blending whimsical story lines with outrageous songs. It also helps that she had some high-class set designers and talented ranks of children join her in making **The Rainy Day Adventure** and **The Extra Special Substitute Teacher.** The plot of **Rainy Day** has frightening overtones for very small children, especially those who fear being alone: Three latchkey children lose their dog in a thunderstorm that also causes a blackout, leaving them alone, in the dark, connected only by phone to their mother, and worried about their dog. But Joanie saves the day: She steps in when things look darkest, retrieving the dog, finding magical ways to turn on the power, and, with songs and silliness, energizing the kids, who become entranced with her as she calms their fears during the storm. Mom and the kids believe she's the babysitter sent in by a service. You have to wait until the very end to find out whether she's mortal or magic. In **Substitute Teacher,** as in her first video, Joanie mysteriously appears to take kids on a musical adventure (without leaving their environs, of course). By unlocking their imaginations through songs, she takes the students on trips to the Jurassic age ("Dinosaur Rock and Roll"), Mexico ("La Bamba"), and even Mars ("Do the Martian Rock"). More entertaining than educational, the tape does manage to name the planets, teach a little geography, and demonstrate American Sign Language. Joanie and her supporting cast are enthusiastic, but this title has a weaker story line and more contrived reasons to sing than her earlier release. Kudos, though, for Bartels' closing comments encouraging viewers to study hard and treat the people around them with respect.

Joe Scruggs: Joe's First Video (Shadow Play, 51 m., 4–6)

Here's a performer who looks as if he could be anyone's next-door neighbor. Scruggs, who dresses in tropical casuals, doesn't hide his receding hairline or his spare tire, and that helps him achieve the natural look that draws kids to him. The sheer variety of formats he packs into this concert is astounding. One minute, kids will be engaged in a sing-along; the next, they'll be up dancing and clapping. Scruggs tells stories and jokes with his audience and shows kids how to use their imaginations when he dons costumes to illustrate characters in his songs. Few other singers attempt to exercise as many mental muscles in a concert format.

many of his simple songs; you may find you can't get "Brush-a, Brush-a, Brush-a Your Teeth," sung in the style of an Italian folk song, out of *your* head! There's a pleasant balance of instruction and fun in each tape, and you'll probably appreciate that each video ends with a quiet, relaxing song to settle kids down.

Fred Penner (BMG Kidz/The Children's Group/Oak Street Music, 3 tapes, 2–8, stars Fred Penner)

Penner, star of Nickelodeon's *Fred Penner's Place,* has released three videos so far. **Circle of Songs** (40 m.) is a concert in an intimate setting. Penner performs his original tunes—including "Grandma's Glasses," "Rock a Little Baby," and "I Had a Rooster"—but his audience is there to listen more than to participate. In **The Cat Came Back** (45 m.), also the name of Penner's signature song, he performs in another stage setting, but here he encourages some interaction from his audience. His variety-show style even includes a Navajo greeting in sign language: "May the Great Spirit work sunshine into your heart." The most lively of his three videos is **What a Day!** (28 m., stars Penner, Al Simmons, Rocki Rolletti, Charlotte Diamond), in which he's supported by a cast of flexible, talented players who each perform a song. The crux of the story is a magical photo booth in a train station. While he awaits his train, Penner enters the booth, but instead of having a photo snapped, he's transported to a different destination to meet a diverse group of people. Penner's uplifting concert number "Proud" closes the video. You can tell from the intricate web of laugh lines around his eyes that Penner knows how to have fun, and knows how to teach kids to let loose and have fun, too.

Greg and Steve: Live in Concert (International Film & Video, 800-366-5902, or Youngheart, 800-548-4063; in CA 213-663-3223, 50 m., ages 2–10; stars Greg Scelsa, Steve Millang)

Printed right on the box is the reason this live performance video is so worthwhile: The theme is "Educate, Motivate, Enrich, Entertain." Greg and Steve are a talented children's entertainment duo who excel at motivating their audience of children, parents, and teachers to participate, laugh, and sing. Witness their first of twelve musical numbers, "If You Feel Like Rockin'," which has the audience dancing up a storm. The pair then invite a few dozen children on stage to invent dance steps for the rest of the audience to mimic in "The Body Rock." Participation programs are rarely as successful as this (see how few of the audience members *aren't* on their feet), and parents will appreciate the multitude of interactive activities for children. As an added value, the video is packaged with a songbook. A second program, **Greg and Steve: Musical Adventures** (30 m.), compiles nine skits based on Greg and Steve's audio releases. Listen to their rockin' versions of "Three Little Pigs" (set to nostalgic footage of old cartoons), "This Old Man," and "Bingo," among other tunes, and judge for yourself their exceptional talent for transforming familiar tunes and nursery rhymes into darned good kiddie rock. The tape closes with an environmental message and a discussion that continues as the credits roll.

In Search of the Wow Wow Wibble Woggle Wazzie Woodle Woo (A&M/Noazart Productions, 1990, 60 m., 4–12; stars Tim Noah)

Noah is an energetic, talented performer who got his start as a children's entertainer with the group **Tickle Tune Typhoon** (see later in this chapter). Essentially a one-man show, this fantasy adventure takes place in a boy's bedroom (Noah's) as he imagines himself sucked into his closet and whisked off on a quest for a mythical creature. With boundless energy, singer/musician Noah takes on the adventure of a lifetime (well, he is, after all, portraying a kid) and sings his way through a difficult day, surviving on the power of his boundless imagination. His actions and songs dispel boredom and emphasize that anyone who can imagine should never be bored. His costumed characters, including Musty Moldy Melvin and Greasy Grimy Gertie, are comical enough that you might see one or two at your door one Halloween. And his voice is really compelling; parents probably won't mind listening to his audiotapes several times as their children grow even fonder of this creative individual.

It's Not Easy Bein' Green (1994, Buena Vista, 37 m., infant–6, puppets)

This tape is only one in a collection of Muppet mania, from *Fraggle Rock* episodes to classic segments from the zany *The Muppet Show*. It's here to represent the whole, since it showcases Kermit's theme, one of the most poignant songs ever sung by a frog. This tape compiles thirteen tunes from various episodes of *The Muppet Show* and from the Muppets feature films. And the variety of musical

styles helps children appreciate different kinds of music, from and roll to jazz and the blues. The Muppets' wacky interpretat of cover tunes, including "Octopus's Garden" and "Heat Wave," great fun, but the original tunes are just as wonderful and za interpreted by the off-the-wall minds behind the Muppets. Ea song's lyrics scroll across the screen, making it simple for even t youngest of viewers to follow—and help preschoolers with wo recognition. Look for the brand identified as "Jim Henson Vided and you'll unlock a treasure chest of music, silliness, games, som facts, and lots of fun.

Jazz Time Tale (Family Home Entertainment, 30 m., 4–up, animated narrator Ruby Dee)

Renowned animator Michael Sporn magically weaves a tale in which a young girl meets the legendary pianist Fats Waller as he begins his musical career. This production crosses cultural bound aries in much the same way music itself does, and effectively de scribes the birth of jazz. Waller got his first big break playing th piano and organ in a theater that showed silent pictures and hoste vaudeville entertainers. Especially engaging is Sporn's animated i terpretation of a silent film to highlight how important a role mu played in early theaters, adding dramatic highlights and punctuat the plot with piano or organ music. After watching this lovingly t exciting story, young viewers will be hard-pressed not to develo appreciation for the spontaneity of jazz, a musical genre that vates with its bouncy rhythms and bursts of energy and pas This is one of those animated programs that every member family can truly enjoy.

Joanie Bartels Simply Magic Videos (Discovery Music/BMG tapes, 45 m. each, 4–10; directors Sidney J. Bartholomew, Dominic Orlando, stars Joanie Bartels, Kenny Mirman Warden)

Bubbly Bartels has a secret: If you use your imagination go anywhere, be anyone, and do practically anything you v if you're housebound during a storm or trying to learn in class. The enthusiastic children's performer made an sition from her *Magic Series* of audiotapes to video, th zany sense of humor, her dedication to showing childre

Kidsongs (Warner Reprise, 14 tapes, 30 m. each, 2–7)

This series of lavishly produced music videos has proved its dependability since its introduction to the home video market in 1985. The Kidsongs Kids are a talented, multiethnic group of preteens who sing, dance, and obviously enjoy being in front of the camera; but they're also very well coached and not spontaneous. Unlike the **Wee Sing** series, this collection relies on the music more than the stories for the glue that holds each program together. The series includes **A Day at Camp** (1990), **A Day at Old MacDonald's Farm** (1987), **A Day at the Circus** (1988), **A Day with the Animals** (1986), **Cars, Boats, Planes and Trains** (1988), **Good Night, Sleep Tight** (1987), **Home on the Range** (1988), **I'd Like to Teach the World to Sing** (1986), **Let's Play Ball** (1989), **Sing Out, America** (1986), **Ride the Roller Coaster** (1990), **Very Silly Songs** (1991), **We Wish You a Merry Christmas** (1992), and **What I Want to Be** (1991). Each tape contains a series of songs strung loosely together by a theme and interwoven with humor. Not every tape will appeal to the same age group; **Cars, Boats, Planes and Trains,** for instance, will appeal to a wide cross section of kids interested in vehicles, while the lullabies and fairy tales of **Good Night, Sleep Tight** will appeal more to the younger children in the recommended age range. Test a few, and know that whichever you choose will entertain your children with nondiscriminatory scripts and fair, if corny, performers. Children who enjoy Barney the Dinosaur will probably cotton to these tapes.

Lyle, Lyle Crocodile, The Musical *The House on East 88th Street* (Hi-Tops, 25 m., 2–10, animated)

When a new family moves into an old New York brownstone, they discover they're not alone: There's a crocodile in the bathtub! What's more, he can clean, is a gourmet chef, and loves to babysit children with no other motive than enjoying the attention. His previous owner then comes to claim him for a career in show biz. The family who found him has grown too attached, and their parting is difficult, but the ending is sweet. With some real "show tunes" punctuating the plot, this is a beautifully produced comment on appreciating what you have before it's gone.

Mister Rogers Home Video series (FoxVideo, 2 tapes, 60 m. each, 2–6, live action/puppets; stars Fred Rogers)

Dependable Mister Rogers proves his value to parents and his love for children in musical videos that feature his adorable puppets from *Mister Rogers' Neighborhood*. The series actually includes five tapes, but only two are suited to this musical theme of this chapter. (You'll find **Mister Rogers: When Parents Are Away** in Chapter 5; the other two titles, **Dinosaus and Monsters** and **What About Love**, are not reviewed here but are also wonderful programs.) **Music and Feelings** (1986) explores how music is woven into many aspects of our lives and helps children gain an appreciation of the various moods music can inspire. **Musical Stories** (1988) contains two stories that help preschoolers appreciate who they are and who their families are. In "Potato Bugs and Cows," a cow realizes she's better off as herself than wishing she were someone else. And in "Granddad for Daniel," Daniel Tiger learns how special family ties are.

Mother Goose Rock 'n' Rhyme (Media Home Entertainment, 1990, 96 m., 6–up; director Jeff Stein, stars Shelley Duvall, Teri Garr, Dan Gilroy, Jean Stapleton, Cyndi Lauper, Howie Mandel, Little Richard, Gary Shandling, Paul Simon, Ben Vereen, Cheech Marin, Debbie Harry, Elayne Boosler, Bobby Brown, ZZ Top, Woody Harrelson, more)

What are all these celebrities doing in a children's feature-length film about a missing Mother Goose? Trying to find her, of course, and responding to Duvall's siren call about having fun and making children smile while working on a high-quality production. Duvall has a knack for developing highly original—okay, off-the-wall—programming that enchants viewers of any age. This is one of those special programs, although it's a bit long for a child to sit all the way through in one shot. But once you take a look at it, you'll find yourself laughing at the double entendres, sight gags, and celebrity cameos that are intended for adults anyway. Mother Goose's son Gordon Goose (Gilroy) and Bo Peep (Duvall) launch the countrywide search of Rhymeland, meeting all the characters along the way who, if they don't find her soon, will begin to disappear themselves. You'll have just as much fun as your children, if not more fun, watching this and picking out familiar faces under outrageous wigs, overblown makeup, and bizarre costumes.

Mouse Soup (Golden Book, 1992, 30 m., 2–8, stop-motion animation; voice of Buddy Hackett)

A mouse who's on a weasel's menu for dinner cooks up a seemingly endless supply of stories and songs to "season" the soup, of which he is to be the main ingredient. Of course, the weasel becomes more than a little befuddled by Mouse's inventions, which saves Mouse for another day. All-original songs (among them, "A Boo-Boo on My Finger," "Do-Di-Dadingo," "Ain't Got It," and "Feelin' Good") add zest to the tender stories, whose subjects run the gamut from magic thorn bushes to dancing stones. Children will delight in the odd little stop-animation figures, and you might find young viewers inventing their own stories after watching Mouse work his magic. If you and your child like this type of program, Golden Books has released a series of stop-animated treasures from director John Matthews at Churchill Films that were originally available only to the education market. Here are a few of the titles, though they are not reviewed here: **Uncle Elephant, Frog and Toad Together, Frog and Toad Are Friends, Just Me and My Dad** and **The Adventures of Curious George** (all based on books).

Music & Magic: Positive Music for Today's Kids (Bright Ideas Productions, 30 m., 4–8; stars Kevin-Anthony)

Producer/songwriter Lisa Marie Nelson has written seven original tunes that parents are sure to find uplifting. Combined with engaging visuals and Kevin-Anthony's wholehearted delivery, the effect is positive, whimsical, and enchanting. See if the titles of several songs don't entice you: "Doing the Best We Can," "Potential!," "Shining Star," and "What You Love to Do." The style and theme are similar to Rory's (see **The Rory Story** in this chapter) message of improving self-esteem. (If you enjoy Nelson's style, check out the **Karate for Kids** tapes in Chapter 5; she served as producer on both.)

Nonsense & Lullabyes (Family Home Entertainment, 1991, 2 tapes, 27 m. each, 1–6, animated; director Michael Sporn, narrated by/or stars Karen Allen, Linda Hunt, Eli Wallach, Courtney Vance, Heidi Stallings, Phillip Schopper, Grace Johnston, Diane Cherkas)

Each of the two tapes in this brief series features a large number of very short segments, ideal for the brief attention spans of very young children. A few of the fourteen segments on **Poems for Children,** including Hillaire Belloc's story of Matilda, who was burned to dust when she told one lie, and Heinrich Hoffman's "Story of Augustus," who died because he wouldn't eat his soup, could be potentially frightening to the under-4 group. Older children in this age group may think the scary stories are a scream, but if you have an impressionable toddler, preview this tape first. **Nursery Rhymes** is more appropriate for the diaper set; it features eighteen soothing lullabies and animated interpretations of familiar, nonthreatening nursery rhymes.

Original Tales & Tunes (Video Treasures, 3 tapes, 1992–93, 30 m., 2–8)

From Backyard Productions, the group responsible for bringing the magic of **Baby Songs** to home video, comes another creative foray into children's entertainment. Music plays an integral part in this video, which also includes stories, animation, and comedy sketches. Post–**Baby Songs** tots join K.J., the Muppet-like "Kids Jockey," as he introduces each of seven segments and listens to an off-camera mom ask him to do his chores. Viewers can participate in a "Chain Story," where every player gets to add outlandish plot twists and characters; watch the animated "William Small," a boy who shrinks to the size of a thumb; cheer for "Eddie Cinders," an updated version of Cinderella, as Eddie, with the magical assistance of his Fairy Garbage Man, wins a basketball game and a girl's heart; rock out with a preteen who, when her mom encourages her to stop watching so much MTV and "Do Something," grabs the camcorder and turns her little brother into a rock star; "Sing a Song" with Karen Benjamin in a music video; "Listen to Your Feelings" as Chic Street Man (whom you'll see on other **Baby Songs** tapes) explains in reggae/calypso style that it's okay to feel emotions; and get to know shapes in nature in "Our World." Two other tapes in this series, **Silly Tales & Tunes** and **Spooky Tales & Tunes,** are equally entertaining. The producers are successful and dependable, and you'll feel they've tested everything they've created on their own children.

Pete Seeger's Family Concert (Sony Kids' Music/Sony Wonder, 1992, 45 m., 4–up)

What better way to introduce children to a performer their parents listened to in their younger days than with a gentle, folksy video? Folk musician Seeger delivers an environmental message in an outdoor concert filmed on the banks of the Hudson River. His environmental concern extends to this video's box art, on which he lets buyers and renters know how a donation to his charity, the Clearwater Foundation, will help clean up polluted rivers. Seeger's evergreen strengths are old standby favorites, including "Skip to My Lou" and "This Land Is Your Land," which viewers will find fun to sing along with. He also shines in his original story/song, "AbiYoYo."

Raffi in Concert with the Rise and Shine Band (1988), **A Young Children's Concert with Raffi** (A&M, 1986, 50 m. each, 2–8)

The Canada-based singer of Egyptian extraction charms children like no one else. Viewers at home and at his concerts are drawn into his performances with his gentle delivery of songs both original and familiar. Like Mister Rogers, Raffi has that mannerliness that does not work kids into a frenzy; he manages to hold their attention through powerful storytelling and captivating singing. He has a wide selection of audio releases, so the videos can be supplemented with listening fun, as well as with his songbooks (*Raffi Songs to Read: Shake My Sillies Out* and his *Everything Grows Songbook* are but two). **A Young Children's Concert** contains live renditions of eighteen Raffi favorites, such as "Shake My Sillies Out," "Bumping Up and Down," and "Baby Beluga," taped at one of his sold-out Toronto concerts. **Raffi in Concert,** another live performance, covers both Raffi's older and newer material, such as "Apples and Bananas," "Tingalayo," and "De Colores" for a multilingual experience. Although he previously announced his retirement from children's performances in favor of finding other ways to help the planet, his heart is still with children, and he has resumed a tour schedule. Consider his admonition not to let your children overuse this or any other video.

Rock Along with Bo Peep (Morris, 1992, 45 m., 3–6, puppets; stars Kandra Inga)

Rivaling the detailed costumes and intricate movements of Jim Henson's Muppets, this group of puppets shows that working together is really the best way to get things done. A group of animals sets out to produce a musical play about Little Bo Peep. The cast of characters includes producer Mac the beaver, director Fleeter the mouse, agent Travis the fox, and his newest rising star, Shermi the sheep. The only human in the production is the woman who portrays Peep. Fleeter wants to star in as well as direct the production, Shermi is painfully shy about performing, all-business Mac tries to compromise to get the show on the road, and Travis has more than a few tricks up his sleeve. Woven into the story are a number of musical segments that incorporate terrific tunes from the fifties and sixties. Of all the lessons this video touches upon, probably the most lasting is that through teamwork and putting aside one's ego, almost anything is possible. This was intended as the first release in a twenty-six-program series, so stay tuned for more productions. Packed inside each video are stickers that feature the puppet characters.

The Rory Story (Sony Kids' Music, 1990, 55 m., 4–up; live-action/puppets, stars Rory)

Gentle Rory, an East Coast children's performer, stars in her own story; well, if the Muppet-like creatures were real, it would almost be a biography. Like a distaff Raffi, Rory mesmerizes viewers with her soft, mellifluous tones, even when she's performing a rock-and-roll number. The tale begins when she meets her sidekicks, the Piglets, whose interest in performing is waning as Rory's grows; Rory, playing new to the business and a little shy, discovers her own voice, and sings "I'm Gonna Be Somebody." She has a positive outlook, which young viewers will pick right up on, but since her delivery is soft, the message isn't always as powerful as it could be. If you like her style, look for her collection of audio versions, such as *Rory's Little Broadway,* as well as her videos. Recipient of a 1992 Parents' Choice Award.

Rosenshontz (Lightyear Entertainment, 2 tapes, 30 m. each, 3–6; stars Gary Rosen, Bill Shontz)

The duo who perform as Rosenshontz are funny and even a little funny-looking, and that's often enough to captivate children. These two grown men, who never lost their childlike wonder, have maintained a deep appreciation for teddy bears, as you can tell by the names of their videos: **The Teddy Bears' Picnic** and **The Teddy Bears' Jamboree.** The former is a story told with songs about the infamous day the bears have their picnic and how a child who's sick can attend by using his or her imagination. (An aside to parents: The video was created as a premium offer for Children's Panadol and features the cold remedy's mascot, Pandy, a costumed panda bear.) **Jamboree** is a terrific concert-performance video culled from the duo's 1993 performances; it compiles fifteen of the dynamic duo's greatest hits. When your child's in the mood for upbeat music, or needs a little cheering up, either of these programs will fill the bill.

Sesame Songs Home Video series (Random House, 8 tapes, 30 m. each, infant–6, Muppets)

Trust the folks at Children's Television Workshop to continue on video what they began 25 years ago on PBS-TV. CTW's cautious approach to what they produce and how it's marketed has earned them not only awards but also a permanent place in most parents' hearts. True to its name, this sing-along series praises the diversity of Muppetdom, from aardvarks to monsters. Each video comes with a lyric sheet that can be used as a poster. Elmo, the toddler-aged Muppet, holds **Elmo's Sing-Along Guessing Game,** a trivia game that gets him so riled up he can't help but answer the questions before the contestants do. **Sing Yourself Silly** features Ernie and his beloved rubber duckie leading monsters and Muppets in zany tunes from *Sesame Street.* **Dance-Along!** features a disco-clad Grover leading children in an array of crazy dances. In **Sing-Along Earth Songs,** lovable Grover chaperones young hikers through Monster State Park, where they meet talking mountains and singing fish who remind children to keep the environment healthy. Make sure you sit in for Oscar the Grouch's Frank Sinatra homage, "Just Throw It My Way." **Monster Hits** features Cookie Monster and his otherworldly buddies in songs that showcase how different each monster or person is. **Sing, Hoot & Howl with the Sesame Street Animals** is a cacophony of sound and fury, courtesy of the immense variety of inhabitants of Muppetdom. In **Rock and Roll!,** it's Animal's turn to be in the spotlight, as he and his band play old-time rock and roll that even parents may want to join in on. **We All Sing Together** celebrates the cultural diversity in our world as only the globally conscious and diverse Sesame Streeters can: with jubilant Muppet mania.

Shari Lewis' Kooky Classics (MGM/UA, 1984, 54 m., 4–8, live action/ puppets; director Walter Painter, stars Shari Lewis)

Dated? Maybe. Fun? Definitely! Lewis's aura of enthusiasm is absolutely contagious when she does what she does best: converse with Lamb Chop, perform musically, and show children a multitude of ways in which they can have a grand old time. Here, Lewis introduces viewers to musical classics, including "The Minute Waltz," the "William Tell Overture," the opera *Carmen,* and Brahms' "Hungarian Waltz." Younger children in this age range will guffaw with glee at Shari's silly humor, geared just for them, while older children and the rest of us jaded adults just roll our eyes and remember when *we* used to tell such silly jokes and puns. But the magic is that she succeeds at getting young viewers to listen to beloved music, and maybe spark some genuine music appreciation. You'll find more of her videos in Chapter 6, which also features an interview with Lewis.

Sharon, Lois and Bram (A&M, 12 tapes, various running times, 2–12)
This Canadian trio has some of the best chemistry among children's performers, and it's evident in their cable TV series, *The Elephant Show,* as well as in their live performances, some of which have been preserved on video. Even with well-rehearsed stage shows and a terrifically scripted TV show, they manage an irresistible air of spontaneity. **Sharon, Lois and Bram Sing A to Z** (50 m.) artfully combines snippets of *The Elephant Show* with live concert footage to create a highly entertaining series for preschoolers. Other videos compile complete episodes from the TV show, often with new footage added, and they're all equally wonderful: **Live in Your Living Room, Back by Popular Demand . . . Live!, Sleep Over, Soap Box Derby, Treasure Island, Who Stole the Cookies?, Radio Show,** and **Pet Fair** are each one entire episode from the trio's TV show (30 m. each). **Making News, Summer Fun** (both distributed by Cineglobe Video in Canada), and **Mysteries** (from MCA/Universal) all compile two episodes on each video (60 m. each). You'll also find most of the trio's music on audiocassette and CD.

Sing-Along Story Songs with Don Cooper (Random House, previously titled **The Video Music Box: Story Songs**, 1987, 30 m., 2–6, live action plus animation/puppets; stars Don Cooper)
Before launching his more successful tapes from Wood Knapp (see **Don Cooper** entries in this chapter), Cooper tried a stint as the

Video Music Box Man. As the title indicates, each song is a story. For example, along with standards like "The Three Little Pigs" and "The Tortoise and the Hare," Cooper tells viewers about "Fuzzy the Caterpillar," who eats his way through the garden among a multi-racial group of kids. Earnest and serious, Cooper later developed themes for each video and honed both his craft and his stage persona, but here you can see he was already well on his way to establishing himself as a solid children's entertainer.

Songs and Finger Plays for Little Ones (Clever Productions, 408-449-9141, 30 m., 2–5; host Mary Clever)

Clever is a day-care provider based in California, and her years of experience and genuine concern and love for children illuminate this well-conceived production. As the title indicates, the purpose of the program is to teach children some of the familiar ditties like "Itsy Bitsy Spider" and "Where's My Thumbkin?" that are accompanied by hand movements, great ways to develop a child's memory and motor skills, as well as coordination. Clever keeps a passel of preschoolers following smartly along, singing, rhyming, and learning the hand movements. She also tells parents to be lenient with youngsters who may not follow exactly as instructed; after all, some of the brightest children may develop creative responses. Throw aside your adultness for 30 minutes; this is a great program to watch with your preschooler.

Stories to Remember: The **"Baby"** series (Lightyear Entertainment, 26 m. each, 800-229-STORY, infant–6, animated)

These four musical programs are based on illustrator Kay Chorao's books, which really reach infants and toddlers with gentle rhymes and melodic music. **Baby's Bedtime** (sung by Judy Collins, music by Ernest Troost) contains sixteen soothing, tenderly sung lullabies. **Baby's Nursery Rhymes** (sung by Phylicia Rashad, music by Jason Miles) is adapted from Chorao's *The Baby's Lap Book;* the colors and animation are so appealing, even children up to age six will enjoy the video. **Baby's Morningtime** (sung by Judy Collins, music by Ernest Troost) is complemented by Collins' beautiful interpretation of all-original music that increases in tempo as the day progresses. **Baby's Storytime** (storytelling and music by Arlo Guthrie), adapted from Chorao's *The Baby's Story Book*, is not as compelling as the other entries in this series, despite a valiant effort by Guthrie. You may find it rewarding to have the books on hand to share with your child; the sound tracks are also available on audiocassette and CD. (You'll find an additional six videos in this series under **Stories to Remember** in Chapter 7, Storytelling and Literature-Based Videos, because they contain more story than song.)

This Pretty Planet: Tom Chapin Live in Concert (SonyWonder, 1992, 60 m., 4–up)

This is one of those rare performances that kids will find instantly appealing. Chapin, whose sensitivity and awareness of the curiosity of children is renowned in child-development circles, sings thirteen songs, most of them interactive, for an audience of parents and kids in New York's Hudson Valley. The overall theme, as the title suggests, is respect for Nature and Earth. Chapin hopes to encourage his audience to become involved in protecting the fragile environment. His songs reflect his concern: "This Pretty Planet" is sung as a round for the round Earth, with assistance from Judy Collins; "Good Garbage" identifies good and bad waste and defines "biodegradable"; "The Wheel of the Water" explains the cycle water takes on our planet as the audience provides sound effects; "Someone's Gonna Use It After You" emphasizes that Earth's natural resources are limited and must be conserved and shared. Chapin delivers his message in serious words set to either lighthearted or hauntingly beautiful music, and also includes a few purely fun songs, such as "Accident," "Alphabet Soup," "Cousins," and "Family Tree." Whether you opt to watch this in a single viewing or over several days, it's unlikely that the songs will get old fast. And if even one viewer decides to do something to benefit the Earth on just one day, Chapin will feel his message got through.

Tickle Tune Typhoon (Just for Kids, 818-595-0666, 60 m., 4–up)

The musical group composed of singers and musicians from all ethnic backgrounds and of all abilities translates its award-winning concert material to home video. Included here are twelve upbeat songs that will be sing-alongs after the second rewind. Among the tunes are "My Body Belongs to Me" and "Hug Bug." Powerful messages encourage viewers to open their minds and hearts to every possibility for increasing their knowledge and learning more about others and the world we all occupy together. To give you an idea of the diverse topics this group addresses, a musician in a wheelchair is key to the song "We Are All Differently Abled." For a comparison, see one of the Typhooners go independent: Tim Noah created the musical adventure **In Search of the Wow Wow Wibble Woggle Wazzie Woodle Woo** (reviewed earlier in this chapter) on both audio and video.

The Tin Soldier (Just for Kids, 1994, 63 m., 6–10; stars the Ottawa Ballet, narrator Sally Struthers)

This unusual presentation tells the Hans Christian Andersen tale "The Steadfast Tin Soldier" in ballet form with exuberant orchestral accompaniment. What a wonderful way to introduce children to the magic of dance! In this version, a one-legged tin toy bravely protects the paper ballerina he loves from an evil jack-in-the-box. Scenes alternate between the real child who plays with the toys and the tabletop tableau of the soldier's castle. Spare but effective sets focus viewers' attention on the dancing, while sharp and shiny computer animation updates the solider's trip through the sewers and into a fish, via which he is returned home. Parents who are searching for an entertaining dose of culture will find that Struthers' narration and the troupe's lively dancing make the format accessible for all ages.

Wee Sing series (Price Stern Sloan, 9 tapes, 60 m. each, 2–up)

Colorful sets that any preschooler would love to play in and clever stories make this series consistently entertaining—and often painlessly educational. The children always wind up being drawn into an imaginary landscape in which they sing and learn. Some of the plots and contrived ways of using musical chestnuts come off a bit sticky, like a candy cane, but the programs always try to make a point about using one's imagination. Lyric sheets are included with each release. Titles in the series are the debut title, **Wee Sing Together,** which celebrates friends; **King Cole's Party,** which emphasizes that the best gifts come from the heart; **Grandpa's Magical Toys,** where age is no barrier to having lots of musical fun; **The Best Christmas Ever,** where children visit Santa's workshop and learn that friends can help you surmount your troubles; **Wee Sing in Sillyville,** where magical Sillywhim whisks children to a place where silly things happen; **Wee Sing in the Big Rock Candy Mountains,** which, unlike what its name suggests, features a forest of veggies and two creatures who overindulge in sweets and wind up with tummyaches; **Wee Sing in the Marvelous Musical Mansion,** which promotes self-confidence through uplifting songs; **The Wee Sing Train,** in which children who create a village for their model train are magically transported into it; and **Wee Sing Under the Sea,** in which a woman's magical seascape painting comes alive for her and her grandson, offering a view of the deep and the impact of people on the world's oceans.

Where the Wild Things Are (Home Vision, 40 m., live action, 6–10)

Opera for children? Absolutely! Author/illustrator Maurice Sendak makes it seem like a child's own imaginings, in this, probably his most famous, work. The Glyndebourne Festival Opera dons fantastic costumes to represent Sendak's sometimes immense creatures, and the music is captivating without overpowering young viewers. This company, the parent of Public Media Video (who released on video the **WonderWorks** programs that are reviewed in Chapter 7), is well known in arts circles for distributing some of the best-produced opera and classical music videos. For parents who'd like to introduce their children to music, opera, and the stage, here's one of the most natural ways available on video. CC Studios has released a compilation of Sendak's story-songs in **The Maurice Sendak Library** (Chapter 7: Storytelling and Literature-based Videos).

Other Tapes of Interest on This Topic . . .

Amadeus (Chapter 1, Feature Films)
Baby's Bedtime, Baby's Nursery Rhymes, Baby's Morningtime, Baby's Storytime (See the entry under **Stories to Remember** in this chapter, as well as six more titles listed under **Stories to Remember** in Chapter 7, Storytelling and Literature-Based Videos.)
Fantasia (Chapter 2, Animated Feature Films)
Rappin' 'n' Rhymin' (Chapter 5, Sports, Safety, Health, and Fitness)
The Red Shoes (Chapter 7, Storytelling and Literature-Based Videos)

Chapter 4

■

DISCOVERY AND LEARNING:
Science, Nature, Geography, Society

What will you discover in these pages? Frogs and snails, birds and bees, geography and history, pets and money, garbage and knowledge. If you want to develop in your toddler an appreciation of nature, or communicate to your child how interesting different cultures and places can be, or encourage your preteen to be environmentally aware or responsible with his or her finances, this is the chapter for you.

This is "edutainment," a word coined to cover the wide variety of videos that aim to teach gently as they entertain a child. Choosing videos from this genre is like programming your own personal PBS station: several nature and wildlife shows, a few travel documentaries, maybe some exploration of ancient sites. Granted, some of the programs are more successful than others, and some take longer than others to grow on you, but all the tapes presented here merit a look—if they meet your needs or address a topic you'd like to broach with your children.

Educator George Maxim discusses ways parents can make a video session educational without becoming didactic.

George Maxim teaches early childhood education and elementary education to prospective teachers and to graduate students at West Chester University in West Chester, Pennsylvania. He has published three books in multiple editions: two on early childhood education, the other an elementary-education social studies methods text. Parts of his courses show aspiring teachers how to use video in the field, both preproduced programs and self-produced videos.

"Video is one of the most underutilized technological resources in the classroom," Maxim acknowledges, "mainly because oftentimes teachers just don't have the time to preview videos, or to videotape somthing they might be able to use in the classroom. That's often paralleled with parents, who also don't always have the time to preview everything their child watches."

Finding the time is something most parents will just have to do, but Maxim says video is definitely a worthwhile investment of your time and money. Despite being one of the cheapest forms of entertainment, it's able to draw children into discussions, open new avenues of interest, supplement classroom work, and broaden a viewer's horizons. If you have very little time but still want to sample a video, Maxim suggests that you try watching the first ten minutes, skip to a portion in the middle, and then fast-forward to the end.

Does a child learn better or more quickly from video rather than standard teaching formats? Answers Maxim, "The research is really divided on that. There's some research that says if you do it well, then it does result in enhanced learning with students at all levels. As with anything else, if you don't do it well, then you don't see much growth from it. I've found that video does present a very worthwhile experience with students, primarily because it can offer them some insights into things that they wouldn't otherwise be able to observe directly. As a vicarious experience, it's terrific, especially if you prepare the students well, let them know what the objectives are, give them an overview of what the video is about. If you don't do it properly in terms of accepted educational practice, then the benefits of using video are minimal."

Maxim, as a specialist in social studies, says social studies and science are two subjects that demonstrate well the ability of video to bring people and places into the classroom or home, since many children may never travel to Africa or the moon.

With video, adds Maxim, parents can censor in the good programming and censor out violence or adult situations. "Parents have to be concerned about the roles they see people playing in videos: gender roles, violence, etc., and whether people from other cultures are being stereotyped. It's awfully hard for parents to be that discriminating when they're just showing their child something." That's why previewing is important.

What can a parent do to enhance a child's video sessions? Ac-

cording to Maxim, "There are three key elements parents can incorporate to make a video viewing session more meaningful: (1)
motivation (letting your child know you are as excited about the
video as the child should be); (2) making time for good quality,
relaxed viewing (not after a child has watched several hours of TV);
and (3) having a good quality discussion afterwards."

When you're watching a video that you want to supplement your
child's schooling, Maxim suggests thinking of reading as a parallel.
"I think a lot of the things that go on with early reading and books
should be applied to how parents use video. So many parents who
might not be aware of the potential of video treat it as a babysitter,
putting the children down in front of the TV and saying, 'Look what
I got for you today.' I think that kind of thing has very little benefit
at all unless children are highly self-motivated and sit down and want
to get something out of it, especially if it's an educational video.

"One of the things that I respect a lot is the 'lap' technique with
reading: If children can attach warmth to the situation, then they'll
get a lot more out of it. By the 'lap' technique, I mean you cuddle
up with a child on your lap or next to you, and there's a warmth
related to the experience, and the parent is asking questions and
interacting with the child as the experience unfolds, and the child
feels this closeness and warmth and transfers it to the book. And
that's the magic of how reading develops. Parents should have the
same kind of approach with video: They should know what the video
is all about first, so they can sit down and say to that child, 'you
might be interested in looking at this because . . .' and communicate
that purpose and that interest; say 'I've seen this before,' or 'I talked
to so-and-so's parents,' or 'I know you're studying this in school and
thought you might like to see this'—whatever the purpose might
be, get the child excited about the video, and let the child know
you're interested in what it's about, and don't just leave it there."

Just leaving a child alone with a video usually won't cause any
harm, but there are so many missed opportunities, continues
Maxim. "It's interesting that video is pretty powerful in terms of the
concepts that students can develop as a result of watching, but it's
very weak in terms of promoting critical thinking. Very often, children are left alone to watch it, and although their attention is directed toward it, no one is around to really talk with them and say,
'What did you like best and why?' 'What would you have done dif-

ferently?' 'How did this change your attitude toward. . . ?' Parents don't have to act like a teacher preparing a list of questions; just think of it as though you were seeing a movie, walking out and realizing something touched you very deeply. Follow the child's lead and have a little talk: 'Gee that was an interesting video; let's talk about it.' " And if the video is particularly interesting to the child, it may come up again over dinner with the parent who may have been at the office earlier.

Always follow up a video used for schooling, Maxim recommends, by relating it to and comparing it with other information sources: "Attach a real value to what video is; let the child know this is something important, not just something you'll plop them in front of, just to pass time."

Is it healthy for a preschooler to latch onto a video or TV character (like Barney)? Maxim feels the attachment is normal, "as long as the characters they attach to are positive characters. We have to realize that's a normal developmental stage they go though, then we have to accept it. Preschoolers are often in a fantasy world, and they often are unclear on where that line exists between fantasy and reality. We have the Easter Bunny and Santa Claus, which are so real to some of these kids. We try to make them grow up too fast; they'll have their imaginary friends. That's why we have to be careful with characters who are randomly violent."

Adventures in Willoughby (Imaginary Friend, 800-242-7961, 1993, 3 tapes, 30 m., 2–8)

There's something appealing about model trains and the world you create around them that's as timeless as a holiday afternoon. Like *Thomas the Tank Engine*, this clever video series sets up models of trains, villages, and countryscapes and creates characters and stories around these miniature environments. But unlike Thomas, in **Willoughby,** the humans have the lead speaking roles, and the trains play mute supporting characters. The programs present an engaging combination of tall tales and mini-vacations to famous North American sites west of the Mississippi. In **Familiar Faces and Faraway Places,** visits to Dinosaur National Monument, the Mayan pyramid at Chichen Itza, Mexico, and the bats in Carlsbad Caverns are interspersed with stories about imaginary Willoughby. **Stories and Travelogs Just for Kids** takes viewers to the Grand Canyon, Mount

Rushmore, and Mesa Verde while the residents of Willoughby gear up for a balloon ride and encounter a bear. A real-life balloon ride is filmed for the third installment, **Trains, Planes and Other Fun Things,** as are trips to Newspaper Rock in Utah, Devil's Tower in Wyoming, and the Georgetown Loop in Colorado.

Astrodudes (Golden Book, 1992, 2 tapes, 35 m. each, 6–12, live action)

What a motivated team of elementary-aged children we find here: Five amateur astronomers are so fascinated with the worlds beyond ours that they produce their own underground TV show about space and attempt to beam it from their attic-based newsroom to the nearest star, Alpha Centauri. They figure they'll tell Alpha Centaurians about the U.S. space program (relaying only the good news, of course) and let the aliens know Earthlings are a friendly, intelligent bunch. Among the curious tidbits the children discover as they conduct their research prior to the broadcast is the name of the astronaut who smuggled a corned beef sandwich aboard one mission. Although one of the Astrodudes appears to be about 4 years old, this program will best appeal to children 6 and up, who can understand the concept of space flight and will enjoy watching their peers put a fun spin on adult responsibility. Perhaps young viewers will take a cue from these ingenious role models who investigate topics by interviewing experts, gathering news, and working as a team. There are two tapes in the series: **Shooting for the Moon** documents the efforts to put men on the moon up to 1970, while **The Solar Mysteries** features footage and information gleaned from the unmanned space probes Voyager, Magellan, and Explorer, as well as computer images of the surfaces of various planets, courtesy of NASA.

Astronomy 101 (Mazon Productions, 800-332-4344, 1994, 25 m., 7–12, live-action; stars Kira Spencer Hesser, Julie Crossen, Sam Saletta, Ken Metz)

Here's an activity most families can share: stargazing. It's amazingly simple, states the 11-year-old host, Michelle (Hesser), considering that amateur astronomers need nothing more than a pair of binoculars to pick out craters on the moon. This high-quality tape from the producer of **I Dig Fossils** (also reviewed in this chapter) features the same family and is a terrific primer on exploring the heavens. Michelle shares her love of the heavens with her mother; together, they use an amateur telescope on clear nights to scour the sky for planets, nebula, constellations, and details of the moon's surface. They're so serious about their avocation that they've taken a beginner's astronomy course and often set the alarm for the wee hours to catch a glimpse of various planets in the night sky. Don't be put off by the volume of technical information Michelle spouts at the beginning of the tape about distances to stars, definitions of the types of telescopes, and such; her zeal might just whet the curiosity of a young viewer. At the end of the tape is a handy on-screen list of resource books, magazines, and organizations catering to amateur astronomers. This is one of the only tapes that teaches beginners how to pick out various phenomena in the night sky, but if your child is keen on astronomy, look up **Astrodudes** and **Lift Off! An Astronaut's Journey,** both reviewed in this chapter.

The Baby-Sitters Club: Dawn Saves the Trees (A*Vision/KidVision, 1993, 30 m., 6–16; director Noel Black; stars Melissa Chasse, Meghan Andrews, Avriel Hillman, Meghan Leahy)

Familiar to readers of Ann Martin's tremendously popular books for young girls, the teenagers who form the Baby-Sitters Club find causes, solve problems, and in general perform lots of Goody Two Shoes–type deeds. In this installment, nature-loving Dawn finds herself pitted against a new boyfriend over the development of local parkland. She is distressed that developers want to cut down healthy old trees to put a road through the park; her impassioned plea at a public hearing, though defensive and irate, draws the attention and admiration of the council chair—her boyfriend's mother. Together, the two work on a compromise development plan that allows for a road to circumvent ancient trees. Savvy young viewers will learn how decisions are made for civic improvements and may feel empowered by witnessing a teenager's success in voicing her opinion —and getting adults to listen. The program was filmed at Flat Rock Brook Nature Center, an educational and park preserve in Englewood, New Jersey, which, like the fictional park in the video, was saved from development in 1962, when citizens organized to conserve it. For other tapes in the **Baby-Sitters Club** series, check out the **Baby-Sitters Club** listing in Chapter 7: Storytelling and Literature-Based Tapes.

The Berenstain Bears (Random House, 1982–1990, 12 titles, 30 m. each, 2–8, animated)

Stan and Jan Berenstain created a parenting treasure with their lovable Bear family; even Papa learns a lesson now and then. There's an extensive series of books and videos, and although the programs are book-based, it seems more appropriate to include the tapes in this chapter to acknowledge the excellent job the Berenstains have done as children's authors addressing today's social and environmental issues, instilling decent social values, and giving video the same moral appeal as many good books. If you find this series really hits home, you may want to experiment with Joy Berry's **The Human Race Club** (also reviewed in this chapter), another book and animated "mini-morality play" video series that helps children realize they're thinking elements in a system that runs best when its parts cooperate. Each of the following tapes contains at least two episodes unless otherwise noted. **The Berenstain Bears and the Messy Room** has Mama Bear turning to Papa Bear after she tries in vain to get the kids to clean their rooms (also contains **The Berenstain Bears and the Terrible Termite**). **The Berenstain Bears and the Missing Dinosaur Bone** presents three short episodes: the title adventure, plus **Bears in the Night** and **Bear Detectives**. **The Berenstain Bears and the Trouble with Friends** finds Sister coping with the new bear cub in town, who's just as domineering as she is (it also includes **The Berenstain Bears and the Coughing Catfish**). In **The Berenstain Bears and the Truth,** Brother and Sister are caught in a lie and are in danger of losing their mother's trust in them when they accidentally break her favorite lamp (also includes **The Berenstain Bears Save the Bees**). **The Berenstain Bears and Too Much Birthday** features Sister's knockout sixth birthday party, for which the whole family gets carried away, and which ends in tears (it also includes **The Berenstain Bears to the Rescue**). In **The Berenstain Bears Forget Their Manners,** Mama decides that rudeness will be punished with excess chores, and the family tries to adhere to her politeness plan. But the chores go undone when the cubs find they actually enjoy being polite! **The Berenstain Bears Get in a Fight** finds Mama mediating when Brother and Sister make a mountain out of a molehill (the tape also features **The Berenstain Bears and the Big Paw Problem**). The family wants to put on a show, but the show may not go on when **The Berenstain Bears Get Stage Fright** (which also contains **The Berenstain Bears Go Bonkers over Honkers**). In **The Berenstain Bears in the**

Dark, Papa comes to Sister's rescue with his childhood nightlight when she can't fall asleep after hearing Brother's scary tale (also included is **The Berenstain Bears Ring the Bell**). **The Berenstain Bears Learn About Strangers** showcases Papa's cautionary talk about the dangers of talking to strangers, which makes Sister suspicious of anyone she doesn't know—but Brother isn't so cautious (also contains **The Berenstain Bears and the Disappearing Honey**). In **The Berenstain Bears Meet Big Paw** (Children's Treasures, 1980, one episode on this tape), Bear legend has it that if a bear becomes greedy, a giant will appear to eat the entire town. The giant Big Paw does appear, but it turns out the legend was wrong. **The Berenstain Bears' Christmas** contains three episodes: **The Bears' Christmas, Inside Out, Upside Down,** and **The Bike Lesson. The Berenstain Bears: No Girls Allowed** is notable for its forward-thinking premise: The boys bar girls from their clubhouse, but that raises too many problems. (An early version of this program also includes **The Berenstain Bears and the Missing Dinosaur Bone.**)

The Best of Beakman's World (Columbia TriStar, 1993, 60 m., 6–16; stars Paul Zaloom)

Scientific experiments and fast-paced, MTV-like snippets define this stylish production from the Learning Channel. Fans of the cable series will applaud the fifteen tricks and experiments that are compiled on this cassette, if only because they can glue a child to an entertaining, educational program. Children will learn tricks like spearing a potato with an ordinary drinking straw, as well as elements of chemistry and physics, such as building a rocket that's propelled by water. There's nothing ordinary, however, about how these activities captivate most children, encourage experimentation, and pique their curiosity. Watch for more of *Beakman's World* to be released on video.

Big Rigs Up Close and Very Personal (Stage Fright Productions, 1992, 30 m., 1–8)

As in the company's earlier video, **Farm Animals Close Up and Very Personal** (see review in this chapter), there's no narration here—just truck noises and instrumental music to accompany footage of trucks doing everything a child can imagine, from being repaired to rolling down the road. That leaves parents and older siblings free to take as interactive an approach as they want: to explain whatever a viewer questions, encourage their children to *ask* questions, even provide their own narration and sound effects and wild guesses at what the different trucks are hauling. Viewers have the pleasure of watching trucks navigating highways, back roads, and truck stops, being washed, being loaded and unloaded, and undergoing engine repairs. The camera zooms in for close-ups of wheels, horns, lights, and hitches. There's even a driver's-eye view from the cab, so the littlest viewers, who have years before they get a driver's license, can pretend they're driving these mighty big rigs. The company has also released **Choo Choo Trains Up Close and Very Personal** (also reviewed in this chapter), and if your child loves this type of program, check out these tapes featured later in this chapter: **There Goes a Firetruck, There Goes a Bulldozer, Road Construction Ahead, Fire and Rescue, Terrific Trips,** the **Here We Go!** series, and the two **Sesame Street Visits . . .** tapes.

Bugs Don't Bug Us! (Bo Peep Productions, 800-532-0420, 1991, 35 m., 2–8)

If your toddler is developing a sense of wonder at the world of nature, then find this tape that uncovers the wonderful world of insects large and small. Viewers will even see a caterpillar transform into a butterfly through the magic of time-lapse videography. A diversity of on-screen children explore insects by touching the ones that are safe and observing them in their natural habitats. The original background music complements the video footage—for example, dulcimer tones enhance Rocky Mountain scenes, as do the fiddles and harps. The video succeeds in gently encouraging exploration without forcing the issue.

Captain Planet and the Planeteers (Turner, 1991–94, 6–12, animated; voices of Tom Cruise, Whoopi Goldberg, Louis Gosset Jr., Ed Asner, Tim Curry, Meg Ryan, Martin Sheen)

Media magnate Ted Turner created the concept for a group of environmentally correct teenagers, the Planeteers, led by the nearly invincible superhero Captain Planet. Although this is a TV series, it deserves mention for its attempt to make young viewers aware that they can be superheroes, too, if they take actions to help the Earth by working to preserve the delicate balance in nature. Among the titles available are **Mission to Save Earth,** the pilot (100 m.), and several 45-minute titles, each of which packs two episodes from the TV series onto one video: **A Hero for Earth** (some of the series' humorous villains are introduced in this series opener: Hoggish Greedly, Dr. Blight, and Duke Nukem), **The Power Is Yours** (the heroes put their powers together to locate a lifesaving plant and battle an alien's deadly plan), **Deadly Waters** (Hoggish Greedly and Verminous Skumm take center stage), and **Toxic Terror** (Duke Nukem, Dr. Blight, and Sly Sludge cause more trouble for the Planeteers). Clever name for villains and the snappy dialogue between the teen heroes make for a punchy preteen series.

Choo Choo Trains Up Close and Very Personal (Stage Fright Productions, 1993, 30 m., 1–8)

From old steam and coal engines to new diesel and electric trains, this video shows viewers what it's like to ride in the cars and cabs of locomotives and, like the song says, work on the railroad. You'll marvel at how a rotary snowplow clears the tracks of huge snowdrifts, see city commuters take it easy while their trains maneuver the train yard, watch workers lay rail and couple and uncouple cars. At the close of the tape, an engineer gently reminds viewers that trains are great fun, but rail yards are no place for children to play. For more information on how to use this type of program, see the reviews in this chapter for **Big Rigs Up Close and Very Personal** and **Farm Animals Up Close and Very Personal.** Rail fans may want to check out **Grandpa Worked on the Railroad** (reviewed later in this chapter). And if you and yours are partial to songs about trains, look up **The Wee Sing Train** video in Chapter 3: Musical Fun.

Clifford series (Family Home Entertainment, 7 tapes, 30 m. each, 2–6)

Scholastic's wonderful Clifford the Big Red Dog is showcased in this series that helps preschoolers and young elementary-school children learn their alphabet, numbers, and size and spatial relationships. Each program was designed by experts from Scholastic, and part of the magic is that each tape also encourages children to accomplish these skills on their own. In **Clifford's Fun with Letters,** the lovable dog is part of the "ABC Message Service," so he has to know how to read to deliver messages. **Clifford's Fun with Numbers** is set during "Clifford's Birthday Surprise," where children learn to count party hats and birthday candles. **Clifford's Fun with Opposites** takes the fun concept to a "Pet Show" to explore relationships. **Clifford's Fun with Rhymes** lets viewers use rhymes to solve riddles in "The Rhyme Cat Rescue." **Clifford's Fun with Shapes** also covers colors as it takes viewers on a "Scavenger Hunt" with Clifford. **Clifford's Fun with Sounds** helps develop listening skills and introduces onomatopoeia when "Clifford Goes to Hollywood." **Clifford's Sing-Along Adventure** is reviewed in Chapter 3: Musical Fun.

Dinosaur! (CBS/Children's Video Library, 1985, 60 m., 4–8; director Robert Guernette, host Christopher Reeve)

The dinosaur mania that ran rampant even before Steven Spielberg released **Jurassic Park** still shows no signs of slowing—and that's healthy for such programs as this live-action and animated program originally shown on TV. The facts presented here may seem too familiar (today's children not only easily pronounce "Tyrannosaurus rex," but condescendingly declare, "*Everybody* knows people and dinosaurs didn't coexist!"), but the program facilely blends humor and education for those who can't get enough of the dinos.

Dinosaurs! (Golden Book, 1980, 30 m., 4–8, live action and Claymation; director Dick Baka, stars Fred Savage)

An elementary-school boy learns science projects come together much more easily if (1) you choose a topic with which you're very familiar, and (2) the subject comes to life via the magic of Will Vinton's wacky, malleable, lovable Claymation art. Dreaming to the strains of the animated rock video "Mesozoic Mind," young Philip lets his imagination run wild, visualized with the help of Claymation dinosaurs demonstrating their stellar eating habits at a table, chasing one another, and generally being adorable. Don't just plug this one in: Sit down and share this highly original, inspiring experience with your child.

The Dinosaurs (Pacific Arts, 1992, 4 tapes, 60 m. each, 8–up)

The facts of the dinosaur world are uncovered—sometimes literally—in this four-tape series that was shown on PBS-TV. The tapes **(Flesh on the Bone, The Monsters Emerge, The Nature of the Beast, The Death of the Dinosaur)** encompass the entire period during which dinosaurs flourished on Earth. Two of the world's most renowned paleontologists, Jack Horner and Robert Bakker (who were consulted by Michael Crichton for his novel *Jurassic Park*), are among the experts interviewed. Each episode is augmented with animation to give viewers an idea of what these creatures may have been like in their prehistoric habitats. Anyone of any age who's seriously interested in learning more about these magnificent, mysterious creatures will find their curiosity satiated by these tapes.

Donny Deinonychus: The Educational Dinosaur (Falcon/Victory, 800-422-6484, 30 m., 3–8, animated; narrators Ruth Buzzi, Richard Moll)

Donny is a parrot who is accidentally transformed by his scientist owner into what may have been his prehistoric predecessor, a dinosaur. The confusion that Donny feels as his brain power is reduced to a dinosaur's level essentially transforms him into a preschooler, so that he learns along with viewers. Two partially animated stories are on this tape: Each features lots of dinosaur facts told in voice-over by children and lovely original songs performed by talented artists, and also teaches viewers about relationships. The songs, complete with words on-screen, conclude each episode and remind viewers that like Donny, "You will never be alone, you will always have a friend." Is this series going to be a winner for your child? Judge for yourself: The program's Film Advisory Board Award of Excellence is prominently displayed on the box and at the beginning of the tape. The series of twenty-six half hours is heard on the Radio AAHs children's radio network.

Eco, You and Simon Too (Centerpoint Distribution, 1989, 40 m., 2–8)

This eco-video merits a mention here for taking a gentle, musical approach toward environmental education, although some adult viewers may find the approach sickeningly sweet. The puppet Eco is a playful sea otter, an animal on the endangered species list. He helps his friend Simon, a child portrayed by an adult, learn about protecting and preserving nature so that everyone can share in its beauties. Simon's joy bubbles over into songs that help viewers learn about life and society and how humans impact the planet. Computer graphics captivate the younger viewers, while older ones in this age range may be able to sing along to the cute original tunes.

Farm Animals Up Close and Very Personal (Stage Fright Productions, 1992, 30 m., 1–8)

This unnarrated program that launched a four-tape series lets children ask questions and provide sound effects and lets parents explain and encourage participation and learning. Children who show an affinity for animals (and there are few children who don't) will replay this tape again and again. Watch a playful horse cavort and snort; see chickens scratch and peck; find out how a pig spends his day; and visit sheep and cows as they nibble and nudge the camera as it zooms in close. The producers also combined some footage from this tape with additional equine footage for a new tape, **Horses Up Close and Very Personal** (1994). Other tapes reviewed in this chapter that are similar include **Big Rigs Up Close and Very Personal, Choo Choo Trains Up Close and Very Personal, There Goes a Firetruck, There Goes a Bulldozer, Road Construction Ahead, Fire and Rescue, Terrific Trips,** the **Here We Go!** series, and the two **Sesame Street Visits . . .** tapes. If this tape causes your child to ask for a pet, look up **Paws, Claws, Feathers and Fins** in this chapter. And for more tapes on animals, see the beginning of this chapter and reviews of **Mother Nature Tales of Discovery** and **Really Wild Animals** in this chapter, as well as entries for **The Bear, The Adventures of Milo and Otis, Bingo,** the **Black Stallion** films, **The Dog Who Stopped the War, Homeward Bound: The Incredible Journey, The Incredible Journey,** and **The Man from Snowy River** (all in Chapter 1); **101 Dalmatians, All Dogs Go to Heaven,** the **American Tail** films, **Charlotte's Web,** the **Dot and . . .** series, **Dumbo, The Fox and the Hound, Once Upon a Forest,** and **Watership Down** (all in Chapter 2); you get the picture.

Fire and Rescue (Focus Video, 800-843-3686, 1993, 30 m., 2–8)

Head out on a firetruck with firefighter Mike, who explains how firefighters receive their training, shows viewers the equipment, and participates in the action (or the "inaction," as is sometimes the case with firefighters) at the firehouse. This is the company that made **Road Construction Ahead,** so you can be sure it's engaging and well made and speaks intelligently about the subject. If this type of program appeals to your child, check out these similar tapes reviewed in this chapter: **Choo Choo Trains Up Close and Very Personal, There Goes** a Firetruck, There Goes a Bulldozer, Road Construction Ahead, Terrific Trips, the Here We Go! series, and the two Sesame Street Visits . . . tapes.

Grandpa Worked on the Railroad (Phoenix Media, 800-700-3153, 1994, 30 m., 2–8)

More than just a close-up look at steam engines (some still in use today), this video packs an educational punch that's pure fun. In a highly entertaining, often musical format, rail fan and singer/song-writer/actor Pete Shoemaker conducts a "musical train school" to teach children about the days when steam engines plied the rails. By opening a "magic" scrapbook that his grandfather (played by folksinger Utah Phillips) created, Shoemaker helps four children learn what it was like for his grandpa to work on the railroad. As the pictures in the scrapbook come alive, a child explains the on-screen action, showing engineers, firemen, and brakemen at work on vintage locomotives. Shoemaker gets all four children involved while they make fun raps and rhymes about how engineers use signals and how steam propels a train; he also takes a serious moment to explain why children should never play near trains. At the tape's close, a woman engineer (subtitled "Mom") steps from the cab of an Amtrak locomotive, and the children encore the songs. Rail fans of all ages will be mesmerized by the amazing mechanical power and industrial grace of these old-fashioned "iron horses." Also look up **Choo Choo Trains Up Close and Very Personal** in this chapter.

Happy Campers with Miss Shirley and Friends (Kids Express, 417-889-2234, 45 m., 2–6; host Shirley Bowers)

What better way to incorporate all of this chapter's "discover" topics than a child's first group hike, a venture into the great unknown beyond the back door! "Miss Shirley," who when off the small screen teaches and runs a preschool in California, encourages preschoolers to become "naturalists" and enjoy and appreciate the natural world around them. Before she sets off on a hike (despite the title, there's no "camping"), she sings to and quizzes her eight charges about safety on the trail, including asking your parents' permission and walking with a buddy at all times. Safety is paramount to her, and she reminds children repeatedly during the program about the rules of hiking; she even makes certain to equip her hikers with things such as whistles so they can make noise if they're separated from their group. Don't rent or buy this video expecting to view a lot of woodland creatures: Miss Shirley is more interested in the fascinating details of nature, such as buds on a tree or a squirrel-nibbled pine cone, and it's a happy coincidence when the group actually spots a bird or squirrel. Being a naturalist, she tells viewers, means "using your eyes like a hawk, ears like a deer, and nose like a wolf" to gather lots of information about what goes on in the woods. One fact that isn't addressed, but parents may already know: Children don't last as long on a hike as adults do, and although the on-screen toddlers exhibit exemplary behavior, that's not typical. Another strike in favor of a video outing!

Help Save Planet Earth (MCA/Universal, 71 m., 6–up; host Ted Danson, guest stars Whoopi Goldberg, Jamie Lee Curtis, John Ritter, Beau Bridges, and more stars)

Environmentally concerned actors make their point about what we've done to the Earth and what it will take to correct our mistakes—and that's a heavy load for a youngster to shoulder alone. In a program that's informative but a bit dry, the stars present viewers with simple steps each person—adult or child—can take to help make the planet a healthier place. Parents who want to instill in their children a responsible attitude toward reducing, reusing, and recycling (and who are willing to practice what they preach) will want to watch along, and maybe discuss what actions the family can realistically implement. A similar program, **The Earth Day Special** (Warner, not reviewed in this book), also features familiar stars sharing their experiences of preserving the planet and making recommendations for viewers.

Here We Go! series (Just for Kids, 1987–90, 3 tapes, 33 m. each, 2–6; host Lynn Redgrave)

The series that started the live-action visit video genre, **Here We Go!** features exemplary production values, great narration, and clear, crisp visuals that really make the viewer feel as if he or she is in the driver's seat. Plus, while Lynn Redgrave narrates only some segments, most segments are narrated by children whose parents operate some of the vehicles. In **Volume 1,** the family takes a helicopter ride over a southern California harbor; watches a bulldozer at work; rides a steam locomotive through a high mountain pass;

discovers how a hovercraft functions; and learns how to steer a blimp. In **Volume 2,** the family travels beyond U.S. boundaries to London and Mexico to luxuriate on an ocean liner; ride a double-decker bus; become familiar with an electric English milk truck; ride a fire engine; and learn about bicycle safety. **Here We Go Again!** features more of the same high-quality, interesting trips. If your children are interested in this type of firsthand visit, there are plenty of other programs available: **Big Rigs Up Close and Very Personal, Choo Choo Trains Up Close and Very Personal, There Goes a Firetruck, There Goes a Bulldozer, Road Construction Ahead, Fire and Rescue,** and **Terrific Trips** (all reviewed in this chapter).

Hey, What About Me! (KIDVIDZ, 1987, 30 m., 4–10; directors Jane Murphy, Karen Tucker, stars Robbie Kalin, Heather Richland-Shea, Cara Garber)

The title of this video aptly conveys the upset that can erupt in the household when a new baby arrives. Nearly every child goes through a range of emotions when first introduced to his or her new baby brother or sister, and as this video commendably points out, even anger is a natural reaction. This program stresses the importance of communication between parents and children, especially to emphasize the positive outcomes of having a new sibling. It helps young viewers to see some of their peers going through the same confused feelings of hurt and disappointment; they'll understand that this is all a part of growing up. And the responsibility of being a big brother or sister is such an honored position that young viewers will come to realize they are just as special to their parents as the new baby. Only two other programs come as close to reality as this program in helping siblings adjust to the arrival of a new baby: **Sometimes I Wonder** and **My Sesame Street Home Video: A New Baby in My House** (both reviewed in this chapter).

The Human Race Club (Just for Kids, 1989, 6 tapes, 30 m. each, 5–10, animated)

Like **The Berenstain Bears,** this video series seems to belong here, rather than in the chapter with its book-based counterparts. Joy Berry's books of the same name have proved invaluable in helping kids develop essential social and life skills such as tolerance of people of all shapes, sizes, colors, and abilities, alternatives to fighting, and coping with death. Five children are the members of the Human Race Club (HRC), and watching how they cope with problems and find solutions will show young viewers that they can find ways to deal with awkward or difficult situations. Berry herself adds some narration and appears briefly to make a few comments. You may find that some video stores stock the older tapes, which compile two episodes on one 60-minute tape; recently, each episode was released on a separate cassette. **The Letter on Light Blue Stationery** addresses self-esteem as Pamela copes with the loss of one of her good friends. In **A High Price to Pay,** Teddy discovers that money can't buy happiness. In **The Fair Weather Friend,** A.J. chooses friends for the wrong reason. **The Unforgettable Pen Pal** discusses the negative effects of prejudice. **Casey's Revenge** deals with fights between brothers and sisters, and teaches that respect beats fighting. **The Lean Mean Machine** addresses how to handle emotions by demonstrating that "there are no bad feelings, only bad ways to handle feelings."

I Dig Fossils (Mazon Productions, 800-332-IDIG or 708-272-2824, 25 m., 5–12; stars Sam Saletta, Ken Metz, Jim Kostohrys)

Father-and-son producers Jay and Scott Doniger turned their amateur passion for paleontology into a video that introduces elementary-school children to the excitement of fossil hunting. Narrated by 9-year-old "Scott," the program explains how and when fossils formed, details how to scout for sites and explore them, and paints the pastime as a terrific family adventure. Young Scott naturally weaves plenty of safety tips into his voiceover and conveys the awe of someone discovering a treasure that's been locked in rock for 300 million years. Though the stars are a boy and his father, the subject matter lends itself easily to exploration by the entire family. A list of fossil-related books for all ages and sources for site maps (such as museums and universities) are included at the end. A separate activity guide is available for teachers, but it is just as useful for parents. For a high-quality introduction to stargazing from this producer, see **Astronomy 101** in this chapter.

Lamb Chop in the Land of No Manners (A&M, 1991, 45 m., 2–10; stars Shari Lewis)

Although you'll find most of Shari Lewis's tapes in Chapter 6, Activity Tapes, Lamb Chop is included in this chapter because she learns some very valuable lessons about how to live with other people. "Guest artist" Mort Gerberg transforms live-action Lamb Chop into an illustrated fable to show how important manners are to the smooth operation of societies. When she's impolite, Lamb Chop is told by Lewis to reflect on her behavior, and while she's alone, Lamb Chop discovers the door to the Land of No Manners. It's guarded by five Dinoslobs: Belcher, Philth, Bumper, Tantrum, and Slobber. Once admitted to their disordered, ugly world, she learns that where no one has any manners, you can't even play softball, because the Dinoslobs don't follow any rules! Viewers will walk away having learned the important lesson that manners are contagious: If you demonstrate to someone that you're agreeable and polite, chances are they'll be just as nice to you. The video also contains a short drawing lesson from Gerberg and a brief tribute to Lewis and her puppets, who, at the time this program was produced, were celebrating their thirtieth anniversary on the air.

Let's Get a Move On! (KIDVIDZ, 30 m., 4–12; directors Jane Murphy, Karen Tucker, stars Clara Sturges, Amanda Hoffman, Eli Freedman, Maurice Johnson)

Did *your* parents move from town to town before *you* were old enough to realize what was going on? Then you may understand how your children feel if you're planning to relocate. This is one of the only tapes on the market that can help your children adjust to the changes moving brings. In it, four middle-class children tell the audience of their excitement, fears, and misgivings about leaving friends, discuss how strange it is to walk through someone else's house and have people walk through yours, and share their feelings about making new friends. What makes this program so appealing is how it involves the children in so many aspects of moving, without letting them get in the way. They help pack their own clothes and toys, and one creates his own imaginary planet to help him adjust, while another buries a tin time capsule so he can return one day and rediscover the treasures of youth. As the wonderful original song the kids sing reminds viewers, "Change is hard but it makes you strong." This is a must-have if you're planning a move.

Lift Off! An Astronaut's Journey (Peter Pan, 1990, 60 m., 3–up; narrator Patrick Stewart)

Shadow a NASA space shuttle crew as they prepare for a voyage, take off, conduct business aboard a shuttle in flight, and safely return to Earth. Listen to the crew's frank assessments of the rigors of training, the fun of zero gravity, and the awe space travel still inspires, even in adults. Official NASA footage enhances this engrossing examination of a career in the space program. Since this video's release, much has been learned about space flight, and shuttle flights have been scheduled more frequently, so youngsters today might consider them more routine than those of us who remember the first moon landing. Still, the video succinctly describes what it's like to be an astronaut and is a thought-provoking introduction for viewers who dream of one day traveling in space. Other programs about space that are reviewed in this chapter include **Astrodudes, Astronomy 101,** and **Patrick Stewart Narrates "The Planets."**

Look What I Grew: Windowsill Gardens (Pacific Arts, 1992, 45 m., 5–10; host Amy Purcell)

The host's engaging personality and commonsense approach are a boon to this program that teaches viewers the rewards of indoor gardening. The projects are uncomplicated enough for a 6-year-old to master, and Purcell, an elementary-school teacher, provides plenty of clear, simple instructions, reasons to do things in a particular way, and encouragement. The projects children will undertake include creating a terrarium, growing vegetables in water and in soil, and documenting gardening activities and progress in a journal, which in itself is a commendable exercise for anyone. (See a review of another tape in the series, **Look What I Made: Paper Playthings and Gifts,** in Chapter 6: Activity Tapes. The series also includes **Look What I Found: Making Codes and Solving Mysteries,** which, although recommended by association, is not reviewed in this book.)

More Dinosaurs (Twin Tower Enterprises, 1985, 30 m., 4–10; director Richard Jones, stars Eric Boardman, Gary Owens)

The original release in this series is still funny, building as it does on Owens' crazy voice and sense of timing. Boardman, playing a modern explorer, discovers a Utah town that calls itself the dinosaur capital of the world, and digs up dino myths and facts as well as bones in his adventure to find out all he can about the extinct creatures. In 1986, Twin Towers produced a second popular title in its

Videosaurus series, **Dinosaurs, Dinosaurs, Dinosaurs,** in which Boardman again heads out of the studio to explore the regions where dinosaurs once roamed. While he's exploring, visiting museums, and learning from experts in the field, Owens is slowly morphing into a dinosaur. Anyone who's ever raged across the living room as a pretend tyrannosaur will get a kick out of the closing scenes in a museum, where an actual "Garyosaurus" is displayed. Another title, **The World's Greatest Dinosaur Video** (1992), is geared toward children up to age 14 who want to learn more about the subject. Here, the hosts travel the globe to unearth dinosaur fact and fiction and marvel at the mysteries of these long-extinct creatures. Live action and animation combine to provide plenty of factual information, and Boardman and Owens have perfected their comic timing and silly puns. Each tape uses film clips from old and current movies to illustrate points and provide some comic relief.

Mother Nature Tales of Discovery (Discovery, 6 tapes, 25 m. each, 4–12)

Depending on the degree of interest in animals your child exhibits, you may want to check out these videos from the Discovery Channel. Each compiles footage from the cable channel's many nature-oriented programs into a shorter format, with content suitable for any age (that means no "survival of the fittest" nature gore for the squeamish). The didactic approach is intended to instill in young viewers a lifelong love and respect for animals, but it makes for a rather dry presentation, despite engaging visuals of animals in action. In the **Forest Habitat** package (which you can buy as a set) are **When Bears Go Fishing, Antlers Big and Small,** and **The Business of Beavers.** In the **Nursery Habitat** series (again, available as a packaged set) are **Babes in the Woods, Bringing Up Baby,** and **Springtime Toddler Tales.** For younger children, see the entry in this chapter for **Farm Animals Up Close and Very Personal.**

My Sesame Street Home Video series (Random House, 14 tapes, 30 m. each, 2–8)

This popular series needs no long explanation to tell you why it's successful. It's a timeless hit with parents who want to expand on the educational impact of the long-running PBS-TV program. Each video culls special moments from the TV show, adding live-action segments to address a specific topic, such as learning the alphabet. There really is no way to go wrong with this series; all the tapes are equally wonderful: **The Alphabet Game, Bedtime Stories and Songs, The Best of Ernie and Bert, Big Bird's Favorite Party Games, Big Bird's Story Time, Count It Higher, Getting Ready for School, Getting Ready to Read, I'm Glad I'm Me, Learning About Letters, Learning About Numbers, Learning to Add and Subtract, Play-Along Games and Songs,** and **Sing Along.**

My Sesame Street Home Video: A New Baby in My House (Random House, 1994, 30 m., 2–8; director Ted May, voices/Muppets Jerry Nelson, Kevin Clash, Martin G. Robinson, Judy Sladky)

The magic of *Sesame Street* is evident in this thoughtful program that helps preschool-aged siblings adjust to the arrival of a new little brother or sister. The plot is a story within a story: Little Alice tests big brother Snuffleupagus's patience when she breaks his favorite toy. Mom helps them both by reading a fairy tale about how a prince behaves when his new little sister arrives. Six musical numbers add *Sesame Street*'s trademark zip. This program is a good stepping stone to a discussion of how babies are made: Both the Muppets and live-action mothers talk briefly but frankly about how a baby develops inside a mommy. There are only a few tapes on the market today that address this difficult adjustment period for children. The package includes a wonderful parents' guide, with suggestions and a song for which you and your child can invent a melody. For two other views about how to handle this topic, check out **Hey, What About Me!** and **Sometimes I Wonder** (both reviewed in this chapter).

Orca: Killer Whale or Gentle Giant? (The Video Project, 26 m., 4–up)

Right from the start, it's obvious that the producers prefer the latter definition (gentle giant) for orcas. Even before the popular 1993 film **Free Willy** (reviewed in Chapter 1: Feature Films), these dramatically marked, five-ton creatures have been drawing more and more of the public's attention. This moving documentary, an informative, entertaining, and beautiful examination of whales' lives, debunks old myths and exposes the creatures as majestic, intelligent, playful, and loyal to their families, or "pods." Photographer Hiroya Minakuchi spent five summers studying and photographing sixteen different pods in the Johnston Straits off Vancouver, Canada. What he caught on film makes for a magnificent video for all ages:

breathtaking close-up encounters; interesting, rarely seen whale habits, such as rubbing on stones; an awesome whale birth; numerous jubilant breaches. Most memorable is Minakuchi's footage of "super pod day," when a great number of pods congregated in one spot. Young viewers will learn a little about, and maybe come to respect, a species fascinating not only because it's rarely seen at close range but also because of its past "mis-history" of killings. Inside each copy of this video is a brochure detailing the Orca Adoption Project of The Whale Museum in Friday Harbor, Washington (206-378-4710).

Patrick Stewart Narrates "The Planets" (BMG Video, 51 m., 6–up; director Don Barrett, narrator Patrick Stewart)

Blast off with Stewart on his guided tour of our solar system, complete with dramatic narration. Part performance, part science lesson, part symphony, **The Planets** captivates viewers with computer animation and NASA space photography that provides fascinating close-ups of all the planets except Pluto (there won't be a space probe launched that can reach that distant planet until at least the year 2000). The video was crafted to fit Gustav Holst's 1916 musical suite "The Planets," which has been updated and interpreted electronically by Isao Tomita. Like **Lift Off!** (reviewed in this chapter and also narrated by Stewart), this video encourages children to explore the outer reaches of their world and their imaginations.

Paws, Claws, Feathers and Fins (KIDVIDZ, 30 m., 4–12; stars Tiffany Pinnock, Kay Yamaoka, Matthew Krouner, Ben Williamson)

Animals are natural companions for children, but if you're not sure about whether or when your child will be ready to take the responsibility, check out this tape. "These are our friends till the end," the opening song tells viewers as the video launches into a celebration of the joys and aggravations involved with pet ownership. Like KIDVIDZ' other successes that are mentioned in this book **(Squiggles, Dots and Lines, Piggy Banks to Money Markets, Let's Get a Move On!, and Hey, What About Me!),** this video features children talking frankly to viewers about their experiences. Before the program offers its tips on pet care, it deals with many of the basics most kids don't consider: What kind of pet do you have time to care for? A dog takes a lot more time than a fish, for example; but even a fish requires a few minutes a day, and three hours every few weeks just to clean the tank. The video estimates time commitments per pet. Research what the care of your pet will cost before you buy or adopt it, the program suggests; go to the library to look up as much as you can about your intended. And consider how much space your family can allot to a pet. Tiffany wants a dog, but her father says no, only relenting at the very end after she's done all her homework and assures him that she'll be responsible for its primary care. Kay cares for her lovely cat, Ben tells viewers about his cockatiel, and Matthew takes wonderful care of his beloved fish; even so, one dies, and he holds a funeral for it. The original songs are good, but the crowning glory is the operatic takeoff of *The Mikado,* appropriately called "The Poop-A-Do" and dramatizing the cleaning up after the critters' "poop, hair, ick and fleas!" One of the KIDVIDZ principals, Jane Murphy, even appears in a cameo with her "grand old lady," the family dog. Among the consultants to this program are the American Veterinary Medical Association, the ASPCA, and the American Humane Society.

Piggy Banks to Money Markets (KIDVIDZ, 30 m., 6–16; director Barry Bransfield, stars Elizabeth Weisman, James "TJ" Thomas, Dian Lefkowitz, Adam Franklin)

Consultants with clout lend this video its credibility (and don't forget that KIDVIDZ is known for its informative, entertaining, high-quality productions): Among the advisers are representatives from the College for Financial Planning, Price Waterhouse, the National Consumer League, the National Council on Economic Education—and the list goes on. This unique tape effectively communicates to youngsters that they can make a little money (*honest* money, the tape emphasizes) and show people that they are responsible. In scenarios featuring four preteen children, viewers will see how one boy takes cans to a recycling plant to earn money; another young pianist plays at parties to earn money to buy a portable keyboard and then earn a little more money; a third has a yard sale so he can raise money to buy baseball cards; the last, 4-year-old Elizabeth, helps Mom in the garden and is rewarded financially. Some of the kids make adult decisions on how to spend their money; others learn the hard way after they spend foolishly. Highlighted with several terrific songs, the program also shows that kids can take charge of their finances if they do a little organization and planning. So watch out the next time your children ask to do something around the house; they may ask to be paid so they can buy you a birthday gift!

Really Wild Animals (Columbia TriStar/National Geographic Kids Video, 1994, three tapes, 40 m. each, 4–10; narrator Dudley Moore)

With the clout of *National Geographic* and the input of the Bank Street College of Education as educational consultants, this series is guaranteed to make a positive impact on both you and your children. Moore is the voice of the animated "Spin," a "globe-on-the-go" that informs viewers about the region they're visiting and throws in plenty of humor about the animals on-screen (for example, crowds of animal herds at watering holes in Africa during a drought become a traffic jam, with attendant sound effects). Not only will viewers see the wild animals of the title, but they can learn about primates from Jane Goodall or swim with dolphins. Like *Sesame Street,* this series uses songs and keeps the comic level fairly high to make the learning more palatable. **Deep Sea Dive** explores what many consider to be our last great frontier, the oceans; **Wonders Down Under** investigates what makes many of Australia's animals so strange; and **Swinging Safari** travels to the African wilderness to learn how its creatures have adapted to the hot climate and how they live. An ad for the children's magazine *National Geographic World* appears at the end of each tape.

Road Construction Ahead (Focus Video, 1992, 30 m., 2–8)

Even big kids will get a kick out of this terrific program that takes viewers behind the scenes of a road-building project in New England. The narrator, George, is a construction foreman who explains what happens as a road is constructed. He shows the view from inside the driver's compartment of various pieces of heavy equipment, and lets viewers watch as the crew dynamites a rock wall—the camera shows the action in real time and slow-motion, as well as forward and backward from a variety of angles. The discomfort of watching trees being destroyed has been avoided: the video picks up after the land has been cleared. Kudos to the producer for reminding viewers that construction sites are highly dangerous places and should be visited only with an adult, and even then, only with permission. If this program interests your child, check out **Fire and**

Rescue, There Goes a Fire Truck, There Goes a Bulldozer, Choo Choo Trains Up Close and Very Personal, and Big Rigs Up Close and Very Personal in this chapter.

Sesame Street Start to Read Videos series (Random House, 4 tapes, 30 m. each, 2–6)

In this terrific partially animated video series based on the popular PBS-TV educational series, Big Bird reads stories as viewers follow the words that appear on-screen. It's a bit like captioning, but the pace is slow so that young readers can grasp all the words as they scroll across the screen. The four tapes are **Don't Cry Big Bird, I Want to Go Home, Ernie's Big Mess,** and **Ernie's Little Lie.** Each video contains three stories.

Sometimes I Wonder (Media Ventures, 48 m., 3–8; stars Colleen Dewhurst, Keri Houlihan, Ian Fried)

Only a handful of tapes help parents address the confusion a child feels when a new baby arrives (the other two are **My Sesame Street Home Video: A New Baby In My House,** and **Hey, What About Me!,** both reviewed in this chapter). But what sets this video apart is Colleen Dewhurst's endearing role as grandmother to two children who feel displaced when Mom and Dad bring a new baby into their home. The children run away to their grandmother's ranch, where they witness firsthand how special a new life is when one of Grandmother's horses foals. Parents who are ready to discuss birth with their children will appreciate the on-screen birth of the foal, which is handled sensitively and with restraint. And as Dewhurst reminds the children, they are just as special to their parents as the new baby is, and their roles as older siblings are very important. Ideally, this is a video to be shared between parent and child, since it will raise many questions.

Step Ahead Videos (Golden Book, 6 tapes, 30 m. each, 2–5)

Golden intended this animated series as a preschool prep course to give your child an extra advantage once he or she gets to elementary school. The exercises lay the groundwork so that viewers will recognize numbers, letters, words, and relationships, and will adjust to learning in the classroom more readily. For example, **Get Ready for Math** teaches preschoolers counting and number-recognition skills through repetition, song, and innocuous animated animals. Also in the series are **Get Ready to Read, Get Ready for School, Get Ready for Math, Know the Alphabet, Working with Words,** and **Working with Numbers.** The last two titles are more appropriate for first-grade children who have mastered the basics and are ready to move on.

Tell Me Why (Prism Entertainment/Paramount, 1989, 18 tapes, 30 m. each, 3–up)

The best-selling book series by Arkady Leokum spawned this wonderful eighteen-tape series that serves as a virtual encyclopedia for curious children. In each volume, children ask approximately fifty questions that are answered with adult narration, colorful graphics, and explanatory film footage. Although many of the questions will be too advanced for preschool and elementary-school children, the information is solid and can be used for years to come. Here's a listing of the titles in the series (in volume order), along with a sampling of the questions answered: **Space, Earth and Atmosphere** looks at our progress in space travel and satellite launching, and answers questions about comets, the planets, eclipses, and the moon. In **Water and Weather,** meteorologists explain the cycle of seasons and weather patterns and answer questions about why the oceans are salty, why ice floats, and how lakes are created. **Flowers, Plants and Trees** answers questions about why trees change color in the autumn, the difference between conifers and deciduous plants, and how flowers produce their blooms. **Gems, Metals and Minerals** explains how gems are formed, discusses the natural forces that create mountain ranges, examines fossils, and defines atomic weight. **Insects** studies creepy-crawlies and explains how insects are hatched and born, the life cycle of butterflies, and why mosquitoes buzz. **Americana** is a history lesson that encompasses how the United States was established, who the founders of our country were, and why America bought land such as Alaska from other countries. **Life Forms, Animals and Animal Oddities** will captivate viewers with footage of strange creatures like the platypus and the armadillo and explains why animals hibernate, how snakes and worms crawl, and the differences between warm- and cold-blooded as well as vertebrate and invertebrate creatures. **Birds and Rodents** showcases rodent family members and explains how birds fly, how eggs are laid, and what keeps waterfowl afloat. **Mammals** explains why the dolphin and the bear are both mammals, looks at vampire bats, and explains the purpose of the camel's hump. **Animals and Arachnids** looks at some incongruous creatures: examined are why cats have whiskers, how spiders spin webs, and how a scorpion stings. **Fish, Shellfish and Other Underwater Life** explains why fish have gills and how they work, defines the mollusk family, and examines what makes some jellyfish sting. **Prehistoric Animals, Reptiles and Amphibians,** sure to be a hot title with dinosaurs still all the rage, looks at present-day descendants of the dinosaurs, showcases the largest and smallest reptiles, reveals how a frog croaks, and describes the life cycles of turtles. **A Healthy Body** explains what composes a healthy diet, how the bloodstream works, and why the body needs minerals and nutrients. **Anatomy and Genetics** looks at the human body from the inside out to illustrate why we need a skeleton, muscles, and organs to function, and discusses plants and animals to explain hybrids. **Medicine** explains in simple terms the causes of various diseases, some known cures, and how researchers and doctors use medicine to find cures and treat ailments. Chicken pox, asthma, and cancer are addressed, but this video was produced prior to significant public efforts on AIDS education. **Sports and Games** begins with the Olympics, the oldest organized sports contests, and shows how various sports like soccer and football are related. **Science, Sound and Energy** uses natural and lab-produced phenomena to define sound waves, science, and energy. It includes an introduction to basic physics and chemistry in explaining elements and atoms. **Beginnings: Civilization and Government** explains the source of society's customs and institutions by identifying where and, in anthropologists' hypotheses, how the first city was built. It also examines how various forms of government were established, how the American legal system evolved, and how humans discovered uses for fire.

Terrific Trips (GoodTimes, 4 tapes, 30 m. each, 2–6)
Children or a unique narrator explain all the action in a firsthand manner in these four tapes: **A Day at the Zoo/A Trip to the Post Office, A Hot Air Balloon Festival/A Trip to the Aquarium, Down on the Farm/A Trip to the Amusement Park,** and **Touring the Firehouse/A Trip to the Magic Show.** For example, a farmer's children take viewers on a tour of the farm, while the firehouse outing is "narrated" by a Dalmatian. This is fun, good-quality, informative programming. And if your young

viewers are still hungering for more videos of this ilk, look up these tapes in this chapter: **Sesame Street Visits the Firehouse, Sesame Street Visits the Hospital, There Goes a Fire Truck, There Goes a Bulldozer,** and **Zoo-opolis.**

There Goes A . . . (A*Vision/Kid*Vision, 9 tapes, 35 m. each, 2–8; host Dave Hood)

This series (titles include **There Goes an Airplane, There Goes a Boat, There Goes a Bulldozer, There Goes a Fire Truck, There Goes a Police Car, There Goes a Race Car, There Goes a Spaceship, There Goes a Train, There Goes a Truck**) is called **Live Action Video for Kids,** and it's intended to give viewers a behind-the-scenes look at big equipment, jobs, and places that kids may not otherwise have the opportunity to investigate. For example, in **There Goes a Fire Truck,** an actor admits to his secret wish to become a fireman and plays "Fireman Dave" to demonstrate to young viewers what the life of a firefighter is like. Although there's a wealth of interesting information on the tape, viewers may be confused when the visuals skip back and forth between different pieces of firefighting equipment without an explanation. And extended musical segments without narration don't add anything—unless you as a parent are around to encourage some questions and to discuss what's being shown on the screen. The fire department that's profiled here is Los Angeles City, which also has a bomb squad, as well as fireboats and divers. Commendably, one fire chief gives viewers a list of safety tips, and the host reminds viewers never to play with fire. You can buy each video singly, or packaged with a die-cast metal toy for a slightly higher price. If this series interests your child, check out **Sesame Street Visits the Firehouse,** as well as these videos that show lots of heavy equipment: **Road Construction Ahead, Choo Choo Trains Up Close and Very Personal,** and **Big Rigs Up Close and Very Personal** (all reviewed in this chapter).

3-2-1 Contact Extra: The Rotten Truth (Golden Book/Children's Television Workshop, 1990, 30 m., 4–16)

Without preaching to viewers, laying on the guilt, or resorting to scare tactics, this episode from the PBS-TV series presents the basic facts about what happens to garbage after we leave it at the curb. Have you ever wondered how long a glass jar lasts in a landfill? You'll find out on this tape—it's a real eye opener that makes you want to recycle as much as you possibly can. Viewers will visit a landfill to discover the dirty truth about how much of what we discard could have been recycled or reused, and since this message is addressed to kids and adolescents who'll inherit our mistakes as well as our improvements, it ends on a hopeful note. Look to the producer, CTW, for trustworthy, accurate information.

Whatever Happened to the Dinosaurs? (Golden Book, 1993, 31 m., 3–16)

When they refuse to close a drawer marked "dinosaurs," four children are magically transported across the miles to learn from paleontologists why dinosaurs no longer roam the Earth. The scientists explain their theories about dinosaurs' extinction in terms most children over 6 will easily comprehend. And viewers who have not studied prehistoric life may be surprised to discover the dinosaurs were not the oldest creatures on Earth. What this video lacks in style it makes up for in information; it's almost as entertaining as it is educational and will certainly interest serious and very curious students.

Where in the World: Kids Explore (Encounter, 1991, 4 tapes, 30 m. each, 5–12; live action)

Can learning geography be exciting? Carmen Sandiego proves it weekly in her PBS-TV series, and this home video series echoes the excitement. In **Kids Explore Alaska,** viewers join the on-screen cast as they pan for gold and learn about sled-dog racing. The video also pays tribute to Native Americans, featuring the carving of a totem pole during a day spent with Eskimos. In **Kids Explore Kenya,** kids discover via a hometown safari how nomadic peoples herd their cattle across the expansive veldt. The children make a movie of their experiences, documenting the importance of family life to the African cultures and their discoveries, including anthropologists' unearthing ancient skulls. In **Kids Explore Mexico,** the gangs gaze in awe at the silent mysteries of Mayan and Aztec temples, share meals with a Mexican family, immerse themselves in birthday and other cultural celebrations, and revel in lively music. **Kids Explore America's National Parks** journeys from the Olympic Northwest to the Everglades, exploring parks, including Mammoth Cave, Gettysburg, Mesa Verde, Grand Teton, and Mt. Rushmore. Each program uses location footage, maps, cultural excursions, native guests, and graphics to tap into other children's lives around the world. High-quality production and an original musical number highlight each tape. Also check out **Adventures in Willoughby** in this chapter.

Woman's Day Presents: Meet The Animals (Worldwide Entertainment Marketing/BMG, 2 tapes, 26 m. each, 1–5)

Produced by the popular women's monthly magazine, these two programs identify a menagerie of critters using colorful animation. In **Volume 1,** viewers meet and learn about the lifestyles of crocodiles, hippos, and chimpanzees; **Volume 2** introduces elephants, baboons, and lions. Even the youngest of viewers will probably prefer live-action animals to these animated ones, but the video is nonetheless admirably educational.

WonderWorks (Public Media, 37 titles, running times vary from 55 minutes to 120 minutes each, 6–up, all live-action)

The **WonderWorks** series is consistently engaging, creative, thought-provoking, conversation-stimulating, and genuinely enjoyable. Most of the programs have won numerous awards from film festivals and such entities as Parents' Choice and Action for Children's Television. They're included in this chapter because their wonderful stories can prove valuable in helping children mature socially. Some deal with death, others with developing relationships or coping with jealousy and responsibilities, and still others address issues such as discrimination and disabilities. For parents and teachers who want to expand on the viewing experience, the company packs each tape with a teacher-written guide called *A Closer Look* that provides questions for further discussion, as well as behind-the-scenes information on the production and background on the topic. Included in the series is the wonderful fantasy saga **The Chronicles of Narnia** by C. S. Lewis, spread out over three two-tape sets: **The Lion, the Witch and the Wardrobe, Prince Caspian and the Voyage of the Dawn Treader,** and **The Silver Chair** (see Chapter 7). **Almost Partners** (with Mary Wickes, Paul Sorvino) teams a New York City detective with a 14-year-old amateur sleuth in a comic whodunit. **And the Children Shall Lead** (with Danny Glover, LeVar Burton) chronicles the children of the civil rights movements facing challenges in Mississippi. **The Boy Who Loved Trolls** (with Sam Waterston, Susan Anton), based on a poem by John Wheatcroft, is about a boy who tries to hold on to his dreams. **Bridge to Terabithia** (with Annette O'Toole, Julie Beaulieu) is based on the Newbery Award–winning book by Katherine Paterson and tells of a farm boy's close friendship with an unusual girl, whose accidental death shakes his spirit. **Brother Future** transports a black teenage street tough into the pre–Civil War South. **The Canterville Ghost** (with Richard Kiley, Mary Wickes, Shelley Fabares) is based on Oscar Wilde's story about friendship across generations. **City Boy** (with James Brolin, Sarah Chalke) adapts Gene Stratton Porter's novel *Freckles,* a coming-of-age, environmental tale set in logging country at the turn of the century. **Clowning Around** and **Clowning Around II** (with Clayton Williamson, Jean-Michel Dagory) follow Sim from Australia to Paris to Montreal and home again, as he pursues his dream of becoming a world-famous clown. **Daniel and the Towers** (with Michael McKean, Alan Arbus) is a fictional tale that revolves around the real building of Sam Rodia's towers in Watts, Los Angeles. **The Fig Tree** (with Teresa Wright, Karron Graves), based on Katherine Anne Porter's Pulitzer Prize–winning story, is about a young girl coming to terms with the death of her mother. **A Girl of the Limberlost** (with Annette O'Toole, Joanna Cassidy) follows a farm girl who's caught between her mother's needs and her own dreams and desires. In **Gryphon** (with Amanda Plummer, Sully Diaz), a magical teacher brings angels to class and transforms the underachievers, particularly one disadvantaged Hispanic boy. In **Hector's Bunyip** (with Scott Bartle, Robert Coleby), the bunyip is a mythical creation that hides a disabled Australian foster child when authorities come to take him from his beloved adoptive family. In **Hiroshima Maiden** (with Susan Blakely, Richard Masur), a Japanese girl who survived an atomic blast changes the life of an American family. **The Hoboken Chicken Emergency** (with Gabe Kaplan, Dick Van Patten) features an oversize chicken in a comic Thanksgiving tale by D. Manus Pinkwater. **Home at Last** (with Adrien Brody, Frank Converse) documents one boy's experiences on the late-nineteenth-century Orphan Trains, which shipped East Coast orphans to Midwest farm families who needed workers. In **The House of Dies Drear** (with Howard Rollins Jr., Moses Gunn), the history of the Underground Railroad comes alive for a modern African-American family. In **How to Be a Perfect Person in Just Three Days** (with Wallace Shawn, Ilan Mitchell-Smith), based on Stephen Manes's book, a 12-year-old boy passes a course in "perfectology" that brings him ridicule in school and at home. **Jacob Have I Loved** (with Bridget Fonda, Jenny Robertson) is based on Katherine Paterson's book about twin sisters and the jealousy between them. **A Little Princess** (with Amelia Shankley, Nigel Havers) is a three-tape series based on Frances Hodgson Burnett's nineteenth-century tale of a wealthy Victorian girl plunged into poverty. The hero of **Maricela** (with Linda Lavin, Carlina Cruz) is a new immigrant from El Salvador who must come to terms with her mother's position in a wealthy household, and finds friendship with the wealthy daughter. **The Mighty Pawns** (with Paul Winfield, Terence Knox) details the real experiences and successes of a chess team from a tough inner-city Philadelphia school. In **Miracle at Moreaux** (with Loretta Swit, Robert Joy), set in Nazi-occupied Europe, a nun protects three Jewish children. The protagonist of **My Friend Walter** (with Ronald Pickup, Prunella Scales) is actually Sir Walter Raleigh, who aids his descendants as they struggle to right old wrongs and save the ancestral homestead in England. **Necessary Parties** (with Alan Arkin, Julie Hagerty) is based on Barbara Dana's book about a 15-year-old boy who files a lawsuit to stop his parents' divorce. **Runaway** (with Gavin Allen, Kevin Artis) follows a young boy who takes refuge in the New York City subway alongside a mildly retarded boy and a disabled Vietnam vet. **Spirit Rider** (with Graham Greene, Tom Jackson) is about the rivalry between two sullen Native American youths who return to their reservation, and their developing relationship as they compete in a horse race. **Sweet 15** (with Susan Ruttan, Karla Montana) isn't so sweet for a Mexican-American girl who discovers her father is an illegal immigrant. **Taking Care of Terrific** (with Melvin Van Peebles, Joanne Vannicola) observes a sheltered boy whose babysitter arranges a special evening for him. **Walking on Air** (with Lynn Redgrave, Jordan Marder) adapts Ray Bradbury's story about a wheelchair-bound boy realizing his dream of walking in space. **A Waltz Through the Hills** (with Dan O'Herlihy, Ernie Dingo) is based on G. M. Glaskin's book about two orphans who journey solo through the Australian outback. **Words by Heart** (with Charlotte Rae, Alfre Woodard), based on the book by Ouida Sebestyen, tells of a black family in an all-white Midwest town in the early nineteenth century. **You Must Remember This** (with Robert Guillaume, Tim Reid) details the relationship between a budding basketball star and her great uncle, a black filmmaker who endured the discrimination of early Hollywood.

The Wondrous World of Weird Animals (MPI, 1993, 32 m., 2–up; stars Gary Owens, Eric Boardman)

Even grown-ups will enjoy this adventure that follows a pair of competing zoologists (familiar from MPI's other silly **Dinosaurs, Dinosaurs, Dinosaurs** videos, reviewed in this chapter) as they vie to find the world's most unusual animals. From the production site in California, they head to London, and along the way encounter such animal oddities as a two-headed snake and an albino koala. Preservation of certain species is discussed; after all, some of the creatures young viewers see today may be extinct by the time they have their own children. Consider this program an apt follow-up to a zoo trip, since it contains footage of creatures few people would otherwise be able to observe.

Zoo-opolis! (Pacific Arts, 1985, 88 m., 2–10)

With the exception of animated hostess Gilda Gorgeous the Giraffe, the animals depicted in this documentary are all live zoo creatures. Gilda explains daily life at a zoo, showing viewers how the zoo residents are fed and cared for, how habitats are cleaned, and what makes zoo animals happiest, such as a polar bear's fantastic dives into cold water. A treat for viewers could be watching baby gorillas cavort and acclimate to their surroundings, and the footage of Lucy the lion as she receives an annual medical exam.

Other Tapes of Interest on These Topics:

The Animal Alphabet (Chapter 3, Musical Fun)
How Can I Tell If I'm Really in Love? (Chapter 5, Sports, Safety, Health, and Fitness)
The **My First . . .** series (Chapter 6, Activity Tapes) includes these tapes that feature activities about nature and science: **My First Green Video, My First Nature Video,** and **My First Science Video.**
Preschool Power (Chapter 6, Activity Tapes)

Sesame Songs Home Video: Sing-Along Earth Songs (Chapter 3, Musical Fun)

Sesame Street Visits the Hospital and **Sesame Street Visits the Firehouse** (Chapter 5, Sports, Safety, Health, and Fitness)

Squiggles, Dots and Lines (Chapter 6, Activity Tapes)

This Pretty Planet: Tom Chapin in Concert (Chapter 3, Musical Fun)

Chapter 5

■

SPORTS, SAFETY, HEALTH, AND FITNESS

Will your children really learn from video how to be safety-conscious? Do they display the same avid fanaticism for video workouts as we adults do? Titles in these categories can be a tough sell: Children are more inclined to sit in front of the TV to be entertained than to learn something—unless you've already instilled in them a sense of active viewing and introduced them to such things as PBS, computers, CD-ROMs, and such. But included here alongside tapes that teach are some that entertain. And a good number of programs in this category feature well-known sports figures or notable entertainment personalities to catch and hold your attention, as well as that of your child.

For those programs that you intend to use to instruct your children, take a moment to familiarize yourself with the tape and its star/host, and determine whether it's appropriate for your child. Ideally, you'll want to watch most of the programs in this chapter with your children. Many of the safety-oriented and coming-of-age programs merit further discussion, or a parent's reassurance that although many bad or uncomfortable things can happen, a child can have the advantage in any situation if he or she is prepared.

Programs are live-action unless otherwise noted.

Ranny Levy, president of the Coalition for Quality Children's Video, hopes the coalition can make children and parents more aware of alternative programs that may exercise their minds, and maybe their bodies as well.

Ranny Levy is a lifelong dancer, so she is interested in providing children with videos that not only exercise their minds, but also might encourage them to try something new and to be active participants in the viewing process.

She is a founding member of the coalition, which was created in 1991 by a group of video industry professionals who were concerned that many high-quality children's videos had not been introduced to mainstream America. Certainly librarians and educators knew how to locate some of this material, but the average consumer had no idea where to find it. And many of the best programs were not only entertainment-oriented but could also be helpful to families in terms of safety, improving their health, and broadening their horizons.

"We felt there was a real need to call attention to outstanding titles that had not found their way into the mainstream marketplace," Levy stresses. "The coalition is meant to give guidance to parents and caregivers who want to choose quality programming for children. To separate what's great [even though it may not be packaged in the most appealing box] from what's mediocre [but looks terrific on the outside], you have to have guidance; that's why we created the Kids First! seal."

The coalition's mission is threefold:

1. Endorsing videos with a Kids First! seal of approval and publicizing them via the *Kids First! Directory.*
2. Establishing public awareness programs by regularly updating the video **Choosing the Best in Children's Video** (previously available only through the American Library Association) and presenting it in workshops to train local, state, and regional organizations representing 60 million people. **Choosing the Best,** Levy says, "is all about creating an awareness with an established constituency. Educating parents is the primary goal."
3. Reaching at-risk and underserved youth and families through the Videotherapy project, which places videos in health care facilities such as WIC (Women, Infants and Children) centers.

Levy believes the VCR has become such an important entertainment element for today's families because "it is a means for viewers to have control over what they watch. It's another means to offer a wide selection. It's not an issue of video versus movies; it's an issue of video versus TV, and it's more about TV's content, what people choose as entertainment. TV is a constant, whether it's watching a video each night or turning on the news."

The VCR has also been accused of being this generation's most visible great divide, one of the many things that separates the "haves" from the "have nots." Yet Levy and the coalition have used the VCR as a tool to reach underserved youth: In 1993, Levy established a program to provide the New Mexico WIC program with videos as a means of violence prevention for at-risk families. A number of New Mexico WIC clinics have the opportunity to use both Kids First!–endorsed entertainment programs that demonstrate positive modeling behaviors and parenting education programs to reach underserved families. With the WIC program, the coalition reaches beyond those people who can usually afford to go out and buy videos, to those people for whom a video purchase, and even regular video rentals, may not be economically feasible. In this way, the coalition is bringing smiles of wonder and amusement to nearly 45,000 women, infants, and at-risk children at fifty-three New Mexico sites each month.

Parents can use the same criteria the coalition's screening committee uses in judging whether to include videos from any genre in their collections. Jurors evaluate each tape's content, appeal, production quality, and overall benefits. Levy defines these elements as common to high-quality children's programs: presentation, quality, humanistic values, creativity, learning potential, children's response, and packaging. The Kids First! seal on a video's packaging should help parents identify high-quality product. "The coalition is here to guide parents in selecting outstanding programs: The Kids First! seal provides high visibility for outstanding programs, guiding parents toward quality and value. The seal is how people will recognize who we are."

Levy launched the initial Kids First! collection in late 1992 and has been adding to it annually. (You can find a partial list of coalition-approved videos in the index, while the coalition's address is in the Resources section at the back of this book.)

The American Junior Workout (Good Times/Kids Klassics, 1987, 29 m., 6–16)

This program adapted the concept of the once-popular "29-Minute Workouts" for use by children. In three segments, young viewers will learn the important outline of a good workout (stretches and warm-ups, cardiovascular work, and cool-downs) and very basic information that may encourage them to pursue more vigorous strength training. The program conforms to the guidelines set forth by the President's Council on Physical Fitness. Especially if your children are into certain sports, they may want to supplement their routines with a program such as **Fun Fit with Mary Lou Retton, Curly Neal's Basketball Camp,** or Tamilee Webb's **Teen Workout** (see reviews in this chapter).

Baby Songs: Follow Along Songs (Golden Book, 1992, 30 m., 2–6)

Music, toddlers, action! The **Baby Songs** series (which you'll find reviewed in its entirety in Chapter 3: Musical Fun) is dependable, gently educational entertainment for preschoolers, and this tape is no exception. The music of Hap Palmer turns little viewers into active participants in the program as they follow their on-screen peers in marching, rhythm exercises, coordination, and counting games with beanbags. It's infectious. Parents may be called upon to help find appropriate household implements to use for a homemade band, but you can feel comfortable leaving your toddler alone to watch this program.

Baby Steps (Wood Knapp, 60 m., parents of infants; host Patti Gerard)

Gerard, a former world-class gymnast and part of the movement-research team for NASA, has developed a series of movements and "exercises" that help babies develop and help parents identify potential trouble spots or weaknesses. The exercises are very basic indeed: moving a brightly colored ball past an infant's eyes and watching how the child's eyes follow it, rolling a ball across the floor to see how a baby reacts. So much is contained in this program, first-time parents may find themselves and their babies on sensory overload if they try to put all Gerard's suggestions into practice at once. She does, however, remind viewers that babies have extremely brief attention spans and should not be overtaxed with new material. Her recommendation is to try a few of the techniques, then just play with and cuddle your baby.

Child Safety Outdoors (Kids Safety of America, 800-524-1156, 40 min., 3–10; host Bob Chesney)

In this age when children are bringing weapons to school and facing an onslaught of violence both real and in entertainment, can parents be too cautious even in their own backyards? This program will help you judge when it's appropriate to be overcautious and when to rely on more than just common sense. Chesney narrates, giving parents instructions and suggestions while showing scenarios in which children appear to be at risk but are not. He covers such topics as safety in crowded public places, safety on the playground, safety while on the street and in or around cars, and safety while biking, roller-skating, and skateboarding. He suggests techniques to prevent accidents, as well as training tactics for children, and offers statistics that prove how dangerous unsupervised outdoor activities can be for children under age 8, who are often oblivious to their surroundings. Commendably, the video offers an extended segment on how to administer child CPR, which is quite different from the techniques used on adults. Any young person who's ready to make a few dollars babysitting, as well as new parents, will benefit from watching this instructional program. (Another tape, **Child Safety at Home,** is also available, though not reviewed here.)

Curly Neal's Basketball Camp (MGC/Studio 6 Productions, 1991, 60 m., 6–up)

Today's young sports fans may not be familiar with this bald-pated star of the Harlem Globetrotters, but certainly those of us who came of age in the sixties and seventies will not have forgotten his on-court antics. In this video, however, he gets serious with children who want to get serious about their game. Not only does he demonstrate some of his tricks and tell some of his personal history, he also gives a succinct explanation of how basketball is played and always encourages his players. Neal divides the children into two groups: 6- to 10-year-olds and high-schoolers, and gives each group instructions appropriate for their ages and the inspiration for enjoying the game throughout their lives. He's easy to listen to and learn from; in fact, you might want to compare his teaching style to Spud Webb's in **Reach for the Skies with Spud Webb** (reviewed in this chapter). The most valuable aspect of this program, however, is Neal's advice to viewers: "Stay in school and practice."

Cycling for Success (Fox Hills/Media, 1987, 50 m., 12–up; director Kelly Dole, host Brian Drebber)

This video is a virtual encyclopedia of bike-related information, from choosing the right size bike to advanced racing techniques, such as efficient cornering and "drafting," the technique racers use to reduce wind resistance by riding in a teammate or opponent's wake. Anyone who's serious about cycling, whether competitive or simply recreational, will appreciate the tips on proper diet and muscle massage. If you're concerned about commercialism, though, be forewarned that the team sponsors' names and logos are quite obvious for much of the program.

Dance Workout with Barbie (Buena Vista, 1991, 30 m., 4–up, live action/Claymation)

Girls who are addicted to Barbie dolls will enjoy this production, although in truth it's less of a workout than an excuse to show off Barbie. Unlike a real workout, there's very little in the way of instruction, and even less explanation of the various steps used. If young girls have trouble following an instructor simply by doing, they'll be frustrated with this tape. Although Barbie gets the authentic Claymation treatment from Will Vinton Productions, the animators used her real, plastic head, and her mouth doesn't move when she talks to the camera. So even though Barbie raises her arms and legs to do aerobics, it looks like an invisible hand is reaching down to "play Barbies." That gives the production an artificial flavor, instead of the hilariously metamorphosed contortions the Vinton team has made other characters, like the California Raisins, perform. That hasn't hurt Barbie's popularity, however, and preteen girls have made this tape a strong seller. Since it encourages young girls to be active instead of passive viewers, it's worth a look.

First Aid and CPR for Infants and Children (Wood Knapp, 1994, 40 m., 12–adults)

This video capitalizes on the frightening fact that each year approximately 30,000 children are permanently disabled as the result of accidental injuries. Children who are just embarking on a part-time babysitting job can benefit as much as parents from watching this informal, informative video that equips viewers with the necessary techniques to act sensibly in emergency situations. Produced by the National Safety Council, this tape is about as complete and professional as an instructional video can get. The three uncredited hosts (a parent and day-care provider who's joined by two EMTs) dispense information in a very natural, straightforward, demystifying manner that does not wax clinical; viewers will grasp the material quickly and recognize that anyone can perform basic rescue techniques. Both children and adults role-play in simulated emergencies, and the EMTs describe the adaptations for infants, demonstrating those techniques on an infant CPR mannequin. There are a number of other videos that demonstrate CPR for children, or help parents and families babyproof homes and cope with emergencies, but this is one of the most well-produced, well-written, and enjoyable programs available on the subject.

The Fitness Express (USA Network/Pumping Iron America, 1993; available from USA Network, two episodes on one cassette, 60 m., ages 6–16)

Arnold Schwarzenegger, who headed up former President George Bush's Council on Physical Fitness, says "Hasta la vista to flabby kids" with these two programs. To help parents and teachers understand how easy and inexpensive fitness can be, Arnold joined forces with USA Network to make certain plenty of families could get access to either the cable show or the home video. He's a tough taskmaster, telling kids there's no such thing as "nothing to do." Punchy dialogue, crisp, MTV-like video effects, and Arnold himself will hold both kids' and parents' attention. More than conducting a workout, Arnold gives parents and teachers an instruction manual for terminating the bored attitudes and flabby physiques of many of today's video-reared kids. The first volume is geared toward children 6 to 12 or fitness neophytes. Arnold teaches a group of fourth-grade students how to build a gym in their school with such basic items as milk crates, a board, basketballs, and jump ropes. He arranges five "stations" at which the kids perform exercises to develop cardiovascular fitness, flexibility, strength, balance, and sports skills. In the Q&A session at the tape's close, Arnold reminds kids that if you like your body and take care of it, there's no reason to abuse it with drugs and alcohol. The second installment carries an age range of 6 and up, but since teens are the hosts and it features a structured routine, kids 10 and up are more likely to use and enjoy it. There's no fancy equipment, just aerobic and strengthening exercises demonstrated by two girls and a boy. Arnold intones that he's watching, and, through creative video wipes, his eyes occasionally "blink" above and below the teens. Though he's not in the same studio, his instructions and demos are woven throughout the workout.

Fitness Fables (Monterey, 3 tapes, 30 m. each, 3–6; narrated by Tony Randall)

Preschoolers might enjoy this quiet approach to fitness, which marries storytelling with interactivity for viewers in a nonsedentary storytelling format. Like mimes, the two actors, Alan Mintz and Lavinia Plonka, "pull," "push," and "move" the credits across the screen. Once viewers have cleared a spot in front of the TV, they're encouraged to join in the action they see on the screen. Volume 1 contains two nature stories: "The Cat Who Had to Be Best" shows a cat stretching and a tree bending in the wind. To follow along, kids have to know left from right. The second tale, "A Very Special Nut," works muscles isometrically as it tells of Sheldon the squirrel and his unsuccessful attempts to crack a very interesting nut (it's actually a marble). Kids pretend to crack a nut, jump and balance, and do little push-ups and abdominal crunches. In both cases, the number of repetitions is not as important as following the story and helping to tell it by performing the exercises. Children will also be able to follow the action in Volume 2 ("Cowgirl Cat Meets an Alien"—doesn't that title make you want to explore how viewers will "exercise"?—and "Detective Squirrel and the Mysterious Missing Tree") and Volume 3 ("Movie Star Monkeys" and "The Monkey Who Only Watched TV"). There's a moral to each tale; for example, the titular cat of the first tale learns that if you do your personal best, it doesn't matter who's perceived as *the* best, while Sheldon learns that good things happen to those who don't give up. This series is an altogether admirable use of video for preschoolers.

Fundance Kids with Sue Zaliouk (a.k.a. **Sue Zaliouk and the Fun Dance Kids**) and **The Complete Teen Workout** (Family Express, 45 m. and 60 m., 3–10; star Sue Zaliouk)

An accomplished dancer and former performing artist with the Royal Ballet in London, Zaliouk has a rapport with children that makes her programs stand out. In **Fundance Kids,** she takes simple games and makes them even more fun for children 2 to 8 by incorporating them into an extensive exercise routine. For example, "red light, green light" becomes "freeze" while music plays and the children dance furiously, hoping to be caught in impossibly silly frozen positions. Without calling this an exercise video, Zaliouk manages to get her audience involved and learning about their bodies (muscle control, spatial awareness, motor skills, active listening, and sequential memory are utilized) in a fun way. Her second program, geared for teens 12–up and executed by teens under her guidance, focuses on a dance-oriented workout that comprises stretching, cardiovascular work, and some strength training. It's a balanced workout and it's not so difficult that beginners will be put off by the exercises. Zaliouk's warmth pervades each program and invites viewers at home to participate without reservation.

Fun Fit with Mary Lou Retton (Warner, 1985, 30 m., 6–up; host Mary Lou Retton)

The petite Olympic dynamo shows children how to stick to a healthy routine and, in clips from her Olympic gold medal performance, shows the payoff. There are no difficult dance steps or pressure to keep up, just encouragement from Retton to do your best. She intersperses information on health with the exercises and keeps children's attention with her magnetic personality and winning smiles. Although the star is older now and new gymnastic champions have come and gone, this program is an excellent primer on why even a moderate fitness program can work to any child's advantage.

Funhouse Fitness 1: The Swamp Stomp (Warner, 1990, 30 m., 3–8; stars J. D. Roth, hosted by Jane Fonda)

Jane Fonda tries her hand at meeting the physical fitness needs of youngsters with two tapes (see next entry for the one for an older age group). Roth leads a group of studio kids in a series of dance step exercises designed to keep those couch potatoes from getting too soft. He gets some help from a group of adults dressed up as jungle animals and led by the Jungle Princess, who teaches kids the basic step, the "Swamp Stomp." A warm-up and cool-down are included, and many of the movements are fun, though a few are choreographed a little too quickly for the youngest of viewers. The problem lies in overwhelming children with advanced moves or too many repetitions: Can you imagine your 5-year-old trying to do fourteen push-ups? A confusing aside is that while the box cover recommends the tape for kids 3 to 7, in her intro, Fonda says it's for kids 4 to 8; gauge the readiness of your own children accordingly, and make sure you consult your pediatrician before allowing your kids to go hog-wild with these exercises. The tape's close includes plenty of shots featuring the Fun House and the advice to "Eat right! Make your house a Fun House!" Take it at face value: Fonda has done something worthwhile, and if it encourages children to exercise more than their joystick hand in front of the small screen, all the better.

Funhouse Fitness 2: The Fun House Funk (Warner, 1990, 30 m., 7–up)

Jane Fonda's second effort to help kids embark on a healthy life targets elementary-school viewers age 7 and up. An instructor from Jane Fonda's Studio has put together a complicated set of aerobic steps and a lot of push-ups, so viewers have to be fairly well coordinated to engage in the exercises shown on this video. More than anything, young viewers will probably gather a lot of ideas for use on the dance floor from the interesting steps shown here. In fact, the light show at the tape's close makes it look like a disco. Fonda hints at the perils of modern living with the admonition "Eat right, stay clean and have fun!," but children are never too young to hear that caution.

Gary Coleman: For Safety's Sake (LCA, 1986, 40 m., 6–12; director Leslie Martinson, stars Gary Coleman, Amy Foster, Bobby Jacoby)

Two children talk to their peers about unsupervised situations that could be dangerous and how to behave when adults aren't around. Parents of children who watch this tape should stick around to answer questions. The factual, straightforward manner in which the information is dispensed makes the program even more valuable to parents trying to instill confidence in their children without frightening them out of their minds. Among the helpful hints are tips for "latchkey" kids on first aid, fire safety, responding to the doorbell or phone if you're alone, and knowing where to find the fuse box, water shutoff, and other essentials in your home. Thanks to this tape, parents have an outline of items children should know about in order to be competent, confident, independent children. A safety guide is included with each tape. Overlook the fact that in recent years Gary Coleman has had his share of problems; here, he's straightforward and makes an admirable host.

Hip Hop Animal Rock (PolyGram, 1992, 30 m., 6–up; host Jennifer Lynn)

Right from the start, this tape advises interaction between parents and children with the disclaimer "Your supervision and your participation with your children will ensure that everyone gets the maximum benefits from this program." Four commonsense guidelines accompany the routines it demonstrates: (1) Drink plenty of water; (2) wear the proper footgear; (3) make your exercise area safe; (4) stop if you feel faint or queasy. The exercises were developed by fitness expert Gilda Marx and are led by teenager Lynn, while the animated Dee Dee Dodo Bird narrates and tries in a dissolve-animation style to follow along. Both boys and girls participate, and it's great to see them having fun on-screen while they learn steps that could easily be adapted to dancing. Because of a complicated progression of initial aerobic steps, however, children over 6 may derive more benefit; younger ones may just become frustrated, but they should be encouraged to persevere, since children of any age can master the rest of the program. The host is adept and accessible, the brightly costumed children are adorable and hip, and the seven original songs keep the pace snappy.

Home Alone: A Kids Guide to Being Safe When You're on Your Own (Hi-Tops/Video Treasures, 1987, 30 m., 6–12; director Scott Barrie, stars Malcolm-Jamal Warner)

Young viewers seem to learn more quickly from peers, so chances are they'll pay more attention to Warner than to an older authority figure. Warner offers elementary-school viewers plenty of sound advice for times when they find themselves alone at home, such as never telling someone at the door or on the phone that your parents aren't home. Viewers get the feeling that Warner has been through some of these situations, and his enthusiasm for helping children is wonderfully evident. Also notable in this vein is **Gary Coleman: For**

Safety's Sake (reviewed in this chapter) and **Barney Safety** (Chapter 3, Musical Fun)

How Can I Tell If I'm Really in Love? (Paramount, 1986, 55 m., 10–16; stars sibling actors Justine and Jason Bateman, Ted Danson)

When is sex love? How can you tell if you're in a mature or an immature relationship? How can you avoid having sex if you're not ready but someone's pressuring you? Teens and preteens will find answers as fellow high-schoolers comment on their experiences. The big draw, however, is not the hosts or the peers but the comedic presentation by Dr. Sol Gordon, a California-based sex educator who's addressed more than his share of high school assembles. In his unique, disarming manner, he shares advice and comfort with teens coping with peer pressure and concerns about their first sexual encounters. Disregard the first segment of the program (it's so cute you may be tempted to zap it), and hang on for the rest of the informative, enlightening, reassuring facts. The program is frank and addresses various methods of birth control, but it was produced before AIDS was recognized as an epidemic, so it does not broach that topic.

How to Raise a Street-Smart Child (HBO, 1987, 43 m., 10–17; hosted by Daniel J. Travanti)

By the title alone, you can see this is not a tape intended for young children. It is appropriate, however, for children when they're accompanied by parents, since it offers interviews with children of all ages. Be aware that this tape contains graphic descriptions of child abuse and molestation; the best way to handle a tape with such serious content is to screen it first, then watch it with your children. There are moving interviews with police officers, a man whose son was kidnapped and killed, and a convicted child abuser. Among the many suggestions the tape makes are how to teach your children to distinguish between "good" and "bad" touching and to use the telephone effectively in an emergency. Even dealing with such a "heavy" topic, this video assures that children who are prepared need not be afraid. The production is based on the book by Grace Hechinger.

It's OK to Say No to Drugs (JCI, 1988, 40 m., 6–16; narrated by Arte Johnson)

Familiar teen stars Shannen Doherty, Jason Hervey, and others speak out against drugs in interstitial shorts woven into this story of peer pressure. Two new kids in town, Scott and Pam, want to be accepted by a certain clique, but its members use drugs. The more they see of how drugs affect their friends, the less they want to be part of that group. If young viewers get nothing else out of this program, it will be worthwhile if they question whether what their peers are doing is really cool. The message is powerful: It can be cool to abstain from using drugs. This program and **Kids Have Rights, Too!** (see review later in this chapter) are part of a series based on the Playmore books *It's OK to Say No!* Though it's disappointing to acknowledge that we have to teach children these survival tactics, it's comforting to know there are so many resources—from video and books to instructional classes and support groups—to help them adjust to living in an increasingly confusing and dangerous world.

Jim Booth's Bubbly Baby Swim Video (New Market Sales, 800-242-7961, 1993, 30 m., parents of infants and preschoolers; host Jim Booth)

If you want your child to become comfortable and confident around water, you'll find plenty of encouragement in this program. Host Jim Booth, who has 20 years' experience teaching thousands of parents and preschoolers to swim, says the secret to a positive first experience in the water is to keep the learning fun and games, and once you relax, so will your child. Viewers will note his disarming and comforting home video–like approach to teaching children to respect and be safe around water. Although several older children are featured, the focus is on initiating babies into water play. And the on-camera children—including infants who appear no older than 8 months—prove he's right by laughing and even snoozing in the water in their parents' arms. Despite an extended segment in which there is no narration or instruction, the tape is well conceived, and the parents accurately demonstrate Booth's safe system. The disclaimer at the beginning of the tape also reminds parents that "no child can be made water-safe," and the only way to ensure children are safe is to watch them constantly while they're in or near the water.

Karate for Kids series (Bright Ideas Productions, 3 tapes, 30 m. each, 6–up)

Lisa Marie Nelson, the artist/performer who created the award-winning **Music & Magic: Positive Music for Today's Kids** series of audio and video releases (reviewed in Chapter 3: Musical Fun), produced these programs with the same energetic, positive attitude that wins loyal viewers, as well as awards. The original tape, **Karate for Kids** (hosted by Ted Nordblum), emphasizes self-improvement and self-esteem over competitiveness and is suitable for 6- to 10-year-old beginners. Children who watch this program may come away a bit wired from the exciting action of karate, but they'll also gain an understanding for the value of patience, practice, and persistence. There's a commendable concern for safety and health: Everyone warms up and stretches, and Nordblum, a first-degree black-belt instructor, even touches on healthly habits. The original music helps pace the action and keeps the instruction fun. In **Karate for Kids II: Intermediate Instruction and Exercise,** host Brandon Gaines, an 18-year-old black belt, continues the impression left by the first program, helping young viewers develop a positive attitude, take an interest in fitness, and learn self-discipline and perseverance. It's encouraging to see a young man so dedicated to his sport work so easily and comfortably with children. Viewers learn in this program that karate is as much a mental exercise as a physical one. The second tape is recommended for children who have already had some basic karate instruction; the most suitable age range is 8 and up. **Karate for Kids III** demonstrates practical applications for the karate techniques. Host Kenn Firestone, a sixth-degree black-belt and international karate champion, helps participants build confidence as they learn how to defend themselves in potentially dangerous situations, such as abduction or abuse. Rather than frightening young viewers, the tape gives children tools they can use to prevent becoming victimized. In a step-by-step approach, Firestone teaches children how to block an attack, break free, run away, and, most important, yell for help. Firestone also gives his three young costars a pep talk about the importance of trying in any sport. All three programs are terrific confidence boosters and great basic training in the sport of karate.

Kids Have Rights, Too! (JCI, 1988, 28 m., 6–12)

Children have to be more alert now than ever before, and a video

like this can help them distinguish when they're really in trouble—
it might even be able to prevent trouble. A tremendous cast of young
kids convenes a mock "Kids' Rights Hearing" to define their rights
in light of their experiences. Their bill of rights includes their right
to privacy (concerning their space and their possessions), the right
to say "no" to anything they think is wrong (from shoplifting to
drugs), and the right to protect their bodies (from unwelcome
touches). They are encouraged to keep their wits about them even
when confronted with dangerous situations, and when they are prepared, the outcome will usually be in their favor. There are only a
few other videos available that address this issue, and none that lets
the children themselves be the moderators. JCI also released **It's OK
to Say No to Drugs** (reviewed earlier in this chapter) to help children
cope with that eventuality. These and many other videos featured
in this chapter can help children develop the survival skills necessary to make their way through a dangerous, often confusing world
that forces children to grow up much more quickly than many of
us would like.

Kids in Motion (FoxVideo, 1987, 67 m., 3–6; director Eugene Tana-
sescu; stars Scott Baio, Julie Weissman)
   Baio really appears to be enjoying himself—and that's a big draw
for youngsters who need an exuberant host. He and his cohost encourage and instruct their charges in simple movements that will
get viewers thinking about a lifetime of fitness. True to MTV-style,
the tape features plenty of segments geared toward youngsters with
short attention spans, perfect for kids beginning to develop their
concentration powers. And everything is fun, from imitating animals
in "Animal Action," to dancing in "Poetry in Motion." There's a brief
aerobic section, and some very basic dance moves are introduced,
but most segments emphasize balance and coordination. Most of
the exercises also incorporate a mental workout; for example, kids
contort into various numbers during the "Count Bounce." Even this
long after its production date, it's still a viable introduction to fitness
for kids.

Kids for Safety (Monterey, 1990, 25 m., 4–up)
   Do kids teach other kids the right things to do in an emergency?
Believe it or not, the youngsters on this tape are hip and informed

about how to proceed in a crisis such as a fire or an accident. From the opening song ("Play it safe, play it smart") to the closing credits, this admirable tape packs a wealth of information into an entertaining format. Topics include bike safety and the rules of the road (complete with a pop quiz); fire safety, from smoke detectors to family escape routes; and personal safety, which is a broad topic in itself. The most logical piece of information falls into the personal safety category. Not only do kids learn to say no, they learn to say when: "No one has the right to touch you anywhere your bathing suit covers. Tell them to stop. Don't let fear stop you." The serious stuff is interspersed with catchy music videos; the producers, Martha, Tom, and Tony Mazzarella, put their concerns right in the open for all parents to share. If parents need to discuss such serious subjects with their children, viewing this tape could be an easy introduction. The subjects are presented in an empowering way, not a victimizing way; young viewers should gain plenty of confidence watching this.

KinderKicks: Kinder Fun on a Rainy Day (Healthy Young Children Enterprises, 30 m., 3–6; stars Linda Leszynski)

"Ms. Linda," the Ohio-based star of interstitial programming on some PBS-TV stations across the country, produced this video to convince toddlers and their parents that establishing a healthy diet and exercise routine can be fun. When it's raining outside, she helps a small group of preschoolers through some playground-related exercises. The children pretend they're on a merry-go-round, riding bicycles, jumping rope, or rowing boats; they learn that stretching and learning about fitness aren't difficult or intimidating, but very natural. Most important, Ms. Linda provides a sturdy triangle of fitness to follow for the rest of their lives: Eat right, play safe, and get plenty of sleep. This woman has a magical way with the on-screen children that oversteps the boundaries imposed by television: She really reaches her video audience because she's honest and treats toddlers with genuine respect.

A League of Their Own: The Documentary (Columbia TriStar, 1992, 27 m., 8–up; director Mary Wallace)

Containing nostalgic newsreel footage in a retrospective of the "Diamond Girls" who substituted for the men on major-league baseball teams during World War II, this documentary tells the story of the women who inspired the feature film **A League of Their Own** (Chapter 1: Feature Films).

Little League's Official How to Play Baseball Video (MasterVision, 1990, 70 m., 6–16; director John Gonzalez)

You may be parent to one of the more than 2.5 million children playing Little League baseball in one of the 7,000 leagues every year. If so, take a look at this professional yet accessible program that teaches skills and offers information on equipment, training, and teamwork. Under the auspices of the Little League organization, the producers of this video capture all the basics of winning ways in children's baseball. Gonzalez, from NBC's Game of the Week, incorporates slow- and stop-motion effects to catch every angle of proper technique for hitting, bunting, pitching, etc. The Little League motto, "Character, courage, and loyalty," is evident in the emphasis on sportsmanship and the promotion of friendship through sports. The young players who demonstrate their skills are natural in front of the camera. As an added value, you might be able to find it as it was packaged in 1990: along with the book of the same name.

Looking Good! The Fun Teen Fitness Program Featuring Tempestt Bledsoe of *The Cosby Show* (CBS/Fox Video, 1987, 40 m., 8–12; host Tempestt Bledsoe)

Fourteen at the time she starred in this workout video, Bledsoe also toured the country as a spokesperson for Nancy Reagan's "Just Say No" campaign and on behalf of the President's Council on Physical Fitness. Bledsoe and a group of teens try to follow some fairly complicated exercises; it may encourage kids that even Bledsoe can't keep up with every step. Between the exercise segments, she portrays three types of teens who eventually convert their lazy mindset to a pro-fitness attitude: a valley girl, a brat, and a tough street kid. One of the first videos to address the alarming "fit-lessness" of American youth, **Looking Good!** started a quiet trend that even Arnold Schwarzenegger got into (see **Fitness Express** in this chapter). Although this tape is fairly weak by today's standards, if your child wants to see how celebrity kids get fit, this and the Alyssa Milano tape (**Teen Steam,** reviewed in this chapter) are the two to watch.

McGee and Me! Skate Expectations (Tyndale House Publishers, 1989, 30 m., 4–10)

The series **McGee and Me!** is a beautifully produced, well-written, and competently acted series that illustrates Christian (or even more broadly, humanistic) principles such as demonstrating kindness and fairness to all people (religious overtones are evident in both songs and images). McGee is an animated character who acts as young Nick's conscience. In this episode, Nick is distressed when he witnesses a bully picking on a younger child, so McGee suggests a skateboard race to try to level the playing field. Frightened by the prospect of a dishonest opponent and unsettled by the amount of responsibility he's taken on, Nick prays for strength, and finds it when he resists the temptation to cheat, which becomes the bully's downfall. Young viewers will be treated not only to lessons about fairness and good sportsmanship but also to the underlying Christian principles.

Mister Rogers: When Parents Are Away (Playhouse/CBS, 1987, 65 m., 2–7; director Paul Lally, stars Fred Rogers)

Even royal children become anxious when parents are away. So before you send your preschoolers off to day care, let them take a look at how King Friday's son deals with separation via that comforting host Mister Rogers. Rogers reminds viewers that it's all right to feel mixed emotions, and it's even more comforting to talk about those feelings with the people who love us. As he does on his TV series, Rogers spends some time visiting his neighbors, including a day-care center and a cracker factory.

NFL Kids: A Field of Dreams (PolyGram/NFL, 1992, 45 m., 5–up)

Although this program, set up like a series of fantasy interviews, is not a tape that is strictly oriented to sports/health and fitness/safety, the skills and values it emphasizes could easily be used to enhance kids' sports development. Four children at a sleepover party are magically transported to a football "field of dreams" to hear directly from football heroes how they made it to the pinnacles of their careers. Boomer Esiason talks to the kids about self-confidence and leadership; Christian Okoye tells children to embrace life's learning experiences and not be too timid about learning from them; Michael Irvin, one of seventeen siblings who overcame the mean streets of his youth, imparts some words of wisdom about keeping out of trouble by staying focused and working hard; and Ronnie Lott explains that teamwork is crucial to success. Game footage helps illustrate each player's points. Motivational and inspirational, this tape gives sports fans and players a chance to reflect rather than just hit the field with no thought about the outcome.

Once Upon a Potty (Barron's Films, 1993, 30 m., 2–4 and their parents)

This video is based on the parenting books by Alana Frankel that have become very popular in recent years. Like the books, the video comes in two versions, his and hers, and if you can find it, is also available packaged with a doll and the appropriate book. Its humorous approach to the trials and tribulations of toilet training is disarming and welcome during what can prove to be a very stressful transition for parents and children alike. Another video that addresses this subject, although it's not reviewed here, is **It's Potty Time** (TPW, 1993, 30 m., 2–4 and their parents).

The Pistol: The Birth of a Legend (Sony Wonder/SVS, 1991, 101 m., G, 6–up; director Frank C. Schroeder, stars Adam Guier, Nick Benedict, Millie Perkins, Boots Garland)

This heartfelt film captures the essence of an inspirational young man's love of sports and, most important, the bond between father and son. It's the story of the youngest basketball star to be inducted into the Hall of Fame, "Pistol" Pete Maravich, whose untimely death in 1988 stunned the sports world. Set in 1960, the film traces the roots of Maravich's championship abilities under the careful guidance of his father. Guier, who was 12 at the time of the film's production, was handpicked by Maravich before the latter's death; the young actor adeptly plays an innocent yet determined future champion with ingenuous insight. Another message the film conveys is how difficult is to be exceptional at something, whether it's sports, studies, or a skill, and to be accepted by one's peers. At the time of this video's release, Maravich's record as the nation's leading college scorer still stood.

Playtime with the Motion Potion Kids (Best Film & Video, 30 m., 2–7; stars Fyllis Nadler)

Imagination-firing activities and exercises fill this program, designed by dance and fitness instructor Nadler. Even preschool TV staple *Romper Room* has used Nadler's techniques to help children learn coordination as they explore their imaginations. Her winning way with children has them experimenting in a "magic kitchen," planting silly flowers in a pretend garden, and exploring rhythm and body awareness with creative movements and dramatics. And it's all in fun, since everything is whipped up from the minds of Nadler and her on-screen children. The beauty of Nadler's terrific techniques is that everything pretend is okay—all it takes is a little imagination.

Rappin' 'n' Rhymin' (Hanna-Barbera/Turner, 1991, 30 m., 6–up)

Future "fly girls" and "fly boys" will cotton to this program that converts rapping into an exercise. There are raps that count, raps that showcase rhyming words, and raps that just motivate kids to get up and move their feet. Other children's exercise videos that try to be as hip as this one often don't succeed; this one does, thanks to talented young performers who are obviously having fun learning dance steps that turn into exercise steps. A song sheet is included so young viewers can eventually exercise their vocal cords along with the rest of their bodies.

Reach for the Skies with Spud Webb (Sony Wonder/SVS, 1990, 60 m., 8–12)

Despite standing only 5'7", Anthony Jerome "Spud" Webb has a vertical leap of 42 inches and captured the NBA Slam Dunk title in 1987 for his team, the Atlanta Hawks. Serious young basketball players will appreciate the pointers Webb gives on dribbling, passing, shooting, and playing defense, but his main focus is inspirational: Stand tall no matter what life hands you, and you'll find that anything is possible. When this program was released, Webb requested that a portion of the proceeds from its sale be donated to the Boys Clubs of America, reflecting his devotion to guiding children and teens through the difficulties of life. You might want to compare Webb's instructional style with that of former Harlem Globetrotter Curly Neal (see **Curly Neal's Basketball Camp** reviewed earlier in this chapter).

Say No to Drugs (Twin Tower, 1986, 45 m., 8–16)

In fictional vignettes and real-life interviews, parents discuss and dramatize ways to reach their children before and if they encounter drugs. The emphasis is on mutual communication, building a child's self-esteem to offset peer pressure, and helping children adjust to increased responsibility, especially where their own actions are concerned. This is one of the few videos that arms children with comebacks; for example, if a child is cajoled with "Everybody does drugs," he may shoot back, *"I* don't do drugs, and *I'm* somebody!" The key to videos such as this and **It's OK to Say No to Drugs** (reviewed earlier in this chapter) is to initiate a discussion after you and your child watch the program.

Sesame Street Visits the Firehouse (Random House, 1990, 30 m., 3–up, live action/Muppets)

As usual, the masterminds at Children's Television Workshop find a disarming way to address a topic that may frighten young children. Elmo, the Muppets' representation of your average, inquisitive preschooler, gets to investigate what goes on at the firehouse after a firefighter rushes to Sesame Street to put out a "fire" in Oscar's garbage can. (Oscar was just overzealous at the barbecue that day, and he's now the proud owner of a new smoke detector.) Big Bird, Gordon, and a young visitor to Sesame Street learn the consequences of playing with matches and receive instructions on how to stay safe if a fire threatens. The important tips: Yell for help, go to the firefighter (even though he or she may look like an alien), and practice fire drill exits in your home.

Sesame Street Visits the Hospital (Random House, 1990, 30 m., 3–up, live action/Muppets; guest star Robert Klein)

The hospital is one of the most frightening places to children, and even to some adults. But who better than the benevolent Muppet cast of *Sesame Street* to impart to preschoolers the news that hospitals help heal people? Comedian Klein guest-stars as the doctor who treats an unhappy and unhealthy Big Bird, victim of "pneumo tweetitis canariansis." While Big Bird recuperates, his buddies come to visit him and comfort him when the hospital staff continues to "take things" from him, like his temperature and blood pressure. One of the songs that should make perfect sense to children advises,

"You have to be patient when you're a patient so the sickness will go away." This is another of those rare videos that addresses an issue so many other videos have not, so if a hospital stay for you or your children is imminent, check out this comforting program.

Sports Bloopers for Kids (ESPN/WEA Corporation, 1993, 30 m., 6–16)

There are a slew of sports bloopers tapes on the market, but this is one of the few that's oriented toward children and their peculiar sense of humor. When nothing else will cheer you up, sometimes looking at someone else's humanness (the gift of making mistakes) works wonders, especially when it's all in lighthearted fun. Sports mascot the Phillie Phanatic graces the video's cover and races through the program on his motor scooter like he does at Phillies games. He's joined by wacky characters inspired by real sports footage: Blooper Man, a player who can't seem to take a step without a stumble; Coach Dweeb, a man who doublespeaks until his audience is in stitches; First Base Fred, who, like a base in baseball, winds up stepped on more often than not; and Howard Cantspell, who introduces his "Animal Olympics," complete with animal bloopers. If this tickles the fancy of you and your children, check out ESPN's other bloopers videos, including **Sports Blooper Awards** and **Amazing Anything Goes Sports Bloopers** (neither is reviewed here).

Sports Cartoons (Avid, 50 m., 3–10, animated)

Interstitial programming that really captures your eye is rare, but here's one shining example. Avant-garde animation brings to life the humorous side of sports, from the incongruous concept of hippos playing basketball, to crocodiles facing off against cats in hockey— just about anything silly can and does happen, and the smart-aleck cats are usually the ones on the short end of the stick. It's light-hearted and silly, just the thing to perk up children when inclement weather may prevent them from playing real sports. Taken all at once, it's like an overdose of harmless inanity; interspersed with other videos, it's snippets of pure delight.

Strong Kids, Safe Kids (Paramount, 1984, 45 m., 4–8, live action/animated; director Rick Hauser, stars Henry Winkler, Mariette Hartley, John Ritter)

One of the earliest programs to deal with the prevention of child abuse, this tape offers suggestions in a sensitive, caring way. Even animated characters pipe up to help children take control of a frightening situation: how to yell for help, how, when, and why to say no, what kind of touching is bad. Parents will want to be present during viewing: There's a segment that quizzes them on how to be a "askable" parent. A bit rough around the edges, this program and a few others helped launch a trend in programming geared to the prevention of child abuse.

Teaching Kids Speed for All Sports (Excel Sports Science, 800-288-4403 or 503-485-5265, 1990, 51 m., 6–12; stars Carl Lewis)

Olympic gold medal winner Lewis helps children who are determined to improve their performance in any sport learn how to be quicker and more agile. Certainly some people are built more for speed, but Lewis helps adjust each child's body position and mental attitude to develop better body awareness, psych themselves up for an improved performance, and get the most from what they were born with. He frequently reminds the children that they are in sports for the fun of it and encourages them to keep a positive mental attitude. Among the preteen kids on the tape are a 12-year-old girl runner, a 7-year-old girl soccer player, a 7-year-old boy football player, and a 10-year-old boy baseball player. Licensed sports psychologist Scott Pengelly offers parents and coaches some important hints for working with children without discouraging them by being too demanding. Though it *is* fun, especially if a child can reap some benefit from increased speed, this is very specific instruction, aimed at children who are serious about their sports; watch it with your child so you can remind him or her of Lewis's techniques during practice and exercise.

Teen Steam (J2 Communications, 1988, 45 m., 10–14; stars Alyssa Milano)

More a celebration of being a teenager than a fitness program, this video attempts to get kids to work up a sweat and then apply some of the moves they've learned in dances. Young Milano, who also sings the theme song, can't be compared with Jane Fonda or Kathy Smith, but her efforts are earnest, and many teens would rather watch someone their own age than an adult whose business is fitness. Those girls who enjoy some silly interludes along with some fun dance moves will like this program; if you're looking for a workout program with a more structured routine, try **The Teen Workout** (reviewed below), or **The Complete Teen Workout** (see **Fundance Kids** in this chapter).

The Teen Workout (Random House, 1989, 35 m., 13–19; stars Tamilee Webb)

The disclaimer at the opening of this video emphasizes that this workout is *not* for preteens; it was designed for older girls, especially those who are already familiar with exercise routines. Webb divides her workout into three segments: warm-up and stretch, low-impact dance aerobics, and strengthening/toning. This is a serious exercise regimen from a woman who's made a name offering high-quality, worthwhile workouts for adults, and her foray into the children's fitness arena is welcome. Webb explains how to take your heart rate, and while she uses weights in some of the exercises, the girls working out with her do not. The credits include two doctors as fitness consultants.

Time Out: The Truth About HIV, AIDS, and You (Paramount/Arsenio Hall Productions, 1992, 40 m., 8–16; director Malcolm-Jamal Warner, hosts Earvin "Magic" Johnson, Arsenio Hall)

When Paramount released this video, it announced that all proceeds from its sale were donated to the Magic Johnson Foundation and earmarked for organizations that focus on research, education, and care for people with HIV and AIDS. Magic and Arsenio decided that the goal of the program would be to wipe out ignorance in today's youth. You'll probably want to preview this program to determine whether or not your child is ready for the factual and straightforward approach to the devastation of AIDS. Addressed in the program are who can contract AIDS (anyone); how it's transmitted; and how to protect yourself. Admirably, the tape takes a pro-abstinence stance and encourages youths who have not yet become sexually active to abstain as long as they can. The hosts also recommend that anyone who's sexually active be tested. A study guide is included with each video (if you're taking it out as a rental, however, ask the retailer if he or she can locate one of the guides). If your child is more interested in Magic's basketball life, FoxVideo has two tapes (not reviewed in this book): **Always Showtime** and **Put Magic in Your Game.**

Too Smart for Strangers with Winnie the Pooh (Disney, 1985, 40 m., 2–8, animated; director Philip Messina, voices of Hal Smith, Will Ryan)

Like **Strong Kids, Safe Kids** in this chapter, this early attempt to produce a tape focused on the prevention of child abuse relies on sensitivity and gentleness to broach its tough subject. Innocuous Pooh Bear helps elementary-school children learn to say no to strangers, run for help, and always tell someone. Tigger gets in on the act to help keep the tone upbeat, even if the subject matter is scary and serious. Also check out **The Berenstain Bears Learn About Strangers** (see Chapter 4, Discovery and Learning) and **Touch** (reviewed below).

Touch (Media Ventures, 1987, 32 m., 2–10; host Lindsay Wagner)

Illusion Theater of Minneapolis created this theatrical adaptation to help children understand good versus bad touching, recognize the differences, and give them ways of coping with the unwanted aggression that is sexual abuse. The program has won kudos from the National Council for Family Relations, the Chicago International Film Festival, and the Information Film Producers of America. **Touch** is a terrific tool to use as an adjunct if you need to address the topic of sexual abuse with your child; it dramatizes in a factual, non-threatening way the potential dangers and the tactics children can employ to defuse an explosive situation. Parents should be aware that proper anatomical terms are used for body parts, so some preparation with your child before viewing the tape might be beneficial. This is *not* a tape a child should watch on his or her own; it's best accompanied by a discussion with your child.

What Kids Want to Know About Sex and Growing Up (Pacific Arts/Children's Television Workshop, 1992, 60 m., 8–12)

For parents who may find it tough to discuss the topic of sex education, here's a refreshingly straightforward approach certain to generate healthy family discussion. Sex educators Dr. Robert Selverstone and Rhonda Wise direct discussions with a studio audience of preteens, who ask questions about changes boys and girls experience during puberty, desires, fears about the act of making love, and peer pressure. Selverstone takes care of boys' questions, while in a separate session Wise discusses growing up with the girls. CTW guaranteed this program extra exposure when it first was broadcast on PBS-TV and was motivated to produce it not by the AIDS epidemic but by the misinformation, rumors, and myths being repeated by kids to CTW researchers.

What about Sex? and **If You Can Talk to Your Kids about Sex, You Can Talk to Them about Anything** (BMG, 1993, 44 m. each, 10–up; host Lennie Roseman)

Parents of teenagers may find these two programs, which complement each another in subject matter and approach, reassuring. The first, subtitled "Teens Speak Out About Parents, Peers & Personal Responsibilities," helps parents recall how teenagers think and contemporizes the situations and speech. The teens speak frankly about their experiences, fears, values, decision making, and communicating with one another and with their parents. With researcher Roseman leading the workshop, the on-screen teens receive honest, practical information and provide support for one another. The second program focuses more on parents and features a group of on-screen parents who discuss various ways of communicating with their children as they broach difficult subjects. Both teen and parent viewers will garner enough information to make a rental worthwhile, despite the clinical approach that even the warmth of a focus group cannot dispel.

What's Happening to Me? A Guide to Puberty (Starmaker, 1987, 30 m., 10–16, animated)

The confusing, often embarrassing moments of puberty and the physical changes that accompany adolescence are explained in a straightforward way, even for an animated program. Authors Peter Mayle (Mayle also coauthored **Where Did I Come From?**; see below) and Arthur Robins have successfully translated their book of the same name to video in nonthreatening, animated form. **What's Happening to Me?** deals honestly and comfortingly with all the details of young adulthood, from menstruation to erections, pimples to body hair. When accompanied by a little light humor, as this video proves, a potentially unsettling topic becomes quite familiar and is more easily understood by preteens going through such changes.

Where Did I Come From? (Starmaker, 1985, 27 m., 6–10, animated)

In this video based on the book of the same name by Peter Mayle and Lyle Stuart, characters animated in a very simple style emerge from a bathtub naked, and if you aren't expecting it, you'll be surprised by how frank and honest this program is at dealing with the subject of lovemaking. Although correct terms for body parts are used, the material is presented in a very simplistic manner. There's a graphic but tasteful description of lovemaking that lingers on the beauty of the act when it's done in love and happiness. Making this a successful video experience depends on your child's readiness for the topic, although because of the sensitive nature of the material, you may want to look at it first without your child. This program reaches a younger demographic, 6- to 10-year-olds, than its counterpart **What's Happening to Me?** (see above) to explain the loving mystery of conception and birth.

Workout with Mommy & Me and **Workout with Daddy & Me** (FHE, 1991, 30 m. each, 2–6)

Unlike many other programs that purport to be "workouts" for preschoolers, this pair of videos is actually fun for both parents and their kids. These tapes take the "work" out of workout and leave behind a relaxing stretch-and-tone session that exercises the imagination as well as the body. (Parents who expect a more concentrated exercise program should look elsewhere.) In **Mommy & Me,** host Barbara Davis invites mothers and toddlers to "fly" to far-off Africa, courtesy of make-believe and a bit of computer wizardry for background images. Then they're imitating various jungle animals, "swimming" deep under the sea, and rocketing to the moon. Most of the songs are familiar, such as "Itsy Bitsy Spider." **Daddy & Me** finds another group of preschoolers and their fathers using their imaginations while pretending to battle an evil giant. The workouts have been employed in some YMCAs, day-care centers, and other community organizations, and they're great for a day when kids can't play outside.

Other Tapes of Interest on These Topics:

The Berenstain Bears and the Truth and **The Berenstain Bears Learn About Strangers** (Chapter 4, Discovery and Learning)

Breaking Away (Chapter 1, Feature Films)
Don Cooper: Musical Games (Chapter 3, Musical Fun)
Hoosiers (Chapter 1, Feature Films)
The Human Race Club (Chapter 4, Discovery and Learning)
The Karate Kid (Chapter 1, Feature Films)
Let's Get a Move On! (Chapter 4, Discovery and Learning)
National Velvet (Chapter 1, Feature Films)

Chapter 6

■

ACTIVITY TAPES

From play-alongs to craft tapes, a blossoming trend in video is to help children develop their innate curiosity into lifelong skills and pastimes and to get preschoolers started developing such basics as coordination and motor skills. It's especially true now that consumers have begun to adapt to interactive media such as CD-ROM and CD-1. And as Shari Lewis points out in her interview here and demonstrates in all her videos, regardless of how much information a producer tries to impart, an activity tape is worthless if its goal is not to entertain and encourage children to participate.

The wonderful thing about videos that teach crafts or magic tricks or skills such as guitar playing is that if a child can't follow the procedure as quickly as the demonstrator, the rewind button is close at hand, and no instructor ever becomes impatient with the class participants' individual speed or mistakes. Although many other programs claim to be "interactive," these tapes are classic examples of the marriage of video to teaching and experimentation.

Many of the activities shown on the crafts tapes listed here employ scissors, so parents will want to supervise or have an older child do so. The magic in all these tapes is that they capture children's imagination and empower them not only in the operation of a VCR but in learning tasks, skills, and hobbies that they may be able to use to make gifts for holidays and birthdays.

Unless otherwise noted, all programs are live-action.

Shari Lewis lets families in on the secret of her "evergreen"
appeal: It's all in the doing, not simply the viewing.

If Shari Lewis were a corporation, under her logo would be the motto "turning viewers into doers." Her parents, who were both teachers, instilled in her the magic of learning by doing, and even her earliest television performances asked viewers to participate. Today, her PBS-TV show, *Lamb Chop's Play-Along,* carries her tradition into current mindsets and has endeared her to millions of parents.

Despite a career of over 30 years, Lewis can't be called "vintage," thanks to that interactive angle, which helps keep her videos appropriate to today's lifestyle. Her programs are frequently referred to as "evergreen" because they never seem to go out of style. Why? In addition to encouraging a viewer to respond, Lewis uses contemporary music (remember, she's an orchestra conductor as well as a ventriloquist), speaks in familiar nineties-speak, and treats her onscreen child costars, as well as her puppets Lamb Chop and Charley Horse, with respect. "Being evergreen is in the eye of the beholder," she says, dismissing the compliment. "It's a lot of *fun* to keep up with the hip stuff because it *is* fresh, and it's refreshing to me as well as to the children."

And quality never goes out of style: "My father's collection of activities is **101 Things for Kids to Do;** he taught me all of those things." She suggests that if parents want to collect the best in children's entertainment, they should "look for participation, and remember the classics never fail. My advice would be to go to the library; they have a secret treasury, and you can borrow tapes before you decide whether to buy them."

Using the local library in this way may also help parents screen out tapes that contain questionable material, such as violence or adult themes. "We were raised in a different era, with shows like *Gunsmoke*; it's difficult for a child today to understand and reconcile what's going on" in many current television shows, Lewis says. Young viewers are bombarded with so many different messages, and some of what they see on TV contradicts what their parents tell them, or how their friends or older siblings are acting: be cute, stay young, grow up, be responsible, be free, don't drink or do drugs, but have a good time with your peers, murder is bad but it's depicted all over the media. . . .

"Having an alternative medium [to TV programming] is exceptionally important," says Shari, who raised her own daughter B.V. —in the time Before Video. How much TV did Shari allow her to watch? "Very little. I'd schedule a scout event or art lessons; you see, Saturday-morning TV was such a disaster then." Video and VCRs, she continues, "represent the 'instead' medium: Parents can use video instead of watching mindless sitcoms or violent action shows."

Not every video you choose for your children *has* to include an interactive segment or encourage them to be active; but the pleasure in seeing children learn skills, jokes, or crafts—essentially by themselves—is its own reward.

Then how can parents chose the best activity tapes? Lewis has several suggestions: "Don't look for performers who just want to show off; a good interactive video takes someone who is a natural teacher who became an entertainer instead, and that's true of the best children's performers. You really have to work to get the kids involved. Evoking a response has to be your target, your primary focus. The most important message to give to children is 'You *can* . . .': You *can* follow instructions, you *can* remember; you *can* do things you've never attempted before; you *can* surprise yourself with your abilities."

Try some of the programs included in this chapter, and see if your children don't come away with the understanding that they *can*.

Bonjour Les Amis (Monterey, 3 tapes, 50 m. each, 4–9, animated; narrators Annie Courbier, Jay Benedict)

This language tape is listed in the activity chapter because it treats its subject more like an informal, fun activity than a difficult lesson. And if you'd like your preschooler or young elementary-school child to get a handle on French, this may get your child started in the right direction by making foreign languages seem less foreign. Language expert Marie-Pierre Moine's disciples teach viewers rudimentary French through the repetition of various phrases and one song on each cassette. Each tape sets up a scenario with the friendly cat Moustache, whose animated adventures help young viewers gain an understanding of how French is used in everyday conversation. The worst this tape could do is have your children shouting "Bonjour!" incessantly or singing "Frere Jacques" nonstop; the best it could do would be to inspire them to pursue formal language classes. The series also imparts to American youngsters a sense that French children aren't so different from them: Just like their American counterparts, they have meals with families, attend school and church, play and sing, and love animals.

Care Bears Rainy Day Activity Tape (Fries, 1990, 45 m., 2–8, live action/animated)

When "It's Raining, It's Boring" is the theme song, you know you're in for a change of pace. The super-sweet animated Bears appear in four segments that teach specific crafts: The first shows how to make potato prints (have an adult cut the potato, the Bears advise!) and paper airplanes; the second suggests what toddlers can do if they have to spend a day without toys, such as play shadow puppets and make-believe and use bakers clay; the third features "Gram's Cooking Corner" and a real gingerbread recipe viewers may want to try; the fourth examines food facts and fables, such as how the sandwich was invented. Less exciting and engaging than any of Shari Lewis's programs, this is still a decent entry in the activity genre, and it uses familiar children's characters to hammer home a point softly: Even young children can entertain themselves with a few inexpensive household items.

Don't Wake Your Mom (A&M, 45 m., 1990, 3–10)

Shari Lewis, the activity maven whose PBS-TV series *(Lamb Chop's Play-Along)* has proven an evergreen staple for toddlers, gives parents a few moments' rest with this tape designed to give very young children a sense of independence, responsibility, and consideration for their family. Like her earlier activity tape (see **101 Things for Kids to Do)**, this program provides a slew of quiet crafts, tricks, and mind benders that help keep rambunctious Lamb Chop occupied until Shari wakes up. When she does awake, Shari sings a raplike poem about Rip Van Winkle, and best of all, reminds viewers in song that they are their own best friends.

Drizzle and the Rainy Day (Western, 818-889-7350, 45 m., 5–up)

If crafts are what your kids enjoy in their spare time, this independent production could keep them occupied for quite a while. It features a puppet rain elf who encourages housebound, live-action kids to use their imaginations on a boring, rainy day. The brother and sister who learn to combat their boredom in this production are talented at crafts and very natural before the camera. Since the program is somewhat long and filled with a variety of activities and crafts, younger children will find that it's best viewed in chapters or installments. Some of the craft items children on the tape make are boats from half-gallon milk cartons, a construction paper forest, and a snow globe. Nearly all the projects are unisex. Children five and older should find lots here to prevent boredom.

Fun 'n Easy Magic: Quick Tricks (Best Film & Video, 48 m., 6–12; stars Peter London)

What child wouldn't like to astound his or her friends and relatives with a stupefying magic trick that looks impossible but is actually quite simple? Here's one of several tapes that demystifies some tricks so that even young children can master the skills. London, a professional magician, performs eight magic tricks, then demonstrates each twice slowly for the camera and viewers. Among the tricks that most 6-year-olds can master are the jumping rubber band and pounding a saltshaker right through a table without leaving a hole. If your child appears frustrated with some of the more difficult tricks, take a step back and encourage him or her to try a simpler trick first; several tricks require more manual dexterity than a 6-year-old has. If your child likes this, take a look at **Secrets of Magic with Dikki Ellis,** reviewed later in this chapter.

The Great Ape Activity Tape (LIVE/Scholastic, 1985, 30 m., 4–10)

This was one of the first videos to address the bored child syndrome; although it looks relatively mundane by today's standards, it has entertained audiences for ten years. Actors dressed as green gorillas communicate to children that they're bored, and the kids take the initiative to develop a series of activities to keep them entertained. In a nice departure from the usual adult as teacher/narrator, the kids have to use their imaginations to keep their childlike charges from becoming bored. Among the basic activities children will learn: creating puppets from paper bags, making paper airplanes and jungles from newspaper, and folding a dollar bill for a cool trick. If this is a hit in your home, check out **Look What I Made: Paper Playthings and Gifts** and **101 Things for Kids to Do** in this chapter.

Jim Henson Play-Along Video (Lorimar, 1988, 6 tapes, 30 m. each, various ages)

Although we have lost Henson's creativity and potential with his death at far too young an age, his family has vowed to carry on. These tapes were made prior to his death; although there are no new volumes in the series, many video stores will still have them in stock. Henson's philosophy was "to entertain without losing sight of the fact that educational messages and social value can be conveyed through entertainment." In **Hey, You're as Funny as Fozzie Bear** (5–up), young stand-up comics get a head start from Fozzie Bear; the viewer gets to star in a comedy act after a rehearsal, complete with applause after the performance. **Wow, You're a Cartoonist!** (5–up) teaches budding artists to draw their favorite Muppet characters. **Sing-Along, Dance-Along, Do-Along** (2–6) proves kids got rhythm if they listen and sing along to various musical styles, from calypso to country. There's no dance instruction here, just a healthy message to get up and let the music move you. **Neat Stuff . . . to Know and Do** (5–up) informs and entertains with such curious facts as how to charm a snake, and fantastic feats like skipping stones and hanging spoons from your nose. **Mother Goose Stories** (2–6) showcases the one and only Mother Goose telling familiar stories to her brood of goslings. And in **Peek-A-Boo** (infant–3), parents are encouraged by a silly Muppet rabbit parent to share video playtime with their children, playing peek-a-boo, laughing, and enjoying music. If young viewers enjoy watching their peers interact with Henson's magical Muppets, this is the series for them.

Juggle Time and **Juggling Star** (JuggleBug, 800-523-1776 or 206-774-2127, 26 m., 5–12; stars Dave Finnigan, Joey Kline)

Don't laugh! Juggling has actually proven (at least some teachers claim) to foster self-esteem in the classroom by improving dexterity, coordination, confidence, concentration, and listening skills. Not only that, but it's inexpensive, it requires little space, and just about anyone can learn the skill. **Juggle Time** launched this two-tape series with instructions even 5-year-olds can follow, and Finnigan (playing the role of "Professor Confidence") demonstrates the tricks with scarves that float slowly so that beginners can pick up the technique more quickly than if they tried with balls. The video even comes packaged with three colorful chiffon scarves to practice with! And Finnigan steps aside to let the children be the stars. (Check out the peer-modeling success here: All the kids can juggle by the end of the tape.) The program imitates *Sesame Street*'s style and features MTV-like editing and musical variety, so it's hip and current, and the eleven songs help build eye/hand coordination in regulated step-by-step progress. The sequel, **Juggling Star,** aims at the 7- to 12-year-old market; it features twelve songs with a variety of beats so that children can progress from juggling scarves to learning to juggle beanbags, and eventually, four balls. Don't pass up either one. On the box is the hint "For your child and the child in you."

Kids Get Cooking: The Egg (KIDVIDZ, 40 m., 5–12)

A pinch of science and a dash of trivia are some of the ingredients in this video that gives kids an overview of what's happening in the average kitchen. Viewers learn about where an egg comes from and other egg-related facts, health tips about using and cooking with eggs, and safety tips for the kitchen. The recipes demonstrated are included in an activity booklet for easy reference. Lovely production values and energetic children spice up this program. The producer, KIDVIDZ, has also released other terrific programming on other topics; reviewed in this chapter is **Squiggles, Dots and Lines,** while you'll find these titles in Chapter 4: **Hey, What About Me?, Let's Get a Move On, Paws, Claws, Feathers and Fins,** and **Piggy Banks to Money Markets.**

Lamb Chop's Play-Along series (A&M, 1992, 8 tapes, 30 m. each, 2–8)

Here she goes again! Shari Lewis is a nonstop dynamo of creativity, and she capitalizes on her talent with more releases that compile scenes from her PBS-TV series of the same name. As the following titles indicate, Lewis concentrates on a particular strength in each video: **Action Songs** lets viewers in on the fun as they accompany Shari and Lamb Chop with silly sound effects. **Action Stories** allows children to add to Lewis's short but sweet stories. **Jokes, Riddles, Knock-Knocks and Funny Poems** compiles skits and funny scenarios from the TV series to bowl viewers over with a plethora of puns and other silliness. **Betchas, Tricks and Silly Stunts** puts viewers on center stage as Lewis teaches them card and magic tricks that anyone can do with basic household stuff. **Do as I Do** encourages children to follow Shari and Lamb Chop's lead as they learn by doing tricks, basic science (magic, of course), and word games. **Jump into the Story** invites viewers to accompany them on an imaginary journey and put their own two cents in whenever they can. **Let's Make Music** features lots of imaginative ways children can make music—and sometimes, they don't even need instruments! **On Our Way to School** might help take the sting out of the first day of school for toddlers, as Shari and her puppets prove that learning can be fun. And that's why Lewis's appeal hasn't faded over the years: Her simple style relies on children's creative, unfettered imaginations, their love of pure unadulterated, un-adult-influenced silliness, and the universal appeal of comedy and music. Thank goodness she'll be available on video for a long, long time.

Look What I Made: Paper Playthings and Gifts (Pacific Arts, 1991, available solo or with Fun Kit that includes craft supplies, 30 m., 5–up; host Amy Purcell)

If you're looking for a craft tape that's a guaranteed winner, this is the one to choose. High production values and a hostess who, as a former schoolteacher, really knows how to transmit enthusiasm to her students/viewers, are two of the reasons this tape has won awards from Parents' Choice, Action for Children's Television, and the Oppenheim Toy Portfolio. Amy Purcell leads viewers into becoming paper crafts experts; among the projects viewers will learn how to make are giant helix snakes, hats, and flowers, all constructed easily from paper and other materials you probably have in the house. Each project is preceded by a rap song that lists the items viewers will need. Any 5- to 10-year-old can follow the simple instructions, and Purcell is obviously having as much fun as the viewers will. Two more tapes in the series are available to keep children busy when it's rainy outside: **Look What I Grew: Windowsill Gardens** (reviewed in Chapter 4), a wonderful tape that teaches basic gardening skills; and **Look What I Found: Making Codes and Solving Mysteries** (not reviewed here), which lets kids in on the secrets of developing code wheels and shows them how to use their senses and talents for careful observation to solve mysteries.

My First Video Series (Sony Kids' Music/Sony Wonder, 1992, 6 tapes, 40–50 m. each, 4–10)

There are so many activities and experiments on these four tapes that if young viewers don't yet know how to use the VCR's pause and rewind buttons, they will by the end of just one tape. The videos,

My First Nature Video, My First Activity Video, My First Cooking Video (complete with safety instructions and a reminder to parents to supervise kitchen activities), **My First Science Video, My First Green Video,** and **My First Music Video** are based on the acclaimed *My First* book series from Britain's Dorling Kindersley publishers. High quality is evident from the start: The box art is colorful yet simple, showing things children will use or make on the tape. And the theme song is performed by children's entertainer Tom Chapin. The tapes compile a series of activities designed to help viewers understand their world by experimentation; these projects make excellent rainy-day activities. Not only is each activity on every tape preceded by a still frame showing the materials needed for that segment, but a flyer included with each tape lists every segment, as well as the tools and materials needed. For example, to make tree and leaf prints, one of the twelve activities on the **Nature** program, parents can refer to the leaflet to help the viewer gather drawing pens, crayons, colored paper, and so on ahead of time; viewers are then reminded of what they'll need on the video immediately before each activity, and instructed to use the pause button to buy time to assemble the materials or complete a task as shown on-screen. One caveat: The instructions are offered in voice-over by an adult, while the tasks are performed by children, many of whom are depicted only from the neck down in order to focus on their hands. It may be difficult for some children to pay attention to a headless peer and clinical instructions from an adult. Although the box art recommends the tape for children "ages 5 and older," some 4-year-olds may be ready to make some of the crafts and to examine nature; judge your own children accordingly.

101 Things for Kids to Do (Random House, 1987, 60 m., 3–10; stars Shari Lewis)

What seems to keep this energetic dynamo young is how quickly she moves. In this video, Shari's own beginning of the best of the rest, there's not a moment wasted as she and her beloved puppets show youngsters some simple but astounding magic tricks, as well as how to make puppets, invent secret codes, tease toddlers with tongue twisters, and do silly stunts like standing under water without holding your breath—just hold a glass of water over your head, silly! With a minimum of materials, Shari provides maximum entertainment—and 99 percent of it is mild enough to be supervision-free (you may have to search the house for envelopes or toothpicks, but nothing that's called for is expensive or unusual). She encourages young viewers to watch several segments, rewind and replay them as necessary, and then stop the tape and go amaze parents, friends, and relatives; don't, she says, watch the entire 60-minute program at once. How can you expect to remember all the terrific things she includes? Random House also has a book with the same title.

Preschool Power (Concept Associates, 800-333-8252, 301-986-4144 in MD, 1991–93, 8 tapes, 30 m. each, 2–5)

The tapes in this series are confidence builders for toddlers, who are encouraged every minute that they can do things themselves because their on-screen counterparts do it all themselves, from tying shoes to baking bread. Each video reiterates the series' theme, "You can do it once you've been shown." Peers demonstrate all the tasks, and adult intervention is brief and rare; you'll see a father slice a loaf of bread so the child doesn't handle a knife, or Mom slide cookies into a hot oven. And look at those kids' faces: They're happy, proud they've achieved something by themselves, and they can't wait to show off their newfound skills. The first volume, **Jacket Flips and Other Tips,** teaches youngsters the "Jacket Flip"—a clever way to don a coat—and health-conscious tips like washing your hands and blowing your nose, as well as making silly faces and cleaning up after yourself. In the second volume, **More Preschool Power,** more health issues are addressed (brushing and flossing teeth, hair care), plus making music on bottles, painting a face on your hand, and creating silly walks. There's a smart song about a girl who role-plays a construction worker, then dresses in frills later. The third tape, **Preschool Power 3,** lets kids instruct kids in how to tie shoes and pour liquids without spilling, and allows lots of comic relief with funny faces and shadow puppets. Songs celebrating the relationship between brother and sister help keep each viewer interested, even kids at the top of this age bracket. **Preschool Power 4** lets kids be magicians, take care of pets, and make up silly sounds and dances. **Preschool Power 5: Even More Preschool Power** adds advice and instructions for parents on making biscuits, demonstrates sand art, and shows the details of the Montessori exercises that use tongs. **Preschool Power 6, 7,** and **8** continue the fun and learning with more easy activities and original songs. What's so charming about the entire series is its focus on kids, as well as outtakes of them just goofing off and having fun—almost like home videos *you'd* shoot.

Secrets of Magic with Dikki Ellis (Burns Media Productions, 716-433-6592, 30 min., 4–12)

Magician, clown, juggler, and wire walker Ellis regales an audience of children with illusions, then shares the secrets of how each trick works, finally letting the children experiment. The host's instruction is tinged with good-humored and practical suggestions, such as perfecting a style of presentation that involves the audience, working on finger and facial warm-up exercises, and in a disarming and charming way, never revealing your secrets. Every trick can be duplicated at home with a minimum of expense; materials include saltshakers, paper napkins, bandannas, toothpicks, rubber bands, and paper clips. Ellis does not, however, show the secrets for *all* the tricks he performs, such as linking five seemingly solid metal rings. Even adults who want to know more about the basics of magic will find this video worthwhile. Also take a look at **Fun 'n Easy Magic: Quick Tricks** (reviewed earlier in this chapter) if your child appears to be a budding David Copperfield.

Squiggles, Dots and Lines (KIDVIDZ, 40 m., 5–12; stars Ed Emberley)

Artist Emberley teaches viewers his "drawing alphabet" of simple shapes that can form just about "anything in the universe" you'd ever want to draw. The kids on the tape demonstrate their newfound talents by making greeting cards and complete books. Emberley has a fatherly appeal and a wonderfully simplified approach to many people's plaintive cry, "But *I* can't draw!" With the very basic tools of the trade, even the youngest viewers will find they're drawing in a matter of minutes. Just have plenty of scratch paper and pencils and crayons on hand. Like other KIDVIDZ videos, this tape boasts exceptional production values and energetic but natural child stars. If you're interested in KIDVIDZ's other releases, look up **Kids Get Cooking: The Egg** in this chapter, and these titles, which are all reviewed in Chapter 4: **Hey, What About Me?, Let's Get a Move On, Paws, Claws, Feathers and Fins,** and **Piggy Banks to Money Markets.** Shari Lewis also includes a brief drawing lesson on her tape **Lamb Chop in the Land of No Manners** (Chapter 4, Discovery and Learning).

VideoCrafts for Kids (Krafty Kids, 515-276-8325, 4 tapes, 35 m. each, 5–up)

In each tight, broadcast-quality episode in this series, a group of four children hop a miniature train called the Train of Thought to Imagination Station, where a pair of adult supervisors encourage them to be creative. "The only requirement in Imagination Station," intones the comic Engineer Ed, "is that you exercise your imagination." And the children do every time, from learning about drama and putting on plays to forming a homemade band. **Will You Be Mime?** is packaged with nontoxic face paint and a sponge and encourages viewers to think in dimensions as they mimic a mime. **Make a New Friend** keeps viewers busy by showing them ways to transform feathers, pipe cleaners, wooden spoons, Styrofoam balls, and other material provided with the video into a variety of puppets. **Makin' Music** lets children create and name their own personalized musical instruments, mostly percussion adaptations of jingle bell tambourines and improvised maracas. And **The Great Pretender** features a female superhero, The Great Pretender, who entertains children on a rainy day by unlocking their creativity with stories and games with handmade parts. What more could you ask for in an activity video than to have packaged with the tape the materials necessary to play along with the program? This company has provided the option of buying the videos with or without the paints, pipe cleaners, and other paraphernalia to complete the projects (the videos alone cost a little less). The series has received honors from the U.S. Industrial Film and Video Festival (a Silver Screen Award), and Parents' Choice has given it a nod. It deserves an A+ for creativity and letting children use their potential.

You Can Do It! (MGM/UA, 1984, 60 m., 2–8, live action/puppets; stars Shari Lewis)

Along with her clever, witty puppets Hush Puppy, Charley Horse, and the omnipresent Lamb Chop, Lewis shows young children that they have all the talent inside them to entertain themselves and learn new things. She shows viewers how to astound and amaze their friends with magic tricks and silly stunts and how to keep the fun going even after playmates have gone home. The format is a lot like *Lamb Chop's Play-Along,* Lewis' PBS-TV series, but the concentration is more on activities than on songs.

The Yo-Yo Man Instructional Video (Wood Knapp, comes with a yo-yo in the original package; also available from Kodak Video, 1988, 30 m., 8–up; stars Dick and Tom Smothers, Daniel Volk)

The infamous Smothers Brothers, forward thinkers that they were when their controversial TV variety show ran in the sixties and early seventies, perform some comparatively mundane stand-up while Tommy demonstrates his repertoire of fascinating yo-yo tricks. You may be surprised at his talent: he's extraordinary! In a spoof of other instructional videos, real-life yo-yo expert Volk teaches the basics of tricks such as The Sleeper and Walking the Dog while also disseminating the "advanced state of yo." Anyone of any age who's interested in getting better at using a yo-yo to amaze friends and relatives will enjoy the comedy and instruction in this well-produced program.

Other Interesting Activity Tapes:

Astrodudes (Chapter 4, Discovery and Learning)

Baby Songs: Follow Along Songs (The entire series is listed in Chapter 3, Musical Fun.)

Hey, What About Me? (Chapter 4, Discovery and Learning)

I Dig Fossils (Chapter 4, Discovery and Learning)

In Search of the Wow Wow Wiggle Wobble Wazzie Waddle Woo (Chapter 3, Musical Fun)

Lamb Chop in the Land of No Manners (Chapter 4, Discovery and Learning)

Original Tales and Tunes, Spooky Tales and Tunes and **Silly Tales and Tunes** (Chapter 3, Musical Fun)

Playtime with the Motion Potion Kids (Chapter 5, Sports, Safety, Health, and Fitness)

Road Construction Ahead (Chapter 4, Discovery and Learning)

Chapter 7

■

STORYTELLING AND
LITERATURE-BASED VIDEOS

With the work of professional storytellers caught in the act on video, like the stupendous, captivating Jay O'Callahan and Rafe Martin, the oral tradition becomes the oral/aural/visual tradition. And videos based on books are one of the easiest ways to link the high-tech video experience with the comfort and satisfaction of familiar books.

That's part of the reason this is one of the heftiest chapters in this book. There's a wealth of films and videos that have been adapted from books, and the ones that I've included here are some of the best in terms of faithfully adapting a book, updating it in a sensitive way, or getting the most out of celebrity narrators, renowned artists, and top-flight musicians.

Since all these productions are based on books, parents can use video as a learning aid by heading to the library (which can probably also lend you many of these book-based videos!) prior to watching the tapes. Hand a child a picture book while the video plays and you may find that he or she will watch the video, turn a few pages, and be delighted that the same images that are dancing on the TV screen are also right at their fingertips.

All videos are animated unless otherwise noted. Where "iconographic" is indicated, tales are brought to life by scanning the pages of a book, not by full animation.

Shelley Duvall, book collector and video producer, shares her view of the future: a "new technology quotient" that encompasses CD-ROM and interactive media.

Shelley Duvall, a woman of the future who cherishes books from the past, adamantly believes that children can learn to read by using video constructively—but that even the alluring phenomena of multimedia will never replace books entirely. An advocate for multimedia, Duvall was one of the first children's video producers to adapt her storytelling expertise to the CD-ROM format (check out *It's a Bird's Life*). "Research shows that you retain 85 percent of what you've seen and read on CD-ROM, versus only 35 percent by reading," she has heard, adding that "the new technology quotient is the most important element of the education equation. . . . CD-ROM marries publishing to video, to games, to computers, and marries entertainment to education. Like CNN opening the world to the United States, CD-ROM will open our minds to the rest of the world. Multimedia is a nonlinear experience that incorporates the linear, whereas most stories are simply linear: beginning, middle, end. Multimedia gives you the opportunity to go off on tangents that will enhance the learning experience."

Duvall's foray into children's entertainment as a producer began with the **Faerie Tale Theatre** series she concocted for cable television in the early 1980s. This is the farsighted woman who cast Mick Jagger in **The Nightingale,** Ben Vereen and Gregory Hines in **Puss in Boots,** and Robin Williams and Teri Garr in **The Tale of the Frog Prince**—all adaptations of fairy tales that have withstood the test of time based on her belief that "it all boils down to one basic thing: Is it a good story? But you can't overlook the important elements all successful children's videos exhibit: content, good humor when humor is called for, and interesting characters that kids can relate to."

A serious collector of antique illustrated books, Duvall is fascinated by the evolution of books from paper through video to computer disc. Environmentally speaking, multimedia and electronic delivery of information will save trees, she notes: "It's not a matter of losing an art, because there's no way children will lose the ability to read or write." In her hopes that "books will always be cherished," she plans to bequeath her collection of more than 2,000 books to a children's library.

In the meantime, Duvall continues to adapt the works of children's authors to video and laser disc for her **Shelley Duvall's Bedtime Stories** collection, and to corral well-known personalities to serve as narrators. Her more recent efforts include **Tugford Wanted to be Bad** and

Little Penguin's Tale, written and illustrated by Don and Audrey Wood; **My New Neighbors,** written by Keith Faulkner and illustrated by Jonathan Lambert, **Rotten Island,** written and illustrated by William Steig; **Moe the Dog in Tropical Paradise,** written by Diane Stanley and illustrated by Elise Primavera; and **Amos, an Old Dog and His Couch,** written by Susan Seligson and Howie Schneider and illustrated by Howie Schneider. Among the celebrity storytellers are James Earl Jones, Ringo Starr, Bonnie Raitt, Christian Slater, John Candy, Martin Short, Richard Dreyfuss, Sissy Spacek, Morgan Freeman, and Steve Martin.

How can video help your child learn to read? "As you watch it with your child, you'll be able to start a dialogue," Duvall insists. "Look for stories based on books." Modern tales like those mentioned above are available in book form at the local library. A video may not contain all of the book, she adds, or it may contain additional information, maybe not exactly as the author intended; this can be positive or negative, but the important fact is you have at least two versions to compare. Her **Bedtime Stories** series, for example, "based on twentieth-century books featuring original stories," is adapted directly from the books, even to the style of animation. But there's plenty of room for other adaptations. The Rabbit Ears series differs, she explains, because they use literature and legend, generational stories. Duvall is keen to do a live-action interpretation of Aesop's fables.

Her productions work well on video because "all fairy tales and tall tales were originally word of mouth. Now we just do it the other way around," she says, and she laughs. Video simply adds another dimension to the storytelling experience. A good storyteller is one who's also a visual performer, using his or her body to articulate the movements of characters. "The oral tradition is audiovisual as well. It's just a matter of using the new technology," Duvall insists. "And because of the expense, there will always be more books than videos. . . . Video is a good way of showing parents what's good out there. These authors [in the **Bedtime Stories** series] have many more books [than those that we're making into videos]. Go out and read them; see if you like their stories, their style, their humor."

Duvall does not discount video games from the learning experience: "Nintendo, Sega, and other video games have served a great purpose: They are a terrific, entertaining way for kids to learn multimedia," she believes. "Kids can learn to navigate the multimedia world by playing video games." These technologies enhance rather than replace schoolbound learning, she feels, circling again to her "new technology quotient." The future classroom, she believes, features a teacher supplemented by a computer hooked up to a TV, and through their experiences with video games, children have already adjusted to the future world.

What does all this forward thinking say about video? Duvall hopes "technology should free us up. I'm still amazed: How did I ever do the first twelve *Faerie Tale Theatres* without a computer?" The same will go for CD-ROM, electronic mail (e-mail), and other new formats as they're developed. Ultimately, Duvall expects children's video to be incorporated into multimedia, providing kids with text, audio (both dialogue and music), and full-motion video in one educational package. Makes you almost wish you were a kid again, doesn't it?

Abel's Island (Random House, 1988, 30 m., 2–10; narrator Tim Curry)

In William Steig's tale of two mice in love, Abel's valiant effort to retrieve his wife's scarf on a windy day takes him far from his beloved but strengthens their love. It's touching, if you can lose yourself in the warmth of the story and the tenderness with which animator Michael Sporn brings them to life. If you find yourself drawn to Sporn's style of animation, check out these tapes in this chapter: **The Amazing Bone, The Country Mouse and the City Mouse, Doctor De Soto, Ira Sleeps Over, A Child's Garden of Verses, The Marzipan Pig, Jazz Time Tale, The Red Shoes,** and **The Dancing Frog.** Not reviewed here is **The Little Match Girl,** narrated by F. Murray Abraham: the tale is uplifting at the end, but very dark in that a little homeless girl nearly dies.

African Story Magic (Family Home Entertainment, 27 m., 4–up, live-action)

By transporting a young boy from the inner-city streets to the shores of the "land of the magic story people," this tape opens youngsters to an understanding of African oral tradition. Young Kwaku, a child of the inner city, escapes from a frightening, imaginary "green man" through the doorway to his imagination—thanks to intervention by a friendly storytelling spirit that appears as a glowing ball. The people of the magic story land share their tales with

Kwaku, each story offering a lesson or a piece of history. For example, an eagle that was hatched in the barnyard and began life thinking itself a chicken must take the plunge to discover it can fly and rule the skies. The cross-cultural tale of the lion and the mouse becomes "Molly Mouse," about a tiny mouse that thinks tall and is the only animal to think of a way to rescue the king of beasts when he's trapped in a hunter's net. The laudable message at the finale is the belief in the land of the story people that "in the land of imagination, all hearts are the same color."

Aladdin and the Magic Lamp (Rabbit Ears/BMG Kidz, 1994, 30 m., 3–10; narrator John Hurt)

Rather than rely on special-effects wizardry and fancy computer animation like the Disney version of **Aladdin,** this interpretation of the tale, part of the **We All Have Tales** series, depends on storytelling magic. Here, the evil sorcerer diguises himself as Aladdin's wealthy uncle and disappears after he seals Aladdin in the treasure cave. Much later, after Aladdin and the Sultan's daughter are married and living contentedly surrounded by splendor whipped up by the genie, the sorcerer reappears as a peddler who convinces the princess to trade Aladdin's tarnished magic lamp for a shiny new one. It's interesting to compare the different versions; you might even want to check out a copy of *A Thousand and One Arabian Nights* to look at how the Persian story has changed over the years. The exotic musical score is courtesy of Grateful Dead drummer Mickey Hart. The sound track is also available on audiotape and CD versions that feature an additional 20 minutes of original music created for the production.

Alexander and the Terrible, Horrible, No Good, Very Bad Day (Golden Book, 30 m., 3–up)

The title alone should tell you this is an interesting production; based on Judith Viorst's book of the same name, it centers on a young boy, the youngest of three brothers. Everybody has a bad day every now and again, but Alexander just can't seem to shake it, so he grumbles that he'll escape it by moving to Australia. But he realised during several songs that being an only child wouldn't be very much fun, and his brothers heartily agree. Anyone who's had a bad day can relate to Alexander's fervent wish at nighttime that "things gotta get better tomorrow."

The Amazing Bone and Other Stories (CC Studios, 33 m., 3–up)

Action for Children's Television praised the animation in this collection when the organization honored the tape with an award. "The Amazing Bone" by William Steig is tremendous fun, displaying more of the animation talents of Michael Sporn in a tale of a naive pig and a magical, talking bone. The iconographic "John Brown, Rose and the Midnight Cat" is based on an ALA Notable Book by Jenny Wagner—also the winner of a Dutch Silver Pencil Award and the Australia Picturebook of the Year honors—in which a newcomer cat struggles with a loyal sheepdog for the dog's mistress's attention. No other storybook character becomes his art as well as the infinitely creative Harold, who, with his purple crayon, draws "A Picture for Harold's Room" in one of Crockett Johnson's fantastic tales. The tape closes with Ezra Jack Keats's iconographic "The Trip," in which young Louie builds a shoe-box diorama and travels through space and time to visit his old neighborhood.

Babar (Family Home Entertainment, 5 tapes, approx. 45 m. each, 2–8)

The beloved creation of Laurent de Brunhoff has made a wonderfully adept transition to the video age. Although there is some cartoon violence between Babar and his enemies, among them Rataxas, king of the Rhinos, as well as human hunters, Babar's stories for the most part try to instill developing minds with a sense of right and wrong, justice and duty, love and folly. Titles from this supplier include **Babar: The Movie** (see Chapter 2), **Babar Returns, Babar: Monkey Business, Babar's Triumph,** and **Babar's First Step.** Another excellent entry in the series is **Babar the Elephant Comes to America** (Children's Video Library, 23 m., 2–8), in which the genteel creature and his well-mannered family visit many of the most famous landmarks in the States and even enjoy a formal dinner at the White House.

The Baby-Sitters Club (A*Vision/Kid*Vision, 13 tapes, 30 m. each, 6–up, live action)

This Scholastic series has captured the hearts of young girls, thanks to Ann Martin's delightful books. Part of Martin's magic is treating circumstances that could be perceived by some viewers as unusual, such as a single-parent household or a teenage diabetic, as commonplace; that levels the playing field, especially when Martin opts not to preach about the situation. This video series, also shown on cable TV, features young entrepreneurs in live-action episodes making money and friends doing after-school jobs. Yes, there are a couple of Goody Two-Shoe girls, but their sweetness is balanced by some wisecracking, lighthearted characters. And the girls aren't perfect; they make plenty of mistakes and often learn by trial and error. But each episode emphasizes the importance of trying to do what's right and best for all parties. The morals are not overbearing, and what's most comforting, the characters could be your next-door neighbors. As a whole, the series is exemplary: an excellent concept brought to video in an excellent manner. Titles include **The Baby-Sitters and the Boy Sitters, The Baby-Sitters Remember** (a collection of the girls' fondest adventures), **Claudia and the Missing Jewels, Claudia and the Mystery of the Secret Passage, Dawn and the Dream Boy, Dawn and the Haunted House, Dawn Saves the Trees** (see Chapter 4), **Jessi and the Mystery of the Stolen Secrets, Kristy and the Great Campaign, Mary Anne and the Brunettes, Stacey's Big Break, Stacey Takes a Stand,** and **The Baby-Sitters' Special Christmas.** Most of the tapes are packaged with extras, such as collector's mini-book or stickers.

The Box (Smarty Pants, 30 m., 3–10)
The animated shorts compiled on this tape represent some of the best from the National Film Board of Canada (see the interview in Chapter 2 for more on the NFBC). Each of the shorts is animated in an avant-garde style and features a story with a message; these are nothing like what you'd see on commercial TV today. The lead story is a tale of growing up and putting aside childhood. Also on the tape are "The Story of Cinderella" and "Mary of Mile 18." For similar programs, see Smarty Pants' other titles in this chapter: **The Cat Came Back, The Dingles, Every Child, Peep and the Big Wide World,** and **Christmas Cracker,** as well as **Fun in a Box.**

The Bremen Town Musicians (Rabbit Ears/BMG Kidz, 1994, 30 m., 3–10; narrator Bob Hoskins)
This German tale in the **We All Have Tales** series opens on a somewhat sad note that only a few children will latch onto: the obsoles-

cence of pets. It's the story of an unlikely quartet of animals: an aged donkey, a decrepit blue dog, a shaky cat, and a past-his-prime rooster, all cast out of their homes when their owners decide they're no longer useful. Hoskins, in his most engaging cockney accent, chronicles the foursome's adventures on the road to join their cacophony of voices with the Bremen philharmonic. The score, by renowned cellist Eugene Friesen, captures each animal's voice with a variety of instruments, much as in *Peter and the Wolf.* Their discordant voices and peculiar shortcomings combine to make not only music but an effective burglar alarm when they're confronted by a bumbling band of comical crooks who believe the animals are the devil himself, with claws and feathers, hooves and fangs. The story is available in most of the fairy-tale collections by the Brothers Grimm, and Rabbit Ears has also released the story and music on audiocassette and CD.

The Cat Came Back (Smarty Pants, 30 m., 2–10)

Viewers of all ages will find something to like in this compilation of four award-winning animated short films from the National Film Board of Canada (see the interview that heads up Chapter 2 for more on the NFBC). The first story animates the nonsense song in a sidesplitting manner. Also on the tape are "Blackberry Subway Jam," which hypothesizes what might happen if a subway stop suddenly appeared in your living room, "What on Earth," a 1960s-style look at how Martians might perceive our world; and "The Egg," vignettes about how an egg tries to prevent being cracked. Highly original, this tape and others of this ilk could be an inspiration to anyone jaded by the glut of average cartoons.

Christmas Cracker (Smarty Pants, 30 m., 2–10)

The lead animated short in this compilation tape is one that was nominated for an Academy Award for Short Film in 1965, yet it's still current. **Christmas Cracker** is about one man's dream of topping his Christmas tree with a real star, plucked from the heavens. The tape also includes "The Story of Christmas," an animated version of the Bible story without words so families can fill in the narration themselves; "The Great Toy Robbery," a very American story about an accidental hero who saves the day when all the Christmas toys are stolen; and the wonderful "The Energy Carol," a double-edged message about greed and the overuse of energy. Like other titles from Smarty Pants, this video collects four fantastic, award-winning animated shorts from the archives of the National Film Board of Canada (see the interview in Chapter 2 for more on the NFBC).

Christmas Stories (CC Studios, 30 m., 3–up)

As a change from the proliferation of animated holiday specials on TV these days, why not revert to some excellent book-based animation from a dependable producer known for high-quality product? Four titles constitute this gorgeous production, and the centerpiece is the Michael Sporn–animated "Morris's Disappearing Bag," from the Rosemary Wells book. Little Morris is certainly surprised when the last present under the tree doesn't disappear but can make anything inside it invisible. "The Clown of God" is Tomie de Paola's poignant tale of a once-famous, now destitute juggler, who gives his final performance on Christmas Eve to honor God. In "Max's Christmas," a second Rosemary Wells treasure again brought to life with loving care by Sporn, Max is counseled by his older sister that Santa won't come until Max falls asleep, but Max decides to stay up and wait. The video closes with an airy, soothing, iconographic rendition of "The Little Drummer Boy," sung by the St. Paul Choir School and illustrated by Ezra Jack Keats.

The Chronicles of Narnia (Public Media, 6 tapes, 1991, 7–up, live action)

There are three stories in the WonderWorks TV/video version of C. S. Lewis's marvelous books; each installment, with a total running time of 174 minutes, is available on a two-tape set. The tale features child heroes who assist mythical rulers in a series of quests in which good struggles against evil, and eventually triumphs. In **The Lion, the Witch and the Wardrobe** (stars Richard Dempsey, Sophie Cook, Jonathan Scott, Barbara Kellerman, Jeffrey Perry), four children step through the back of a mysterious old wardrobe and are whisked off to the land of Narnia, where animals talk and the lion king Aslan is battling an evil witch to regain his freedom. In **Prince Caspian and the Voyage of the Dawn Treader** (stars Richard Dempsey, Sophie Cook, Jonathan Scott, Sophie Wilcox), the children help a prince vanquish a sea serpent and a dragon on their way to the edge of the world to defeat a corrupt king. And in **The Silver Chair** (stars David Thwaites, Camilla Power, Richard Henders, Tom Baker), another boy and girl enter Narnia to assist Aslan in locating King Caspian's missing heir. Reading and watching fantasy material this complex should help develop young children's imagination and creativity. Look up other titles in the **WonderWorks** series in Chapter 4: Discovery and Learning.

Corduroy and Other Bear Stories (CC Studios, 38 m., 3–up)
If your children are enamored of their teddy bears, here's a fitting complement to their own imaginative mental wanderings. In this live-action adaptation of Don Freeman's book by the same name, creative Corduroy, still awaiting a little girl or boy, sits patiently on a department store shelf—until he notices that one of his buttons is missing and undertakes a storewide search to find it. "Panama" comes from a fabulous European storyteller, Janosch (see **Janosch** in this chapter), whose stories revolve around two young adventurer friends, Little Bear and Little Tiger. In this episode, the duo discovers a mysterious, wonderful-smelling packing crate labeled "Panama," so they set out to find this "land of their dreams." Robert McCloskey's Caldecott Honor Book, "Blueberries for Sal," closes the video in iconographic style with a nostalgic look at an outing in Maine during which a little girl and a little bear become paired with the wrong mothers. This compilation tape won an Action for Children's Television Award, and "Corduroy" received a Blue Ribbon at the American Film Festival and First Prize at the Birmingham International Educational Film Festival, while "Panama" took First Prize at the Prix Jeunesse International Children's TV Film Festival.

The Country Mouse and the City Mouse: A Christmas Tale (Random House, 1993, 25 m., 2–6; director Michael Sporn, voices of Crystal Gayle, John Lithgow)
Animator Sporn shows how adroitly he can illustrate emotive, animated characters in this adaptation of Aesop's fable. Emily the country mouse is quite out of place in the city, and so is her cousin Alexander when the urban restaurant he calls home lets a cat loose in the kitchen. Together, the two trek back to the country, where Alexander realizes Christmas is more than rich food and fancy gifts. Young reviewers will delight in Emily's resourcefulness on her trip to the city to visit her cousin: She hitches a ride from the farmhouse on a milk wagon, then parachutes from a bridge to a passing New

York–bound train, a la Mary Poppins. Gayle, who plays Emily, sings two original holiday tunes about family and Christmas being "where the heart is." All together, it's a tender message about overlooking differences to share a special holiday, the ultimate message of which is loving one another.

The Dancing Frog (Family Home Entertainment, 1990, 30 m., 2–10; voices of Amanda Plummer, Heidi Stallings)

This is another of Michael Sporn's beautifully animated tales. Making your own way in the world might be tough if you didn't believe in yourself and your abilities, and that's what the odd couple on this tape discovers. A woman whose sailor husband drowns becomes attached to a dancing frog. They tour Europe, but since touring is so exhausting, they take a break, and the woman meets and falls in love with a lord. But she does not break her commitment to the dancing frog, and they complete the tour. The youngest children in this age range will love the animation and the pure whimsy of the dancing frog, while older children will also grasp its message of commitment.

The Day Jimmy's Boa Ate the Wash (CC Studios, 35 m., 2–10)

The first two of the four stories on this terrific tape feature Michael Sporn's sensitive style of animation. The lead story illustrates the hilarious havoc a snake can wreak when little Jimmy takes his boa constrictor on a class trip to a farm. The alligator "Monty" is central to the next tale, in which three animal children use him as a river taxi—until their backseat driving convinces him to take a vacation. A selfish boy who wants to swim alone learns a lesson in "The Great White Man-Eating Shark: A Cautionary Tale." And an aging woman and the family of hyperactive rats who live under her floorboards come to an agreement in "Fourteen Rats and a Rat-Catcher," a European tale. Based on popular children's literature, these stories may entice young viewers to read the picture books or visit their library. Look for other titles in this chapter with the CC Studios brand; all were based on good children's books, and all are worth bringing home.

The Dingles (Smarty Pants, 30 m., 2–10)

The National Film Board of Canada (see the interview in Chapter

2 for more about this organization) has a reputation for collecting the best short films and releasing them here in the States as compilation tapes through Smarty Pants. "The Dingles" is a "Wizard of Oz"–like story about an odd family and a storm, backed by crazy kazoo music. There are three other stories on the tape: "Little Red Riding Hood," a new version of the tale, with a closing disclaimer apologizing "to all gentle and well-mannered wolves"; "The Boy and the Snow Goose," which depicts wordlessly through full animation and music the bond between a little boy and a free bird; and "The Lion and the Mouse," a cutout interpretation of Aesop's fable in which musical instruments give voice to the characters.

Doctor De Soto and Other Stories (CC Studios, 35 m., 3–up)

This is one of CC Studios' most decorated productions, with the title tale nominated for an Academy Award for Best Animated Short Film. While William Steig's book won a Newbery Honor, the filmed version won a CINE Golden Eagle and the title Best Film for Children at the Canadian Animation Festival. The story, animated by Michael Sporn, tells of the clever way a mouse dentist and his wife treat and outsmart a sly fox who's entertaining thoughts of eating them after they work on him. Quentin Blake's "Patrick" brings color, life, and movement to the countryside when he plays his fiddle; the film took the Gold Medal at the Atlanta International Film Festival. H. A. Rey's mischievous monkey, Curious George, has an amazing array of talents he displays by riding bikes and performing in a traveling animal show, among other things, in the iconographic "Curious George Rides a Bike." The video closes with Tomi Ungerer's comical (and CINE Golden Eagle–winning) tale of "The Hat," in which a poor man finds a magical hat and commands it to perform wondrous deeds.

Dr. Seuss Series (Random House, 11 tapes, 30 m. each, 1–10)

This beloved author/illustrator will be sorely missed; thankfully, however, his works appear not just in print but also on video. Random House has the majority of Seuss titles, although not all of them are fully animated. The "Beginner Book Videos," **Dr. Seuss' ABC, Hop on Pop, One Fish Two Fish Red Fish Blue Fish, The Cat in the Hat Comes Back,** and **I Am Not Going to Get Up Today** are adapted directly from the books rather than produced in full animation. They're wonderful nonetheless, especially in helping children identify words, colors, shapes, and relationships, but don't expect the intricacies of the TV specials. The three fully animated videos are Seuss's musical specials, each of which features music by Joe Raposo of *Sesame Street* fame: **The Cat in the Hat Gets Grinched** (this Emmy winner was formerly titled **The Grinch Grinches the Cat in the Hat**), **Pontoffel Pock, Where Are You?**, and **It's Grinch Night** (another Emmy winner that was originally called **Halloween Is Grinch Night**). There's also a set of six "Video Classics," each of which is narrated by a celebrity and contains a bonus story: **Horton Hatches the Egg**, narrated by Billy Crystal; **Horton Hears a Who!**, narrated by Dustin Hoffman; **How the Grinch Stole Christmas**, narrated by Walter Matthau; **Yertle the Turtle**, narrated by John Lithgow; **Did I Ever Tell You How Lucky You Are?**, narrated by John Cleese; and **Dr. Seuss's Sleep Book**, narrated by Madeline Kahn. You've no doubt seen the books, so you know you can trust the videos to entertain and subtly share a message with your children.

Dr. Seuss TV Specials (FoxVideo, 7 tapes, 30 m. each, 1–10)
    Dr. Seuss's appeal seems to extend well beyond elementary-school children, since his puns, his story lines, and even the names of his characters and locations are so clever and often work on a multitude of levels. Certainly you'll remember being allowed to stay up an extra half hour to watch some of these programs on TV when you were young: **Dr. Seuss on the Loose** (now also called **Green Eggs and Ham and Other Stories**), **The Cat in the Hat, The Hoober-Bloob Highway, The Lorax** (one of my favorites), **Halloween Is Grinch Night, Pontoffel Pock, The Grinch Grinches the Cat in the Hat**. Also check out the musical versions of four of thee TV specials from Fox's sister company, CBS Video, reviewed in Chapter 3, Musical Fun.

The Elephant's Child (Random House, 30 m., 2–10, iconographic, narrator Jack Nicholson)
    Illustator Tim Raglin's comedic animal characters, Bobby McFerrin's captivating music, and Nicholson's droll narration will entice viewers to rewind and watch this terrific video, by the experts at Rabbit Ears Productions, again and again. It's the wonderfully inventive Rudyard Kipling at his best, making up tall tales about how certain things came to be in this world. Here he explains how the elephant's nose became an elongated trunk. If you take a fancy to

this artistic style, you might also enjoy the *Storybook Classic* **How the Rhinoceros Got His Skin** (Rabbit Ears) also written by Kipling, narrated by Nicholson, illustrated by Raglin, and featuring McFerrin's music. And if it's even more Kipling you're after, check out **Rudyard Kipling's Just So Stories** (4 tapes, FHE, not reviewed here, but definitely worth a look).

Encyclopedia Brown, The Boy Detective series (6 tapes, various suppliers and running times as listed, 6–12, live action; director Steve Holland, stars Scott Bremner, Laura Bridge)

If you'd rather encourage your children to play at sleuthing instead of slaying, check out this series of tapes based on the books by Donald J. Sobol. Eleven-year-old "EB" is younger and a little less mature than his female counterpart, Sally, so it's really through their teamwork that this pair is able to solve mysteries. They use their sleuthing skills, but they also have some scientific knowledge, and they're always learning something new in each episode. The key to their success is curiosity and open-mindedness: Anything can happen, and the right answer isn't always the obvious one. Adults are portrayed as secondary to the leads and never seem as smart as the kids; EB's dad is Idaville's klutzy police chief, and his mom is a nurse who's so wrapped up in her work, she's rarely if ever shown wearing anything but her uniform. **One-Minute Mysteries** (Hi-Tops, 1988, 30 m.) contains condensed versions of five episodes, each of which challenges the viewer to arrive at a solution before EB does. **The Case of the Missing Time Capsule** (Hi-Tops, 1988, 55 m.), set during Idaville's centennial celebration, finds EB and Sally investigating who'd want to steal a time capsule before it's opened. **The Case of the Ghostly Rider** (Golden Book, 1992, 31 m.) has EB and Sally stymied for a while as they hunt treasure with only one clue. **The Case of the Amazing Car** (Golden Book, 1993, 30 m.) uncovers a cheater in the soapbox derby. **The Case of the Burgled Baseball Cards** (Golden Book, 1993, 31 m.) leads the detective duo to three suspects, but no motives and no fingerprints. In **The Flaming Beauty Queen** (Golden Book, 1993, 30 m.), EB and Sally solve a mystery concerning a series of fires and uncover a scam artist's scheme. Because of EB and Sally's constant interaction as friends and young professionals, both girls and boys should enjoy this well-made, cleverly written series.

Every Child (Smarty Pants, 30 m., 3–10)

If this one doesn't tug at your heartstrings, I don't know what will: It's the tale of an unwanted baby who's passed from one person to another. The film, which won the 1979 Oscar for Animated Short Film, was produced to celebrate UNICEF's declaration of children's rights, which basically states that "the child shall be entitled from birth to a name and a nationality." The video contains three other, more lighthearted animated segments: "Catour" sets some bright animation to equally bright jazz instrumentals; "The Magic Flute" is a mellow tale of how, in the right hands, a bit of magic can brighten the world; "The Log Drivers Waltz" begins as live action and turns into animation as pioneer women admire the loggers who can "birl" down the river, waltzing on white water; "The Town Mouse and the Country Mouse" tells the Aesop's fable in bright colors and appealingly simple animation.

The Ezra Jack Keats Library (CC Studios, 1992, 45 m., 3–up)

Parents may not remember Ezra Jack Keats's name, but they won't forget his illustrative style and the pleasure of reading his books when they were children. Six stories (the first two listed are animated, the rest are iconographic) are included here; some also appear on other CC Studios compilation tapes. "The Snowy Day" takes a look at a little boy's wonder at the magic of a snowstorm. In "Whistle for Willie," Peter wants to learn to whistle so he can call his dog. Peter learns a few things about growing up when his newborn sister comes home in the iconographic "Peter's Chair." The wind plays havoc with a letter in "A Letter to Amy"; will she receive Peter's party invitation? The neighborhood children enter all their pets in the "Pet Show," but poor Archie can't find his pet. Louie uses his imagination and a shoe-box diorama to take a trip to visit his old neighborhood in "Trip" (this short is also included in **The Amazing Bone and Other Stories** in this chapter). At the end of the tape, the author/illustrator himself offers a rare interview in his New York studio, giving viewers a brief look at how he works; the interlude will appeal more to parents than to young viewers.

Faerie Tale Theatre (FoxVideo, 1982–84, 26 tapes, under 60 m. each, 4–14, live action)

Lavish sets, intricate period costumes, surefire celebrity casting,

imaginative staging, plot twists, and humor—must be the work of
Shelley Duvall, champion of children's entertainment. If there's a
beloved fairy tale Duvall did *not* adapt in this terrific series, you will
have a hard time finding it. Count on each program to be well conceived, well produced, and guaranteed fun; in fact, some of the stars
and directors may surprise you: **Aladdin and His Wonderful Lamp** (director Tim Burton, stars Valerie Bertinelli, Robert Carradine, James
Earl Jones, Leonard Nimoy); **Beauty and the Beast** (director Roger
Vadim, stars Klaus Kinski, Susan Sarandon); **The Boy Who Left Home
to Find Out About the Shivers** (director Graeme Clifford, stars Peter
MacNicol, Christopher Lee, Dana Hill, Vincent Price. This one's
cryptic title deserves a brief explanation: A fearless boy takes on the
task of ridding a cowardly king's castle of a pesky ghost.); **Cinderella**
(director Mark Cullingham, stars Jennifer Beals, Matthew Broder-
ick, Eve Arden, Jean Stapleton); **The Dancing Princess** (director Peter
Medak, stars Roy Dotrice, Peter Weller, Lesley Anne Warren); **The
Emperor's New Clothes** (director Peter Medak, stars Art Carney, Alan
Arkin, Dick Shawn); **Goldilocks and the Three Bears** (director Gilbert
Cates, stars Tatum O'Neal, Alex Karras, Carole King, John Lithgow,
Hoyt Axton), **Hansel and Gretel** (director James Frawley, stars Rick
Schroeder, Bridgette Anderson, Joan Collins, Paul Dooley); **Jack and
the Beanstalk** (director Lamont Johnson, stars Dennis Christopher,
Katherine Helmond, Elliott Gould, Jean Stapleton); **The Little Mermaid**
(director Robert Iscove, stars Pam Dawber, Treat Williams, Karen
Black, Helen Mirren, Brian Dennehy); **Little Red Riding Hood** (director
Graeme Clifford, stars Mary Steenburgen, Malcolm McDowell); **The
Nightingale** (director Ivan Passer, stars Edward James Olmos, Mick
Jagger, Barbara Hershey, Bud Cort); **The Pied Piper of Hamelin** (di-
rector Nicholas Meyer, stars Eric Idle); **Pinocchio** (director Peter Me-
dak, stars Carl Reiner, Pee Wee Herman, Lainie Kazan, James
Coburn); **The Princess and the Pea** (director Tony Bill, stars Liza
Minnelli, Tom Conti); **The Princess Who Had Never Laughed** (director
Mark Cullingham, stars Ellen Barkin, Howard Hesseman, Howie
Mandel); **Puss in Boots** (director Robert Iscove, stars Ben Vereen,
Gregory Hines); **Rapunzel** (director Gilbert Cates, stars Shelley Du-
vall, Gena Rowlands, Jeff Bridges); **Rip Van Winkle** (director Francis
Ford Coppola, stars Harry Dean Stanton, Talia Shire); **Rumpelstiltskin**
(director Emile Ardolino, stars Ned Beatty, Shelley Duvall, Herve
Villechaize); **Sleeping Beauty** (director Jeremy Paul Kagan, stars

Christopher Reeve, Bernadette Peters, Beverly D'Angelo, Sally Kellerman, Carol Kane); **The Snow Queen** (director Peter Medak, stars Lance Kerwin, Melissa Gilbert, Lee Remick); **Snow White and the Seven Dwarfs** (director Peter Medak, stars Elizabeth McGovern, Vanessa Redgrave, Vincent Price); **The Tale of the Frog Prince** (director Eric Idle, stars Robin Williams, Teri Garr); **The Three Little Pigs** (director Mark Cullingham, stars Jeff Goldblum, Billy Crystal, Valerie Perrine); **Thumbelina** (director Michael Lindsay-Hogg, stars Carrie Fisher, William Katt, Burgess Meredith).

Family Circle Enchanted Stores series (Best Film & Video, 6 tapes, 30 m., each, 2–10, live-action)

This series of wonderfully simple videos proves that the art of oral storytelling is still alive and well. On each cassette, some of the best American storytellers perform in front of a rapt audience of young children, creating their own worlds and realities. To see the openmouthed wonder, hear the giggles, and watch as children lose themselves in each original tale is to recall when everything was new and wondrous in the eye of a child. The first tape, **The Three Little Pigs,** features Rafe Martin telling the lead story and "The Wooly Mammoth," and Laura Simms telling "The Wooden Box." The next volume contains Jay O'Callahan's **The Little Dragon,** Martin's "The Remarkable Horse," and Simms' "Donkey and Goose." The third volume contains Simms' **The Magic Princess** and "Moon and Otter," as well as O'Callahan's "Superbowl Sundae" and Martin's "The Bird Man." Volume 4 includes Martin's **The Foolish Rabbit,** O'Callahan's "New Years Eve" and Simms' "The King of Togo Togo." The fifth and sixth installments feature all three storytellers combining their talents to relate the stories of **The Silly Grasshopper** and **The Brave Indian Chief.** The talented O'Callahan has a particularly magical way with words, actions, and expressions, and has a true rapport with his audience. If you and your child are fascinated by the storytelling tradition, check out **Jay O'Callahan's** tapes, also reviewed in this chapter.

Five Lionni Classics (Random House, 30 m., 2–10, animated/iconographic)

Leo Lionni's "Animal Fables" are magically brought to life in the same cutout style as the books on this terrific tape. The stories—

"Frederick," "Cornelius," "It's Mine," "Fish Is Fish," and "Swimmy"—are absolutely adorable and should lead children right back to the library to check out the books on which they're based. Another plus about Lionni's fascinating artistic style is that it mimics what a child could produce with the simple materials (crayons, construction paper, scissors, and glue) found in most homes. His characters are clever and cute and invite imitation.

Five Stories for the Very Young (CC Studios, 30 m., 2–6)

Introducing children to the magic of book-based video is simple with such imaginative adaptations as this tape includes. All the tales are animated, with the exception of the iconographic "Caps for Sale," Esphyr Slobodkina's American Library Association's Notable Book about a peddler of hats and the mischievous monkeys that wreak havoc on him. Two creative wooden dolls rearrange a set of blocks over and over inspiring viewers to do the same in "Changes, Changes," adapted from Pat Hutchins' ALA Notable Book. The Harrisburg Film Festival awarded its Grand Prize to "Harold's Fairy Tale," featuring Crockett Johnson's adorable kid with the purple crayon and the limitless imagination (Harold also has his own tape, reviewed under **Harold** in this chapter). Will Peter learn to "Whistle for Willie" so his dog will come when called? Ezra Jack Keats's clever story, another ALA Notable Book, comes to life. (For more of Keats's work, see the anthology **The Ezra Jack Keats Library,** reviewed earlier in this chapter.) "Drummer Hoff" was adapted from the Caldecott Medal Book by Barbara and Ed Emberley (see Chapter 6, Activity Tapes, for **Squiggles, Dots and Lines,** in which Ed Emberley explains his drawing alphabet). This collection of rhyme games, colorful animation, and a lesson in peace was awarded the Golden Plaque at the Teheran International Film Festival.

Follow the Drinking Gourd (Rabbit Ears/BMG Kidz, 30 m., 4–up; narrated by Morgan Freeman)

A song that, for escaped slaves, hid the map to freedom in the North lends its title to this animated entry in Rabbit's Ears' **American Heroes and Legends** series. The gourd of the title refers to the Big Dipper; slaves on the road to freedom in the North used the North Star, at the handle end of the Little Dipper, as a compass. Their days traveling the Underground Railroad were fraught with anxiety and danger, yet escaped slaves who had never even been off their plantations trusted the veracity of the instructions in the song. Their life-or-death adventure, their hopes, doubts, frustrations, and determination are vividly captured in this video's emotive watercolor. Freeman's narration is spellbinding and Taj Mahal's musical stylings are catchy and dramatic where appropriate. This tape joins a select group of videos—among them, **Brother Future** (Chapter 4; see **WonderWorks**), **African Story Magic, Stories from the Black Tradition,** and **The Red Shoes,** all in this chapter, and **Jazz Time Tale** (Chapter 3: Musical Fun)—that honor and enhance African-American history, folklore, music, entertainment, and education.

Frankenweenie (Disney, 1984, 27 m., PG, 10–up, b&w, live action; director Tim Burton, stars Shelley Duvall, Daniel Stern)
This short avant-garde film is a canine version of the Frankenstein legend. Burton, whose dark genius gave us the shadowy romance and fantastic sets of **Edward Scissorhands** and the **Batman** films, produced this short while working at the Disney Studios, years before his breakthrough successes. A budding young "mad" scientist resurrects his beloved dog after it's hit by a car, and although the neighborhood is initially terrified, eventually they warm to the stitched-up pup. If you enjoyed the zaniness of Mel Brooks's **Young Frankenstein,** you'll probably find **Frankenweenie**'s humor, only some of which is black, merrily macabre and mad. It's touching in an eerie way, and may hit home with many people who've lost beloved pets.

Fun in a Box (Made to Order Productions, 3 tapes, 30 m. each, 4–10)
Like the collections from Smarty Pants, two of these tapes compile a group of award-winning short films and concept pieces onto video. **Ben's Dream** leads off with the stunning animated line art by Chris Van Allsburg, following a boy's wordless journey inspired by reading and snoozing on a rainy day; "Your Feets Too Big" is animation inspired by Fats Waller's blues song: and "Fish" is the live-action tale of a girl who hires three detectives to find her missing brother. **New Friends** begins with the classy animated adaptation of James Stevenson's book *Howard*, about a duck who makes lots of new friends when he misses his flight south. The next two segments may be a little removed from what children were expecting: "Metal

Dogs of India" is a hyperactive collage of stop-animation, pulsing colors, and wild images set to a speedy song, while "The Kinetic Sculpture of R. Barlow" is a slow, lingering look at an inventor/artist who may be the next Rube Goldberg. Parents may find these segments appeal more to children 6 and up, and both may prove too mature, too quick, or too slow for some children. Michael Parent's American storytelling segment on "Why Cats Eat First," however, is just right as the ending to **New Friends**. Ultimately, there's something for all ages and tastes included on each video. There is also a third tape in the series, **The Birthday Movie.**

The Gingham Dog and the Calico Cat (Rabbit Ears Productions, 30 m., 4–8; narrator Amy Grant)
Grant lends her voice to an updated version—with a happier ending—of the old-fashioned story of two feuding toys. A toy dog and toy cat are on their way to new homes when they fall out of Santa's sleigh. They come alive so that they can cooperate and find their way to the children who want to love them. The twist is that the feuding is actually between the brother and sister for whom the toys were destined. The animation is exquisite, and the reunion of the toys with their human owners quite touching; it should make a nice holiday classic.

Granpa (Sony Wonder, 30 m., 4–up; narrator Peter Ustinov)
John Burningham's book could not have come more beautifully to life than in this video version. The British accents, the watercolor animation, Ustinov's tender narration, and a song by Sarah Brightman of *Phantom of the Opera* fame combine to create a very special program about the joys of childhood and the magic relationship between a little girl and her loving, imaginative grandfather. Be forewarned, parents: Granpa himself does not make the final curtain call, but the lesson that the death of a loved one is one part of growing up is sensitively presented.

Harold and the Purple Crayon (CC Studios, 27 m., 2–10)
Crockett Johnson's friendly, familiar little boy, Harold, armed with his unbeatable purple crayon, takes on the world in three shorts adapted from Johnson's books. The title tale introduces viewers to the boy with the magic crayon and encourages them in the subtlest

of ways that they can use their imaginations to travel all over (maybe not all over their parents' walls, though). The second short, "Harold's Fairy Tale," finds the toddler artist busy investigating why nothing grows in a garden—until he meets the witch who's responsible. Once he draws it, Harold steps right into "A Picture for Harold's Room," even though it seems to be just a two-dimensional crayon drawing on his wall. In an interview at the close of the tape, renowned animator Gene Deitch, who animated these films, discusses what he learned from author/illustrator Johnson.

I Know Why the Caged Bird Sings (LIVE Entertainment, 1979, 96 m., 8–up, live action; director Fielder Cook, stars Diahann Carroll, Ruby Dee, Constance Good, Paul Benjamin, Roger E. Mosely, Esther Rolle)

Maya Angelou, who's been rediscovered since reading one of her poems at President Bill Clinton's inauguration, recounts her youth in the moving book on which this film was based. Good is exceptional as young Maya, traumatized into silence after being abused, and looking to her strong grandmother (Rolle) for support. Her theme is just as relevant today as it was during the Depression: "In order to lift up your voice, you have to lift up your head."

I'm Not Oscar's Friend Anymore and Other Stories (Golden Book, 1991, 30 m., 3–up)

Here's a collection of fully animated stories, all based on books, that will appeal to most young viewers. The fun begins with the title tale, in which a minor incident seems to separate two best buddies. Not only is it narrated by a child, but it has the same flavor as one of *Sesame Street*'s magical interstitial shorts. "Creole," from Steven Cosgrove's book, imparts the same lesson as the *Beauty and the Beast* legend: Looks are not the most important part of a person's character. Voice characterizations are performed by Georgia Engel, Arte Johnson, and Mickey Rooney. "Hug Me" tells of Elliot the porcupine's efforts to make friends by hugging. (Who else would hug a telephone pole or a parking meter, when no one else will reciprocate?) The illustration style dates the production "Birds of a Feather" (1969), but what sets it apart is the music that serves as the story's narration, since there are no words. An orchestra inven-

tively creates the bright chirps and lilting songs of the birds in the
title.

Ira Sleeps Over (Family Home Entertainment, 1993, 27 m., 2–10)

Anyone who enjoys a good story will enjoy this tale by Bernard
Waber, about a boy who, once he decides whether to take his teddy
bear along, has a grand time during a sleepover at a friend's home.
Animator Michael Sporn again shows his talent for letting animated
characters express themselves through his tender style of animation, and there are plenty of musical numbers. Author Waber also
penned **Lyle, Lyle Crocodile** (see Chapter 3, Musical Fun).

Janosch series (Just for Kids/Celebrity Home Entertainment, 1989,
5 tapes, 2–10)

In a soothing, Old World style, complete with gentle watercolor
illustrations, this "big, fat fabulous bear" and his tiger friend embark
on numerous adventures, predominantly ones that are close enough
to home that they can go home for dinner. The longer tapes are
compilations of many episodes that were produced for European TV,
but taken in small installments, they will be accessible to even the
youngest children. The series includes **Janosch: The Big, Fat, Fabulous
Bear** (116 m.), **Janosch Bear Hugs** (30 m.), **Janosch Bear Tales** (30 m.),
Janosch Fables from the Magic Forest (115 m.), and **The Tiger, the Bear
and the Hare** (115 m.). The themes in each video rotate among kindness, loyalty to one's friends, generosity, and exercising one's imagination and curiosity. Another story from Janosch appears on
Corduroy and Other Bear Stories (reviewed earlier in this chapter).

Jay O'Callahan: Herman and Marguerite (Vineyard, 1986, 28 min., 3–8,
live action)

If you think the art of oral storytelling is old-fashioned, think
again! This magical storyteller has the engaging manner to keep
even the youngest children interested in a tale by incorporating his
entire being into the performance. If you have a chance to see Jay
O'Callahan perform live, take it! He personifies each character in
his stories, from the worm Herman and the caterpillar Marguerite
to the wind and the trees. This original tale finds Marguerite as-
sisting Herman on his first trip to Earth's surface; laster, Marguerite
needs reassurance as she frets about entering her cocoon. Together,

these two tiny creatures have a significant, lasting impact on an orchard that was in danger of dying from lack of pollination by bees and butterflies like the transformed Marguerite.

Jay O'Callahan: Six Stories About Little Heroes (Vineyard, 1986, 38 min., 3–8, live action)

O'Callahan's little heroes depict the significant accomplishments of children and other small creatures. In each of the six stories he recounts here, size is not a factor in whether the characters succeed at their tasks. For example, a little girl successfully extricates a king from inside his bubble prison after his guards have failed. Another tale features a hive full of bees who become productive after one of their number has gorged on too much honey and can do nothing but sing a cheerful song. Children who have trouble concentrating on anything for a long period of time will enjoy these quickly told tales and may be inspired to create tales of their own. Their attention spans may be short, but children—and O'Callahan—are long on imagination.

John Henry (Rabbit Ears/BMG Kidz, 30 m., 3–up; narrator Denzel Washington)

Whether legend or real-life, "natural" man, John Henry has embellished our folklore with the drama of the rivalry between man and technological advances. This is another of the Rabbit Ears **American Heroes and Legends** productions that rivals Robin Williams' **Pecos Bill** rendition. Denzel Washington proves to be a surprisingly adroit narrator who keeps the story entertaining with colloquial color, intonations, and sound effects that children will love. Complementing the narration are Barry Jackson's humorous art (he pays such detailed attention to faces, the characters truly seem real) and BB King's musical support (he'll easily have young viewers singing and humming John Henry's eponymous ditty). And although Henry died after besting a machine, his words live on to inspire anyone: "A man's got a heart inside, and a machine's got nothin' but a soul of cold steel." For another of Washington's winning narratives, check out **Anansi** (under **We All Have Tales** in this chapter), about the legendary Jamaican spinner of stories.

Johnny Appleseed (Rabbit Ears/BMG Kidz, 1993, 30 m., 2–10, partial animation; narrator Garrison Keillor)

Contemporary folk icon Keillor, of *A Prairie Home Companion*, faithfully recounts the tale of John Chapman, the gentle, devout naturalist who, in the early nineteenth century, became known as Johnny Appleseed after he began to plant apple trees across the early wilderness. Settlers from the Ohio Valley and farther west learned of his generosity and thoughtfulness as they ate from his apple trees; those who were fortunate enough to meet him basked in his goodwill and sensible nature. Viewers will discover that Johnny Appleseed not only established orchards but also tended to sick and wounded animals and lifted the spirits of settlers by bringing them news and companionship. Keillor's interpretation is respectful of this American legend, although he does allow a few comic scenes. Lovely watercolor illustrations (by Stan Olson) help bring this warm and loving character to life.

The Little Engine That Could (MCA/Universal, 1991, 30 m., 2–8)

Based on Wally Piper's beloved book, this production has transcended its Saturday-morning-style animation to become a favorite among the preschool set. The reason is that its theme, "I think I can," is universal. Another plus is that "Tilly" the engine is female, and she comes to the aid of another female engine that, until she broke down, pulled the Birthday Train over a treacherous mountain. After all, how do you know whether you can do something unless you try?

Madeline (Golden Book, 9 tapes, 26 m. each, 2–up; narrator Christopher Plummer)

The beloved, timeless creation of Ludwig Bemelmans stars in her own animated series, a very enchanting adaptation of the books. The illustrations, true to the books, evoke the atmosphere of Paris, where Madeline and her school chums live with Miss Clavel. And Plummer's distinguished accent and humorous reading lend a special air to the videos. Here are some of the titles available from this video supplier, all of which are great viewing fun, especially when coupled with the books: **Madeline and the Bad Hat, Madeline's Rescue, Madeline and the Easter Bonnet, Madeline and the Dog Show, Madeline and the Gypsies, Madeline's Christmas, Madeline at Cooking School, Madeline and**

the Toy Factory, Madeline in London. Golden Book has plans to release more Madeline videos, so continue to ask your local video dealer about them.

The Marzipan Pig (Family Home Entertainment, 1990, 30 m., 2–10; narrator Tim Curry)

Another sweet treat from Michael Sporn, this philosophical tape looks at the food chain in a unique and whimsical way. When a piece of candy falls to the floor, its sweetness and loneliness affect the attitudes of all who eat it, or are eaten after eating it. A mouse that nibbles on it notices the loneliness; the owl that eats the mouse feels the loneliness, but also the sweetness as he dances to a taxi driver's trumpet; and the chain continues. Beautiful and poignant, it ends on an open note, allowing the young viewer to invent more ways the marzipan pig could affect others.

The Maurice Sendak Library (CC Studios, 35 m., 3–up)

Three favorite, imagination-stretching stories from the renowned children's author and illustrator are compiled on this tape. "Where the Wild Things Are" and "In the Night Kitchen" are both narrated by Peter Schickele, alias P.D.Q. Bach, who also arranged the music for these silly stories about children who make mischief. "The Nutshell Kids" is a collection of short poems, including "One Was Johnny," "Chicken Soup with Rice," "Alligators All Around," and "Pierre," set to music composed and sung by Carole King. A 6-minute interview with Sendak at the end of the tape helps give some context to his wildly creative stories. This tape, which won the Parents' Choice award, is perfect material for a watch-and-read session.

Maurice Sendak's Really Rosie (CC Studios, 27 m., 3–up)

What a wonderful chance to relive childhood through one of Sendak's most memorable characters! Self-confident to the point of being domineering, Rosie directs all the neighborhood children, the Nutshell Kids, in her make-believe movie. The characters are based on those in Sendak's books "The Nutshell Library" and "The Sign on Rosie's Door." Longer versions of some of the Carole King story/songs from **The Maurice Sendak Library** (reviewed above) appear on this tape as well. The video has been decorated with a CINE Golden

Eagle and a Blue Ribbon from the American Film Festival, and is an ALA Notable Film.

Mike Mulligan and His Steam Shovel (Golden Book, 25 m., 2–up; narrator Robert Klein)

Comedian Klein does a great job narrating this animated gem of a story, based on the book by Virginia Lee Burton. Although the steam shovel Mary Anne may seem an anachronism in our highly mechanized and computerized society, there's a poignancy to this story that transcends the decades—and a lesson about finding new uses for something old. Under pressure from diesel operators, Mike learns his trusty steam shovel just can't do what the new diesel diggers can, so he boasts that he can dig the Popperville Town Hall cellar in just one day. Against all odds, he complete the job as scheduled, but then Mary Anne is unable to get out of the hole, so the residents of Popperville find a new use for her: as the steam boiler for their town hall's heating system. This animated version of the classic book won a 1992 Parents' Choice award.

Mose the Fireman (Rabbit Ears/BMG Kidz, 1994, 30 m., 3–8; narrator Michael Keaton)

Another of the splendid **American Heroes and Legends** series, this tape showcases Moses "Mose" Humphreys, a larger-than-life nineteenth-century New York city fire-fighting hero. It's up to the viewer to decide whether this particular gentleman was a hero, a legend, or both. Michael Keaton tells this tale in a comically thick Bronx accent, beginning with how firefighters found Mose as an infant floating in the East River after a disastrous fire and raised him in their Bowery firehouse. The story credits Mose with more than his share of inventions; for example, he is said to have invented the fire pole when he rescues the woman he loves by vaulting up to her fourth-floor room on a ship's mast and sliding back down with her. He's also credited with laying the groundwork for the city's subway when, during another fire, he single-handedly digs a tunnel to tap the Hudson River. Such far-fetched exploits as these will no doubt leave many young viewers in stitches. There's an additional 20 minutes of music on the audiocassette and CD versions. For similar tall tales, check out **Paul Bunyan** and **Pecos Bill** in this chapter.

The Mouse and the Motorcycle (Strand, 42 m., 5–up, live action; stars Fred Savage, Ray Walston, John Byner)

A young Fred Savage stars in the opener of this two-parter (concluded in **Runaway Ralph)** in which a lonely young boy on vacation befriends a mouse in the old hotel in which his family is staying. Originally made for TV, these clever combinations of stop-motion animation and live action are sensitive, touching, and humorous. In **Runaway Ralph** (Strand, 42 m., 5–up, live action; stars Fred Savage, Sarah Gilbert), the adventuresome mouse rides his motorcycle to a children's camp where he befriends a lonely boy who's been accused of stealing. Ralph has his own problems staying one step ahead of a wily tomcat. Corny but appealing in an old-fashioned way, both programs are based on Beverly Cleary's novels (she also wrote the **Ramona** series, reviewed in this chapter); some video dealers may have the version that compiles both episodes on one tape.

Noel (PolyGram, 25 m., 2–8; narrator Charlton Heston, voices of Roscoe Lee Brown, Romeo Muller, Lee Meredith)

A holiday memento takes on new meaning in this story penned by Romeo Muller, who wrote the "Frosty the Snowman" and "Rudolph the Red-Nosed Reindeer" TV specials. Noel is the name of a simple red Christmas ornament—just a glass globe—that's imbued with the spontaneous joy of a glassblower who received the news that he'd become a grandfather while he was making the ornament. Now part of Noel, that happiness delights a family for years until the ball breaks, freeing the happiness inside to touch all people who share the spirit of Christmas. This sentimental story is not for everyone's tastes, but many children, who hold teddy bears and blankets in high esteem, will probably really enjoy it.

One-Minute Bedtime Stories (KidsKlassics, 30 m., 2–8, live action/puppets; stars Shari Lewis)

Lewis distills twenty-six classic fairy tales and children's stories into versions that last only a minute for those with truly brief attention spans. Somehow she keeps it interesting, although the pace is brisk. In fact, parents of children who insist on a good bedtime story may be inspired to adapt her style and get a good couple of weeks' mileage out of several stories. Another tape with short segments that are great for short attentions spans is **Nonsense and Lullabyes** (reviewed in Chapter 3, Musical Fun).

Paul Bunyan (Rabbit Ears/Columbia TriStar, 30 m., 5–up; narrator Jonathan Winters, partial animation)

This giant of American folklore takes on his rival, Hels Helsen, in a battle that creates most of North America's scenic wonders. How else will young viewers understand how the Grand Canyon was carved, or how Niagara Falls turned into such a mighty force? The story is a bit unsettling from an environmental viewpoint, until Bunyan says he feels guilty that he might have chopped down too many trees and begins to replant them. Like other titles in the **American Heroes and Legends** series, this video features beautiful illustrations, great narration, and catchy music. Another advantage to showing children such tall tales is that they might inspire young viewers to create their own stories.

Pecos Bill (Rabbit Ears/BMG Kidz, 1990, 30 m., 4–up; narrator Robin Williams)

You don't have to be a child to enjoy listening to Robin Williams narrate and ad-lib his way through the Old West in this winner of a 1992 Parents' Choice award. If you heard him as the genie in Disney's **Aladdin,** you know how he can steal a movie without even showing his face. In this entry in the **American Heroes and Legends** series, he does the same, and thankfully, viewers can rewind the tape when his lines fly by too quickly. You may recall that Pecos is the American legend who lassoed a cyclone, among other larger-than-life exploits. And after hearing this tall tale in Williams' words, few viewers are apt to forget much of this story, although they might be inspired to embellish on the details.

Peep and the Big Wide World (Smarty Pants, 30 m., 2–10; narrator Peter Ustinov)

Toddlers will find this program, which parallels a child's development, particularly engrossing. The video follows four barnyard creatures as they are born and begin to explore their environs. Peep the chick, Quack the duck, Chirp the robin, and Tom the cat explore food, friends, and swimming, and with the help of Nellie the adult dog, even learn the difference between day and night—all on their first day. The basic circle/square/triangle/straight-line method of animation echoes the illustration style of many basic infant books. It's tender and sweet, and so simple it's irresistible. **Peep** is one of the award-winning short films from the National Film Board of Canada (see the interview at the beginning of Chapter 2, Animated Feature Films, for more about the NFBC).

Peppermint Rose (PolyGram, 1992, 30 m., 4–8)

Maybe this is what "flower power" was supposed to be all about: If girls were in charge, this video implies, the world would be "sugar and spice and everything nice"—and that's not such a bad prospect. Rose is just an ordinary girl, until a dragon whisks her away to save his homeland. There a rosebush, stolen by a neighboring kingdom of beetles, has the power to vanquish evil by transforming it into good. Despite her lack of magic powers, Rose discovers she has the power to rise to the quest and triumphs by using her own ingenuity, sometimes even riddling and rapping her way out of a jam. Smart and sassy, Peppermint Rose embodies the kind of charisma and brains many of today's young girls will want to emulate. The animation is fairly ordinary, but the story is one of empowerment, and its admirable message is that if you put your mind to it, anything is possible.

The Pigs' Wedding (CC Studios, 30 m., 3–up)

Love and friendship are the themes that run through this compilation of short films adapted from favorite books. Two pigs in love prepare for their wedding by painting on their ceremonial garb in the animated title tale, and even the rain is welcome at the event. The tape also includes the stories "The Selkie Girl" (iconographic), about a seal-woman and the man who falls in love with her; "The Happy Owls" (animated), who know the secret of happiness and share it with their animal friends; "A Letter to Amy" (iconographic), an Ezra Jack Keats favorite about what happens to a party invitation on a windy day; and the everlastingly clever "The Owl and the Pussycat" (iconographic), by Edward Lear.

Princess Scargo and the Birthday Pumpkin (Rabbit Ears/BMG Kidz, 1993, 30 minutes, 2–8; narrator Geena Davis)

One of the nicest things about the **American Heroes and Legends** series is that Rabbit Ears' definition of "American" encompasses Native Americans (see **Squanto and the First Thanksgiving** and **The Song of Sacajawea** in this chapter). In this entry, Geena Davis's tender narration and the boldly colorful illustrations bring to life the story of a young girl's generosity. Scargo is an Indian chief's daughter who possesses a natural rapport with wild creatures, but she's especially enamored of undewater life. On one of her birthdays, a neighboring chieftain gives her what becomes her most treasured birthday present: an immense pumpkin, hollowed to serve as a fishbowl for a pair of every fish species in Scargo's tribe's hunting ground. Later, when a long drought threatens the lives of her tribe, who live on fish, Scargo instructs her people to excavate a lake, and she selflessly sets free her beloved fish when rains fill the lake. Legend has it that her spirit now inhabits that lake, so she can swim with her fish and never be separated from underwater creatures. Like the other titles in the **American Heroes and Legends** series, **Scargo,** with its intense colors and fascinating story line, will delight children and adults alike.

Ramona series (various suppliers and running times as listed, 1987, 4–10, live action; stars Sarah Polley, Lorie Chodos, Barry Flatman, Lynda Mason-Green)

These Canadian productions of Beverly Cleary's books about Ramona Quimby are wonderful for the straightforward way they bring to life an average 8-year-old's concerns. Cleary published her first Ramona book in 1955, yet these productions bring the little girl into the present with very contemporary, everyday situations like learning to prepare a meal, coping with schoolmates, and coming to grips with one's feelings when an older relative gets married. The titles from Lorimar Home Video run 60 minutes each and contain two episodes per video: The first episode of **Mystery Meal/Rainy Sunday** finds Ramona and her sister Beezus cooking for themselves when they refuse to eat the dinner their mother prepares; the second shows what happens when rain cancels a family outing. **Squeakerfoot/ Goodbye, Hello** first finds Ramona as the center of attention at school when her new shoes squeak; in the second installment, the family draws closer together after their beloved cat dies. **Perfect Day/Bad Day** details the wedding of Ramona's favorite aunt in the first episode, while the second chronicles a day in the Quimby household when everything seems to go wrong for everyone. Warner Home Video also released several episodes from the Canadian TV series, each on a separate, 30-minute video: In **New Pajamas,** Ramona likes her new pajamas so much she even wears them to school. **Siblingitis** finds Ramona dealing with mixed feelings, but feeling mostly very grown-up, upon the arrival of her new baby sister. **The Great Hair Argument** focuses on the excitement Ramona and Beezus meet when they go to a hairdresser. And **The Patient** features Ramona fighting off a stomach bug to receive the top grade in the class for her book report.

The Red Balloon (Public Media, 1956, 34 m., 3–up, live action; director Albert Lamorisse)

This wonderful fable is the tender story of a boy who can't seem to get rid of a balloon, and the two become so attached, it follows him everywhere. When he needs assistance, all the balloons of Paris come to his aid for a fantasy ending. Also on the tape, **White Mane** tells of a Camargue horse that defies taming, until a boy gentles it. The cowboys who had wanted it, however, relentlessly pursue them, and the boy and his horse swim off to an island where they will never grow old. Somehow today, even in the faded colors of a 40-year-old film, these classics don't seem to age.

The Red Shoes (Family Home Entertainment, 30 m., 4–up; narrator Ossie Davis)

Renowned animator Michael Sporn does it again: He captures people's emotions, talents, and movements in exquisitely detailed animation. And the background music rarely stops, adding an urgency to the story. Here, the classic Hans Christian Andersen tale takes a decidedly modern turn, set as it is in the inner city, and featuring African-American characters. The updated storyline follows the good and bad that befall Lisa, an elementary-school girl who's a bit selfish, and her best buddy Jennifer, a talented dancer. After Lisa's brother dies, her family wins some money in the lottery, Lisa steals ballet shoes that were being made especially for Jennifer, and her family moves away. Wait till you see the segment in which little Lisa tries on the purloined ballet shoes, and begins her dance-till-you-drop frenzy that dances her right back to her old neighborhood and her best friend. Sporn's contortions will leave you in stitches!

Shakespeare: The Animated Tales (Random House, 6 tapes, 30 m. each, 8–16)

Abridged versions of the Bard's classics may be the easiest way to introduce your children to the beauty, adventure, and drama that Shakespeare created. Award-winning author Leon Garfield joined a team of Shakespearean scholars to abridge and adapt the plays for an HBO TV series. As in Rabbit Ears' videos, the animation style matches the tone of each play, even to color scheme: **Macbeth** is darkly colored, foreshadowing the ominous events that envelop the king; **Hamlet**'s deep, rich blues reflect the pensive prince; the comedies **Twelfth Night** and **A Midsummer Night's Dream** are conveyed in bright colors; **Romeo and Juliet** is drawn in warm tones, representing the pair's passion; and **The Tempest**'s style is a jagged, jumbled cacophony of colors. Each video is lovely in its own way, and both the animation and the brevity make Shakespeare more accessible to children than simply reading the play does. If your child is eager for more sophisticated fare that what these shortened versions offer, screen other filmed versions of the classics, including the **Hamlet** featuring Mel Gibson (reviewed in Chapter 1, Feature Films).

Shelley Duvall's Bedtime Stories series (MCA/Universal, 9 tapes, 25 m. each, 2–10)

If anyone looks as if she just stepped from the pages of a children's book, it's Shelley Duvall, so it's only appropriate that this friend of creative children's programming has produced a series of video stories based on books. The wide-eyed wonder that Duvall exhibits puts children at ease, allowing them to invite her, as a friend, a peer, a character from one of her beloved books into their homes via video. An avid children's book collector, Duvall has gathered two of her favorite tales on each cassette. One of the best is **Elbert's Bad Word/Weird Parents,** for its pleasing adaptations of Audrey Wood's stories, avant-garde animation style, and scintillating narration by Ringo Starr and Bette Midler, respectively. The other tapes, no less wonderful, are: **Elizabeth and Larry/Bill and Pete** (narrated by Jean Stapleton and Dudley Moore, and based on books by Marilyn Sadler and Tomie De Paola, respectively); **Little Toot and the Loch Ness**

Monster/Choo Choo (narrated by Rick Moranis and Bonnie Raitt, based on the books by Hardie Gramatky and Virginia Lee Burton, respectively); **There's a Nightmare in My Closet/There's an Alligator Under My Bed/There's Something in My Attic** (narrated by Michael J. Fox, Christian Slater, and Sissy Spacek, respectively; based on the books by Mercer Mayer); **Patrick's Dinosaurs/What Happened to Patrick's Dinosaurs?** (both narrated by Martin Short and based on the books by Carol Carrick); **Tugford Wanted to Be Bad/Little Penguin's Tale** (narrated by Steve Martin and Candice Bergen, respectively, and based on Audrey Wood's books); **Moe the Dog in Tropical Paradise/Amos, The Story of an Old Dog and His Couch** (the first narrated by Richard Dreyfuss and based on the book by Diane Stanley; the second narrated by Morgan Freeman and based on the book by Susan Seligson and Howie Schneider); **My New Neighbors/Rotten Island** (the first narrated by Billy Crystal and based on the book by Keith Falkner; the second narrated by Charles Grodin and based on the book by William Steig); and **Blumpoe the Grumpoe Meets Arnold the Cat/Millions of Cats** (the first narrated by John Candy; the second narrated by James Earl Jones and based on the books by Wenda Gag). Each one has the potential to lead children to the magical books that inspired them. The series was honored with a 1992 Parents' Choice award.

Shelley Duvall's Tall Tales and Legends series (FoxVideo, 1985–87, 6 tapes, 52 m. each, 2–10, live action)

Here Duvall adapts both books and American legends for a really engaging series that's often at once hysterical and historical, at least in the legendary sense—some liberty is taken with facts. **Annie Oakley** (director Michael Lindsay-Hogg, stars Jamie Lee Curtis, Cliff De Young, Brian Dennehy) tells of the infamous lady sharpshooter of the late nineteenth century. **Casey at the Bat** (director David Steinberg, stars Elliot Gould, Carol Kane, Howard Cosell) dramatizes E. L. Thayer's beloved poem about the man from Mudville. In **Darlin' Clementine** (director Jerry London, stars Edward Asner, Shelley Duvall, David Dukes, Gordon Jump), Clementine, a klutz with a heart of gold, falls in love with Levi Strauss, but when he leaves to open his tailor shop in San Francisco, she's heartbroken. **Johnny Appleseed** (stars Rob Reiner, Molly Ringwald, Martin Short) follows the gangly environmentalist as he traverses the Midwest with early pioneers. **Pecos Bill, King of the Cowboys** (director Howard Storm, stars Rebecca

DeMornay, Steve Guttenberg, Martin Mull) focuses on the legend of the man who marries the governor's daughter, only to desert her to hide out in Mexico after he robs a stagecoach. **The Legend of Sleepy Hollow** (director David Steinberg, stars Ed Begley Jr., Beverly D'Angelo, Charles Durning) is a wonderful adaptation of Washington Irving's tale of the lengths some people will go to for love. It's interesting to compare these live-action versions with some of the animated versions—for example, those from Rabbit Ears (mostly in the **American Heroes and Legends** series); even the stories are interpreted differently.

Sign-Me-a-Story (Random House, 1987, 30 m., 4–up, live action; stars Linda Bove, Ed Waterstreet, Tim Scanlon, Elaine Bromka)

Bove, of *Sesame Street* fame, makes sign language accessible for all on this one-of-a-kind video. She is articulate and caring, one of those special people who turn what some might consider a disability into sheer ingenuity. Here, she performs two fairy tales, "Little Red Riding Hood" and "Goldilocks and the Three Bears," using her acting and signing talents, while narrator Bromka vocalizes the story for hearing viewers. Communication like this encourages viewers to put aside differences and learn something new about one another and themselves in the process. And if it breaks down a few barriers, dispels some misconceptions, and teaches a new language, so much the better.

Simple Gifts (PBS, 65 min., 2–up, animated/still photography; director R. O. Blechman, host Colleen Dewhurst)

Six poignant vignettes focus on the holiday season and reflect a variety of thoughts about giving. Dewhurst appears at the beginning and end of the tape to set the tone: "A person gives nothing who does not give of himself," she notes, and the first segment, a very brief Maurice Sendak piece, illustrates that concept brilliantly: A ragtag homeless boy slowly and gracefully transforms himself into a decorated Christmas tree, sheltering and giving joy to other homeless children. Next, playwright Moss Hart recalls his childhood in "A Memory of Christmas" (narrated by Jose Ferrer) when, as a middle-aged man, he finally connects with his father; the lovely animation is crafted to imitate sepia photographs. "Lost and Found" is a silly interlude in which a baby is concealed among the discarded holiday wrapping paper and ends up out on the curb. "The Great Frost," based on a passage from Virginia Woolf's *Orlando,* is an animated love story that begins by showing people and animals freezing solid and shattering. It may be best viewed with a parent; there's also an incongruous Punch and Judy puppet show that may confuse young viewers. To its benefit, however, the production was coordinated by Michael Sporn. In "My Christmas," Teddy Roosevelt describes a Christmas on which he receives "two lamps, an inkwell in the ancient Pompeian style, a cravat . . ." Roosevelt's gifts may be too outmoded to strike anything but a chord of laughter in young viewers. "December 25, 1914" is based upon a World War I letter from the Western Front by Captain Edward Hulse, who describes the strange Christmastime events on the battlefield, when German soldiers suggest a momentary end to fighting to sing Christmas carols. A day later, the fighting resumes, and Hulse survived only until March 15, 1915. Each of the shorts included in this wonderful collection is worth a look, and most merit a discussion with your kids.

The Snowman (CC Studios, 30 m., 2–up)

This animated gem, with its powerful music and shimmering animation, needs no narration. The orchestral score, composed by Howard Blake and performed by the Sinfonia of London, is a better complement than words to the animation, though children may feel compelled to supply their own narration. When his snowman magically comes to life, a young boy is treated to a ride through the sky, above glittering cities and countries he's never even imagined. The book won a Horn Book Award from the *Boston Globe,* while this film version won a British Academy Award for Best Children's Drama (it was nominated for an Oscar here) and was named an American Library Association Notable Film. It's well worth the search to find yourself a copy.

The Song of Sacajawea (Rabbit Ears/BMG Kidz, 1993, 30 m., 2–10; narrator Laura Dern)

Only a few women are given much credit in American history, and although Sacajawea was one of the bravest, her story has been treated mainly as a sideline to Lewis and Clark's groundbreaking exploration of the Pacific Northwest in 1805. The explorers, however, owe their lives to this brave 17-year-old Shoshone woman whose determination, knowledge of the wilderness, and wisdom ensured the surveying party's success. Modern children who dream of an adventurous life may be inspired by her true story: In partnership with her French trapper husband and while nursing her infant child, she was responsible for safely leading the party across the spring-flooded Missouri River and the Rocky Mountains and down the Columbia River to the Pacific Ocean. Dern narrates with quiet dignity, and the illustration style in this mostly iconographic program is a fascinating juxtaposition of colorful linoleum prints and photographs of antique tools, maps, and journal entries. This historical adventure is one of the most gripping and beautiful in Rabbit Ears' **American Heroes and Legends** series.

Squanto and the First Thanksgiving (Rabbit Ears/BMG Kidz, 1993, 30 m. 1–20; narrator Graham Greene)

The beautiful **American Heroes and Legends** series again draws on the wealth of Native American history for this moving tale of a man forcibly removed from his home and destined for slavery in Europe. When the friars in Malaga, Spain, take Squanto under their wing, they educate him, and in return he works in their fields. After two years, the friars arrange for Squanto's return to America, where he discovers that his village has been decimated by smallpox. The next white men he encounters are the Pilgrims, fleeing persecution in Europe; they are impressed with his knowledge, and he with their acceptance of him. They begin a lasting friendship as Squanto teaches them how to hunt and fish, plant and build, and survive in the wilderness. Greene's narrative style is sometimes muted by the music, but his eloquence invites the viewer to tune in to this moving story.

The Steadfast Tin Soldier (Random House, 30 m., 2–10, iconographic, narrator Jeremy Irons)

The American Film and Video Festival bestowed its first prize on this beautiful video based on Hans Christian Andersen's heart-wrenching story of unrequited love. Despite having been "wounded" and losing a leg, a brave toy soldier proves his love for a toy ballerina in a series of adventures that take him from a child's room out to the streets and back again. The static iconographic style of animation superbly suits the nature of this video, as it mimics the way children "animate" their toys as they play. This program, as well as **The Elephant's Child, The Ugly Duckling,** and **The Velveteen Rabbit** (all reviewed in this chapter), was produced by Rabbit Ears before the company launched its own video line. The lovely watercolor illustrations by David Jorgensen complement the tale (you can see more of Jorgensen's work in **The Velveteen Rabbit**). For an unusual, lively ballet version of this tale, see **The Tin Soldier** in Chapter 3, Musical Fun.

Stories from the Black Tradition (CC Studios, 52 m., 5–up)

African-American culture is explored in five stories. The fascinating "A Story, A Story" by Gail E. Harley (animated) tells how the art of storytelling was handed down from the African god of the sky. In "Mufaro's Beautiful Daughters," by John Steptoe (iconographic; the illustrations are some of the most intricately beautiful art to grace this company's releases), two sisters are presented with trials, and only one can succeed to become the king's wife. "Why Mosquitoes Buzz in People's Ears" (animated) is explained in this story newly retold by Vern Aardema and narrated with humor by James Earl Jones. "The Village of Round and Square Houses," by Ann Grifalconi (iconographic), is a primitive place where men and women learn to enjoy their separateness and companionship. Finally, in Ezra Jack Keats's "Goggles!" (iconographic), Peter finds a pair of motorcycle goggles, but before he can share them with his friends, some older boys intercept him. The tape was awarded a 1992 Parents' Choice Award.

Stories to Remember series (Lightyear Entertainment, 10 tapes, 30 m. each, 4–11)

Lovingly, lavishly illustrated tales based on books and original stories constitute this series, which, like the Rabbit Ears titles, boasts celebrity narrators, illustrators, and/or musicians. The series is divided into two groups of programs. The storytelling series of six tapes geared for children 4 to 11 include: **Noah's Ark** (narrated by James Earl Jones, music by Stewart Copeland), **Beauty and Beast** (narrated by Mia Farrow, music by Ernest Troost, based on the book by Mordecai Gerstein), **Merlin and the Dragons** (narrated by Kevin Kline, music by Michel Rubini, written by Jane Yolen), **Peg-**

asus (narrated by Mia Farrow, music by Ernest Troost, written by Doris Orgel), **The Snow Queen** (narrated by Sigourney Weaver, music by Jason Miles, based on Hans Christian Andersen's tale) and **The Wild Swans** (narrated by Sigourney Weaver, music by the Hooters, based on Hans Christian Andersen's tale). Each tape in the nursery series (which are explained in Chapter 3, Musical Fun, because they contain more melody than story) is based on one of illustrator Kay Chorao's books. The supplier has also released the stories on audiocassettes and CDs. Parents who want high-quality productions with engaging celebrities narrating classic tales cannot go wrong no matter which **Stories to Remember** title they choose.

The Sweater (Smarty Pants, 1991, 30 m., 4–up)

This collection of stories begins with an animated Canadian story about the national pastime, hockey. Like all children, our young protagonist has a hero, a hockey player, but what happens when his hero loses is something that's probably happened to many of us who choose to show our allegiance. Things take a comic turn in the live-action "The Ride," in which a chauffeur accidentally loses his car—with his oblivious employer nonchalantly reading in the back seat! The final live-action tale, "Getting Started," is a clever depiction of how a procrastinator operates. The music our recitalist performs, when he finally does sit down to practice, is from Debussy's "Children's Corner," and it's a lovely close to this gentle and entertaining video.

The Ugly Duckling (Random House, 30 m., 2–10, iconographic; narrator Cher)

Who better to tell a story about judging a book by its cover than a woman who's known her share of being judged? Paintings by illustrator Robert Van Nutt bring this poignant Hans Christian Andersen fairy tale to life in this production that earned second prize from the American Film and Video Festival. Although there are several versions of this classic story on the market, the pleasing animation makes this one the best by far.

The Velveteen Rabbit (Random House, 30 m., 2–10, iconographic; narrator Meryl Streep)

Margery Williams' beloved tale is not to be missed—a plush toy is so loved by a little boy that it becomes a real rabbit. Of the seven versions available on video, this is the one most decorated with awards and kudos, including a Grammy nomination. Another version that should be almost as well received by young viewers is the one narrated by Christopher Plummer (Family Home Entertainment, 30 m., animated), despite animation that's just a step above that produced for Saturday-morning TV.

We All Have Tales (Rabbit Ears/BMG Kidz, 13 tapes, 1991–92, 30 m. each, 4–up)

These videos from a company that delights in teaming the best illustrators with celebrity narrators and musicians are difficult to categorize. They're part literature, part folklore, part history, and all beautiful. Each is based on a notable story from a particular country or culture. Denzel Washington tells the delightful Jamaican story of **Anansi** the spider, a clever, vain fellow who spins his tales with the help of the story god. William Hurt recounts the Japanese story of **The Boy Who Drew Cats,** whose peculiar talent is sufficient to vanquish a demon. Max Von Sydow narrates the Norwegian tale **East of the Sun, West of the Moon,** about a destitute young girl who's sent to live with a mysterious white bear. Robin Williams plays havoc in **The Fool and the Flying Ship,** a Russian tale about a country bumpkin who wins the hand of a princess. Michael Palin recounts the familiar British story **Jack and the Beanstalk.** Michael Caine tells of **King Midas and the Golden Touch,** a Greek-based story about materialism. Whoopi Goldberg narrates the African folktale **Koi and the Kola Nuts,** about a young prince who sets out on his own to discover his place in the world. Raul Julia tells the South American story of **The Monkey People,** a lesson in the evils of laziness. Sigourney Weaver shares the Japanese story of **Peachboy,** a boy who was discovered in a peach, yet grows to be a mighty warrior. Danny Aiello skillfully characterizes Gepetto and his beloved puppet in the Italian entry **Pinocchio.** Tracey Ullman narrates the familiar French tale of **Puss in Boots.** Kathleen Turner spins the story of **Rumpelstiltskin.** Ben Kingsley narrates **The Tiger and the Brahmin,** an Indian tale of a holy man, the tiger who betrays him, and the jackal who teaches him the ways of the world. The success of the series over time has been its dependable stories and the star talent amassed for each production, from celebrity narrators to respected musicians and renowned illustrators. The action, however, may move too slowly for some children.

What's Under My Bed? And Other Creepy Stories (CC Studios, 36 m., 4–9)

The four stories compiled on this video would make a great non-threatening Halloween selection for young children who really don't want to be terrified. The title tale by James Stevenson is brought to magical life by the careful hand of animation genius Michael Sporn; it tells how a grandfather calms his two young houseguests when they claim there are ghosts, goblins, and who knows what else under their beds. In Tomi Ungerer's "The Three Robbers," which is not frightening at all, a little girl and her trusting manner change the robbers from men who steal gold to men with hearts of gold. "Georgie" (iconographic), Robert Bright's friendly ghost, deserts his living family for new grounds to haunt. "Teeny-Tiny and the Witch Woman," by Barbara Walker, tells of a brave little boy who outsmarts a witch who plans to eat him and his brothers.

The Wind in the Willows series (HBO, 1983, Vol. 1: 78 m., Vols. 2, 3, and 4: 60 m. each, 3–10, model animation; director Mark Hall, stars the voices of Mark Hall, Brian Cosgrove, Beryl Reid)

Kenneth Grahame's treatise on early-twentieth-century society is a telling exposé of our technological foibles and our class structure. Toad, Mole, Ratty, and Badger are fast and loyal friends who never desert one another. But Toad is an uncompromising buffoon: He gets into trouble with his automobile, and his friends are always there to assist and caution him against future problems (though he rarely listens). The animators went to great lengths to build and stop-animate the intricate scenery and characters, which may inspire creative play once your child has watched one of the installments. You might also like to check out the traditionally animated Disney version, reviewed in Chapter 2, Animated Feature Films.

The Wisdom of the Gnomes (various suppliers, 6 tapes, 50 m. each 4–up)

This animated series is based on the Dutch books and adapted from the Nickelodeon series *David the Gnome*. The nature- and animal-loving gnomes spend each episode helping preserve the delicate balance of nature and encouraging others to live and let live. David is a special gnome with curative powers, which he uses when he travels far and wide to help injured animals. Two tapes from Strand Home Video (two stories on each tape: **Vol. 1** contains **Klaus the Judge** and **The Stolen Mirror,** while **Vol. 2** contains **The Gold Diggers** and **Mystery in the Forest**) are supplemented by others released on the Family Home Entertainment label that compile episodes from the TV series onto four tapes: **David the Gnome: Rabbits, Rabbits Everywhere!, The World of David the Gnome, The World of David the Gnome: Kangaroo Adventure, The World of David the Gnome: The Siberian Bear**). Despite its somewhat banal animation style, the series features an admirable message about taking care of other creatures, protecting the environment, and taking time to learn about subjects with which you might be unfamiliar.

Other interesting storytelling and literature-based titles:

The Berenstein Bears (Chapter 4, Discovery and Learning)
A Child's Garden of Verses (Chapter 3, Musical Fun)
The Human Race Club (Chapter 4, Discovery and Learning)
Jazz Time Tale (Chapter 3, Musical Fun)
Nonsense and Lullabyes, two tapes: **Poems for Children** and **Nursery Rhymes** (Chapter 3, Musical Fun)

RESOURCES

List of Suppliers

Should your local video store not be able to special-order any of the programs mentioned in this book, use the following list of children's program suppliers to order tapes directly from the manufacturer or producer. Many suppliers will also gladly send you a catalogue of available titles. The list was as current as possible at press time.

Academy Entertainment
9250 Wilshire Boulevard
Suite 303
Beverly Hills, CA 90212
310-275-2195/800-972-0001

A&M Video
1416 N. La Brea Avenue
Hollywood, CA 90028
213-469-2411

Apollo Educational Video
c/o Aims Media
9710 De Soto Avenue
Chatsworth, CA 91311
818-771-4300/800-367-2467

A*Vision/Kid*Vision
75 Rockefeller Plaza
New York, NY 10019
212-275-2900

Barr Films & Video
12801 Schabarum Avenue
Irwindale, CA 91706
818-338-7878/800-234-7878

Best Film & Video Corp.
98 Cutter Mill Road
Great Neck, NY 11021
516-487-4834/800-527-2189

BMG Video/BMG Kidz
6363 Sunset Boulevard
Suite 600
Hollywood, CA 90028
213-468-4069

Boys Town Videos for Parents
Public Service Division
Boys Town, NB 68010
402-498-1580

Brentwood Kids Company
316 Southgate Court
Brentwood, TN 37027

Bright Ideas Productions
31220 La Baya Drive
Suite 110
Westlake Village, CA 91362
818-707-7127/800-541-9904

Buena Vista Home Video
c/o Walt Disney Home Video
500 S. Buena Vista Street
Fairmount Building, 633F
Burbank, CA 91521
818-562-3883/800-362-4533

CBS/Fox Video
1330 Avenue of the Americas
5th Floor
New York, NY 10019
212-373-4800/800-800-4369

CC Studios
389 Newtown Turnpike
Weston, CT 06883-1199
203-222-0002/800-543-7843

Child Management
507 Thornhill
Carol Stream, IL 60188
708-653-0109

Children's Treasures
c/o Orion Home Video
9 West 57th Street
New York, NY 10019
212-303-1108

Children's Video Library
c/o Vestron Video/LIVE Home
  Video
15400 Sherman Way
Van Nuys, CA 91410
818-908-0303/800-423-7455

Child's Play Video
c/o Cinema Products Video
7410 Santa Monica Boulevard
West Hollywood, CA 90046
213-850-6500

Coalition for Quality Children's Video
535 Cordova Road
Suite 456
Sante Fe, NM 87501
505-989-8076

Columbia/TriStar Home Video
10202 W. Washington Boulevard
Culver City, CA 90232
310-280-7164

Concept Associates
7910 Woodmont Avenue
Suite 1214
Bethesda, MD 20814
301-986-4144

Creative Learning Products, Inc.
3567 Kennedy Road
South Plainfield, NJ 07080
201-755-3666/800-262-2437

Creative Street
3719 Washington Boulevard
Indianapolis, IN 46205
317-926-9671/800-733-8273

Crown Video
201 East 50th Street
New York, NY 10022
212-572-2627/800-752-3396

Discovery Music
5554 Calhoun Avenue
Van Nuys, CA 91401
818-782-7818/800-451-5175

Ergo Media, Inc.
P.O. Box 2037
Teaneck, NJ 07666
201-692-0404

Facets Video
1517 West Fullerton Avenue
Chicago, IL 60614
312-281-9075/800-331-6197

Family Circle Video
c/o Paperback Visual Publishing
145 Avenue of the Americas
2nd Floor
New York, NY 10013
212-727-7500

Family Express Video
44925 Steeple Path
Novi, MI 48375
313-347-4630/800-356-2820

Family Home Entertainment
15400 Sherman Way
Van Nuys, CA 91410-0124
818-908-0303/800-423-7455

Filmation
(See MGM/UA Home Video)

Films for the Humanities, Inc.
P.O. Box 2053
Princeton, NJ 08543
609-452-1128/800-257-5126

Focus Video Productions
RD #5, Box 2108
Montpelier, VT 05602
800-843-3686

FoxVideo
2121 Avenue of the Stars
25th Floor
Los Angeles, CA 90067
213-203-3900

Golden Book Video
c/o Western Publishing
1220 Mound Avenue
Racine, WI 53404
414-633-2431

GoodTimes/Kids Klassics
16 East 40th Street
New York, NY 10016
212-951-3000

Hanna-Barbera Home Video
c/o Turner Home Entertainment
One CNN Center
Atlanta, GA 30348
404-827-3066

HBO Video
1100 Avenue of the Americas
New York, NY 10036
212-512-1000

Hemdale Home Video
7966 Beverly Boulevard
Los Angeles, CA 90048
213-966-5112

HPG Home Video
400 South Houston, Suite 230
Dallas, TX 75202
214-741-5544/800-888-1188

Imagination Tree
c/o Random House
225 Park Avenue South
New York, NY 10003
212-872-8235/800-733-3000

Informed Democracy
P.O. Box 67
Santa Cruz, CA 95063
408-426-3921/800-827-0949

JCI Video
21550 Oxnard Street
Suite 920
Woodland Hills, CA 91367
818-593-3600/800-223-7479

Jim Henson Video
(see Buena Vista Home Video)

Jugglebug
7526 Olympic View Drive
Edmonds, WA
206-774-2127/800-523-1776

Just for Kids Home Video
c/o Celebrity Home Video
P.O. Box 4112
Woodland Hills, CA 91367
818-595-0666

Kid Pics
c/o Amvest Video
937 East Hazlewood Avenue
Rahway, NJ 07065
201-396-3113

Kids Klassics/GoodTimes
401 Fifth Avenue
New York, NY 10016
212-889-0044

Kids Stuff
2999 East 191st Street
Suite 800
North Miami Beach, FL 33180
305-935-3995

KIDVIDZ
618 Centre Street
Newton, MA 02158
617-277-8703

Kinderkicks
P.O. Box 68
Avon Lake, OH 44012
216-933-8905

KVC Home Video
12801 Schabarum Avenue
Irwindale, CA 91706-7878
800-234-7478

Les Productions la Fete
2306 Rue Sherbrooke Est
Suite 1
Montreal, Canada H2K1E5
514-521-8303

Lightyear Video
(See also BMG Video)
Empire State Building
Suite 5101
350 Fifth Avenue
New York, NY 10118
212-563-4610

The Lyons Group
2435 N. Central Expressway
Suite 1600
Richardson, TX 75080-2722
214-390-6000/800-791-8093

Macmillan Publishing
866 Third Avenue
New York, NY 10022
212-702-7815

Made to Order Productions
(See Coalition for Quality
Children's Video)

The Maier Group
235 East 95th Street
New York, NY 10128
212-534-4100

Magic Window
(See Columbia/TriStar Home
Video)

Major League Baseball Productions
1212 Avenue of the Americas
New York, NY 10036
212-921-8100

Mastervision, Inc.
969 Park Avenue
New York, NY 10028
212-879-0448

Mazon Productions
P.O. Box 2427
Northbrook, IL 60065-2427
708-272-2824

MCA/Universal Home Video
70 Universal City Plaza,
Suite 435
Universal City, CA 91608
818-777-5539

McGraw-Hill Video Production
1221 Avenue of the Americas
New York, NY 10021
212-512-4014

Media Home Entertainment
510 W. 6th Street
Suite 1032
Los Angeles, CA 90014
(213) 236-1336

MGM/UA Home Video
2500 Broadway Street
Santa Monica, CA 90404-3061
310-449-3381

Miramar Productions
200 Second Avenue West
Seattle, WA 98119-4204
206-284-4700/800-245-6472

Monterey Home Video
28038 Dorothy Drive
Suite 1
Agoura Hills, CA 91301
818-597-0047/800-424-2593

Morris Video
2730 Monterey #105
Torrance, CA 90503
310-533-4800/800-621-0849

MPI Home Video/VideoSaurus
15825 Rob Roy Drive
Oak Forest, IL 60452
708-687-7881/800-323-0442

Muppet Home Video
(see Buena Vista Home Video)

Music for Little People
Box 1460
Redway,CA 95560
800-346-4445

My Baby Can Read
12021 Wilshire Boulevard
Suite 522
Los Angeles, CA 90025
310-826-1619

New Line Home Video
116 N. Robertson Boulevard
Los Angeles, CA 90048
310-967-6674

Nickelodeon
(See Sony Wonder/Nickelodeon)

Only for Children
c/o Dixie Entertainment
P.O. Box 407
Long Beach, CA 90801
310-491-0332

Orion Home Video
1888 Century Park East
Los Angeles, CA 90067
310-282-0550

Pacific Arts Video
11858 La Grange Avenue
Los Angeles, CA 90025
213-820-0991/800-282-8765

Paramount Home Video
5555 Melrose Avenue
Los Angeles, CA 90038-3197
213-956-5000

PBS Video
1320 Braddock Place
Alexandria, VA 22314
703-739-5000/800-424-7963

Peter Pan Industries/Parade
88 St. Francis Street
Newark, NJ 07105
201-344-4214

Playhouse Video
(See CBS/Fox Video)

PolyGram Video
825 8th Avenue
New York, NY 10019
212-333-8000/800-223-7781

Price Stern Sloan
11150 Olympic Boulevard
Suite 650
Los Angeles, CA 90064
310-477-6100

Prism Home Entertainment
1888 Century Park East
Suite 350
Los Angeles, CA 90067
213-277-3270

Public Media Video
5547 N. Ravenswood Avenue
Chicago, IL 60640
312-878-2600/800-323-4222

Rabbit Ears Productions
131 Rowayton Avenue
Rowayton, CT 06853
203-857-3760

Rainbow Educational Video
170 Keyland Court
Bohemia, NY 11716
516-589-6643/800-331-4047

Random House Home Video
201 East 50th Street
New York, NY 10022
800-726-0600

Rhino Home Video/Kid Rhino
2225 Colorado Avenue
Santa Monica, CA 90404
310-828-1980/800-843-3670

Saban Video
4000 W. Alameda Avenue
Burbank, CA 91505
818-972-4848

Scholastic Video
(See Warner Home Video)

Silo/Alcazar
P.O. Box 429
Waterbury, VT 05676
802-244-7845/800-541-9904

Smarty Pants Video
15104 Detroit Avenue
Suite #2
Lakewood, OH 44107-3916
216-221-5300

Sony Wonder and SonyWonder/ Nickelodeon
550 Madison Avenue
New York, NY 10022-3211
212-833-8000

Stage Fright Productions
P.O. Box 373
227 South Fifth Street
Geneva, IL 60134
708-208-9845

Starmaker Entertainment
151 Industrial Way East
Eatontown, NJ 07724
908-389-1020/800-233-3738

Strand Home Video
3350 Ocean Park Boulevard
Suite 205
Santa Monica, CA 90405
310-396-7011

Tapeworm Video
12420 Montague Street
Unit 8
Arleta, CA 91331
818-896-8899/800-367-8437

Time-Life Video
1271 Avenue of the Americas
New York, NY 10020
212-522-1212

Touchstone Home Video
(See Buena Vista Home Video)

Turner Home Entertainment
One CNN Center
Atlanta, GA 30303
404-928-3066

Twin Tower Enterprises
18720 Oxnard Street, Suite 101
Tarzana, CA 91356
818-344-8424/800-553-3421

Tyndale House Publishers
P.O. Box 80
351 Executive Drive
Wheaton, IL 60189
708-668-8300/800-323-9400

Video Krafts for Kids
c/o Krafty Kids
11358 Aurora Avenue
Des Moines, IA 50322
515-276-8325/800-747-6569

Video Schoolhouse
c/o Video Learning Library
15838 N. 62nd Street
Suite 101
Scottsdale, AZ 85254
602-596-9970/800-383-8811

Video Treasures
500 Kirts Boulevard
Troy, MI 48084-5299
810-362-9660

Video Tutor, Inc.
2516 Highway 35
Manasquan, NJ 08736
908-223-8580/800-445-8334

View-Master Video
c/o Tyco Toys
6000 Midlantic Drive
Mount Laurel, NJ 08054
609-234-7400

V.I.E.W. Video
34 E. 23rd Street
New York, NY 10010
212-674-5550/800-843-9843

Walt Disney Home Video
(See Buena Vista Home Video)

Warner Home Video
4000 Warner Boulevard
Burbank, CA 91522
818-954-6000

Warner Reprise Video
3300 Warner Boulevard
Burbank, CA 91505
818-846-9090

Western Publishing
(see Golden Book Video)

Whole Toon Video
P.O. Box 369
Issaquah, WA 98027
206-391-9064

Wishing Well Distributing
P.O. Box 7040
Santa Rosa, CA 95401
707-525-9355/800-888-9355

Wood Knapp Video
5900 Wilshire Boulevard
Los Angeles, CA 90036
213-965-3509/800-521-2666

Worldvision Home Video
1700 Broadway
New York, NY 10019-5992
212-261-2700

List of Mail-Order Houses

The following mail-order companies were found to be the most responsive.

The Blackhawk Catalog
5959 Triumph Street
Commerce, CA 90048-1688
213-888-2229/800-826-2295

Facets Video
(a subsidiary of Facets
Multimedia)
1517 W. Fullerton Avenue
Chicago, IL 60614
312-281-9075/800-331-6197

Listening Library
One Park Avenue
Old Greenwich, CT 06780
800-243-4504

Movies Unlimited
6736 Castor Avenue
Philadelphia, PA 19149
215-722-8398/800-523-0823

Music for Little People
Box 1460
Redway, CA 95560
800-346-4445

Silo/Alcazar
P.O. Box 429
Waterbury, VT 05676
802-244-7845/800-541-9904

Whole Toon Catalog
P.O. Box 369
Issaquah, WA 998207
206-391-8747

Suggested Reading

Catchpole, Terry, and Catherine Catchpole. *The Family Video Guide.* Charlotte, VT: Williamson Publishing, 1992. A movie-lover's handbook, this book selects some terrific feature films that the entire family can enjoy, as well as some that address certain themes—among them, "Race Relations" and "Science Gone Amok."

Chen, Milton, Ph.D. *The Smart Parent's Guide to Kids' TV.* San Francisco: KQED, 1994. The director of the KQED Center for Education and Lifelong Learning (CELL) culls tips from his experience in communication research and program development for the Children's Television Workshop to help parents make TV viewing an entertaining and educational experience—a concept easily translated to video viewing.

Green, Diana Huss, ed. *Parents' Choice Magazine Guide to Videocassettes for Children.* Mount Vernon, NY: Consumer Reports Books, Consumers Union, 1989. This reference compiles the reviews of some of the country's leading newspaper and syndicated film critics: Ed Bark, *Dallas Morning News*; David Bianculli, *New York Post*; Charles Champlin, *Los Angeles*

Times; Green, *Parents' Choice*; William A. Henry III, *Time*; Noel Holston, *Minneapolis Star Tribune*; and Lee Margulies, *Los Angeles Times*.

Jarnow, Jill. *All Ears: How to Choose and Use Recorded Music for Children.* New York: Penguin Books, 1991. An excellent source for cross-referencing audio performers with their videos, and for seeking alternatives to video.

Levine, Evan. *Kids Pick the Best Videos for Kids.* New York: Citadel Press/ Carol Publishing Group, 1994. The author of the nationally syndicated column "Children's Guide to TV" collects comments from a panel of children ages 3 through 14, and adds one or two per video to her own lengthy synopses. The book focuses not on mainstream movies but on less well-known titles.

Maltin, Leonard, ed. *Leonard Maltin's TV Movies and Video Guide.* New York: Signet, new editions published annually since 1986. Maltin's expertise in the industry is unparalleled, and his eye for details and trivia is refreshing.

Martin, Mick; Marsha Porter, and Ed Remitz. *Video Movie Guide for Kids: A Book for Parents.* New York: Ballantine, 1987. Martin and Porter are coauthors of Ballantine's annual *Video Movie Guide*.

Oppenheim, Joanne, and Stephanie Oppenheim. *The Best Toys, Books, and Videos for Kids.* New York: HarperCollins, 1994. The publisher of the Oppenheim Toy Portfolio describes more than 1,000 children's toys, books, and videos, including her Platinum Award winners. All were reviewed in her quarterly publication. The book includes a chapter on how to adapt terrific toys for children with special needs.

INDEXES

Indexes of Some Award-Winning Videos

To help you find some of the best programming quickly, here are three of the organizations that bestow awards on high-quality children's videos, and a list of some of the videos that have received their awards. The list is intended to help you recognize topflight productions, producers, stars, and suppliers. Take a look at how many of these tapes show up on multiple lists.

This list is far from complete. To list all the children's videos that have won awards would be the subject of another entire book; besides, new awards are handed out from various entities at least four times a year.

The Coalition for Quality Children's Video

The Coalition for Quality Children's Video has compiled a select group of videos, and affixed its Kids First! seal of approval on the boxes for all buyers and renters to see. For more on the Coalition, see Chapter 5: Sports, Safety, Health, and Fitness, for an interview with founder Ranny Levy, and the List of Suppliers for its address. Here's a sampling of videos that bear the Coalition's Kids First! seal, and the chapter in which they appear in this book (this list was current as of press time; the coalition periodically updates its selection).

The Oppenheim Toy Portfolio,

Joanne Oppenheim, a toy and child-development expert, author, and senior editor with the Bank Street College of Education, publishes *The Oppenheim Toy Portfolio*, a quarterly review of children's toys, books, games, and videos. Over the past four years, her list of Gold and Platinum Award winners has included the following videos:

Parents' Choice

The Parents' Choice Foundation seals of approval are probably one of the more well-recognized imprints on videos, as well as on books, toys, computer programs, and audiocassettes, since they are announced each year around Thanksgiving on *Good Morning America*. Here's a partial list of some videos that have won awards or honorable mentions:

General Index

FOR THE BEST IN PAPERBACKS, LOOK FOR THE

In every corner of the world, on every subject under the sun, Penguin represents quality and variety—the very best in publishing today.

For complete information about books available from Penguin—including Puffins, Penguin Classics, and Arkana—and how to order them, write to us at the appropriate address below. Please note that for copyright reasons the selection of books varies from country to country.

In the United Kingdom: Please write to *Dept. JC, Penguin Books Ltd, FREEPOST, West Drayton, Middlesex UB7 0BR.*

If you have any difficulty in obtaining a title, please send your order with the correct money, plus ten percent for postage and packaging, to *P.O. Box No. 11, West Drayton, Middlesex UB7 0BR*

In the United States: Please write to *Consumer Sales, Penguin USA, P.O. Box 999, Dept. 17109, Bergenfield, New Jersey 07621-0120.* VISA and MasterCard holders call 1-800-253-6476 to order all Penguin titles

In Canada: Please write to *Penguin Books Canada Ltd, 10 Alcorn Avenue, Suite 300, Toronto, Ontario M4V 3B2*

In Australia: Please write to *Penguin Books Australia Ltd, P.O. Box 257, Ringwood, Victoria 3134*

In New Zealand: Please write to *Penguin Books (NZ) Ltd, Private Bag 102902, North Shore Mail Centre, Auckland 10*

In India: Please write to *Penguin Books India Pvt Ltd, 706 Eros Apartments, 56 Nehru Place, New Delhi 110 019*

In the Netherlands: Please write to *Penguin Books Netherlands bv, Postbus 3507, NL-1001 AH Amsterdam*

In Germany: Please write to *Penguin Books Deutschland GmbH, Metzlerstrasse 26, 60594 Frankfurt am Main*

In Spain: Please write to *Penguin Books S. A., Bravo Murillo 19, 1° B, 28015 Madrid*

In Italy: Please write to *Penguin Italia s.r.l., Via Felice Casati 20, I-20124 Milano*

In France: Please write to *Penguin France S. A., 17 rue Lejeune, F–31000 Toulouse*

In Japan: Please write to *Penguin Books Japan, Ishikiribashi Building, 2–5–4, Suido, Bunkyo-ku, Tokyo 112*

In Greece: Please write to *Penguin Hellas Ltd, Dimocritou 3, GR–106 71 Athens*

In South Africa: Please write to *Longman Penguin Southern Africa (Pty) Ltd, Private Bag X08, Bertsham 2013*